M000105365

EDITORIAL BOARD

ROBERT C. CLARK
Directing Editor
Distinguished Service Professor and Austin Wakeman Scott
Professor of Law and Former Dean of the Law School
Harvard University

DANIEL A. FARBER
Sho Sato Professor of Law and Director, Environmental Law Program
University of California at Berkeley

SAMUEL ISSACHAROFF
Bonnie and Richard Reiss Professor of Constitutional Law
New York University

HERMA HILL KAY
Barbara Nachtrieb Armstrong Professor of Law and
Former Dean of the School of Law
University of California at Berkeley

HAROLD HONGJU KOH
Sterling Professor of International Law and
Former Dean of the Law School
Yale University

SAUL LEVMORE
William B. Graham Distinguished Service Professor of Law and
Former Dean of the Law School
University of Chicago

THOMAS W. MERRILL
Charles Evans Hughes Professor of Law
Columbia University

ROBERT L. RABIN
A. Calder Mackay Professor of Law
Stanford University

CAROL M. ROSE
Gordon Bradford Tweedy Professor Emeritus of Law and Organization and
Professorial Lecturer in Law
Yale University
Lohse Chair in Water and Natural Resources
University of Arizona

AGENCY, PARTNERSHIPS & LLCs

SECOND EDITION

by

STEPHEN M. BAINBRIDGE

William D. Warren Distinguished Professor of Law
University of California, Los Angeles
School of Law

CONCEPTS AND INSIGHTS SERIES®

FOUNDATION
PRESS

The publisher is not engaged in rendering legal or other professional advice, and this publication is not a substitute for the advice of an attorney. If you require legal or other expert advice, you should seek the services of a competent attorney or other professional.

Concepts and Insights Series is a trademark registered in the U.S. Patent and Trademark Office.

© 2004 FOUNDATION PRESS
© 2014 LEG, Inc. d/b/a West Academic
        444 Cedar Street, Suite 700
        St. Paul, MN 55101
        1-877-888-1330
Printed in the United States of America

ISBN: 978-1-60930-466-9
Mat #41552217

PREFACE

The agency and partnership course once was a staple of the law school curriculum. In the latter third of the 20th Century, however, corporate law mounted a hostile takeover of the business law curriculum. To the extent agency and partnership survived, it typically did so only as a small part of a course on business associations.

Ironically, however, it was during the same period that a new form of unincorporated business association—the limited liability company—was devised and popularized. Since the Internal Revenue Service held in 1988 that limited liability companies could be treated as a pass-through entity for tax purposes, such firms have become a tremendously important phenomenon.[1] By 2001, the most recent year for which government statistics are available, over 800,000 limited liability companies had been formed. In many jurisdictions, the limited liability company is now the business organization form of choice for closely held businesses. This development established a demand for more extensive attention to unincorporated business associations in the law school business curriculum.

The emergence of the limited liability company also rekindled interest in unincorporated business associations among legal scholars. This revival was further stimulated by the multiple revisions made to the Uniform Partnership Act in the 1990s.[2] By lending new intellectual respectability to the study of unincorporated business associations, these developments stimulated the supply side of the curricular equilibrium. Courses on unincorporated business associations have thus sprung up at many law schools. A number of very fine casebooks compete for that market, including one co-edited by the author of this volume.[3]

---

[1] See Rev. Rul. 88–76, 1988–2 Cum. Bull. 360.

[2] The original Uniform Partnership Act (UPA) was promulgated in 1914 and eventually was adopted widely and mostly uniformly. See UNIF. PARTNERSHIP ACT (1914). A new uniform partnership act was first promulgated in 1994. Major amendments to that statute were promulgated in 1996 and 1997. See UNIF. PARTNERSHIP ACT (1997).

[3] See William A. Klein, J. Mark Ramseyer, & Stephen M. Bainbridge, Agency, Partnerships, and Limited Liability Entities: Cases and Materials on Unincorporated Business Associations (Foundation Press 3d ed. 2012); see also Melvin Aron Eisenberg and James D. Cox, An Introduction to Agency, Partnerships, and LLCs (Foundation Press 6th ed. 2012); David G. Epstein et al., Business Structures (West Group 2002); William A. Gregory & Thomas R. Hurst, Unincorporated Business Associations (West Group 2d ed. 2002); J. Dennis Hynes & Mark J. Lowenstein, Agency, Partnership, and the LLC (LexisNexis 8th ed. 2011); Larry E. Ribstein & Jeffrey M. Lipshaw, Unincorporated Business Associations (Anderson Publishing 4th ed. 2009); Gary S. Rosin & Michael L. Closen, Agency,

Law students taking a course in unincorporated business associations are the primary audience for this text, although I hope the analysis also will prove useful to lawyers and judges seeking a fresh perspective on corporate law problems. In addition, students taking a basic course in corporations or business associations may find this volume helpful as a more expansive treatment of the law of agency, partnership, and limited liability companies.

In preparing this volume, I sought to produce a readable text, with a style I hope is simple, direct, and reader-friendly. Even when dealing with complicated economic or financial issues, I tried to make them readily accessible to legal audiences. Hence, this text is neither an encyclopedia nor a traditional hornbook. You will find no stultifying discussions of minutiae (I hope) or lengthy string citations of decades-old cases (or, at least, not very many). A student who wants a section-by-section analysis of the Restatement (Third) of Agency should look elsewhere. My goal is to hit the highpoints—the topics most likely to be covered in a law school course.

In closing, I thank the able reference staff of the UCLA law library for their superb help.

Stephen M. Bainbridge

Los Angeles, California
2014

Partnerships, and Limited Liability Companies (Carolina Academic Press 2000). Although the organization of this text owes much to the Klein, Ramseyer, and Bainbridge casebook, I have tried to ensure that this text is usable with all of the major casebooks in the field.

CITATION FORMS

In general, citations herein follow standard Blue Book form. Having said that, however, I have kept footnotes to the bare minimum. In particular, I generally refrained from using "id.," short form citations, and jump cites. Hence, unlike most modern law review articles, not every statement in the book is footnoted. Instead, I typically provide a source citation and allow interested readers to seek out pinpoint citations on their own. I trust that this approach will help produce a more readable text. Finally, note that frequently referenced texts, statutes, and Restatements are cited in abbreviated form without dates, as follows:

DEMOTT: Deborah A. DeMott, Fiduciary Obligation, Agency and Partnership (1991)

DLLCA: Delaware Limited Liability Company Act, Del. Code Ann., tit. 6, chapter 18.

EISENBERG: Melvin Aron Eisenberg & James D. Cox, An Introduction to Agency, Partnerships, and LLCs (6th ed. 2012)

EPSTEIN ET AL.: David G. Epstein et al., Business Structures (2002)

Exchange Act: Securities Exchange Act of 1934, as amended, 15 U.S.C. § 78a *et seq.* (1999).

GREGORY & HURST: William A. Gregory & Thomas R. Hurst, Unincorporated Business Associations: Including Agency, Partnership, and Limited Liability Companies: Cases and Materials (2d ed. 2002)

KLEIN ET AL.: William A. Klein, J. Mark Ramseyer, & Stephen M. Bainbridge, Agency, Partnerships, and Limited Liability Entities: Cases and Materials on Unincorporated Business Associations (3d ed. 2012)

HYNES & LOWENSTEIN: J. Dennis Hynes and Mark J. Lowenstein, Agency Partnership, and the LLC: The Law of Unincorporated Business Enterprises—Cases, Materials, and Problems (8th ed. 2011).

HYNES: J. Dennis Hynes, Agency Partnership, and the LLC: The Law of Unincorporated Business Enterprises—Cases, Materials, and Problems (1998).

RESTATEMENT (SECOND): American Law Institute, Restatement (Second) of Agency (1958).

RESTATEMENT (THIRD): American Law Institute, Restatement (Third) of Agency (2006).

CITATION FORMS

RIBSTEIN & LIPSHAW: Larry E. Ribstein & Jeffrey M. Lipshaw, Unincorporated Business Entities (4th ed. 2009).

ROSIN & CLOSEN: Gary S. Rosin & Michael L. Closen, Agency, Partnerships, and Limited Liability Companies (2000).

Rule: A rule adopted by the Securities and Exchange Commission under either the Securities Act or the Securities Exchange Act, 17 C.F.R. § 230.100 *et seq.* (1999) and 17 C.F.R. § 240.0–1 *et seq.* (1999), respectively.

RULLCA: Revised Uniform Limited Liability Company Act (2006)

RULPA: [Revised] Uniform Limited Partnership Act (1976, with 1985 amendments).

Securities Act: Securities Act of 1933, as amended, 15 U.S.C. § 77a *et seq.* (1999).

ULLCA: Uniform Limited Liability Company Act (1996)

ULPA: Uniform Limited Partnership Act (1916).

UPA (1914): Uniform Partnership Act of 1914.

UPA (1997): Uniform Partnership Act of 1997 (also known as the Revised Uniform Partnership Act).

SUMMARY OF CONTENTS

TABLE OF CONTENTS

AGENCY, PARTNERSHIPS & LLCs

SECOND EDITION

Chapter 1

INTRODUCTION: A TYPOLOGY OF BUSINESS ASSOCIATIONS

It is useful to think of the statutes governing different types of business organizations as standard-form contracts. When two or more persons enter into a business relationship, they are undertaking an inherently contractual act. They must specify a host of rules to govern their relationship: what are their respective rights and duties, powers and obligations. If the parties choose to structure their relationship as a legally recognized form of business organization, however, much of this work already will have been accomplished. The applicable statute provides a sort of standardized contract, which lowers bargaining and other transaction costs by providing a set of default rules the parties can adopt off-the-rack. At the same time, because most statutory rules in this area are merely default rules, it is possible to modify the standard form contract when and as necessary to more closely tailor the firm to the clients' needs.

Until recently, the only important standard form contracts provided by most states were the corporation, the general partnership, and the limited partnership.[1] In the late 1980s, however, states began adding a fourth standard form contract to this short list of options: the limited liability company (LLC). In more recent years, even more options have emerged in the form of limited liability partnerships (LLPs) and limited liability limited partnerships (LLLPs).

Given the wide array of organizational forms now available to the transaction planner, how does one decide which is the right starting form for a particular client? A very useful approach is to focus on the six key attributes of any business organization: Does

---

[1] A number of minor forms linger on in most states, but are of rapidly diminishing significance. Among these are: (1) The joint stock company, which has attributes of both the corporation and a partnership. The company issues ownership certificates in the form of stock, which its shareholders are free to sell, but shareholders are liable for all debts and other obligations of the company. (2) The business trust, which has continuing importance due mainly to its use by real estate investment trusts (REITs) and mutual funds. The business trust is established under a declaration of trust, just like a standard trust, pursuant to which legal title to the trust assets is vested in the trustees who then issue transferable participation certificates to the beneficiaries. The trust participation certificates resemble corporate stock. (3) The mutual association, which is a form of cooperative in which members receive shares that entitle them to vote on association affairs and receive income in the form of dividends. Many financial institutions, especially savings and loans and insurers, are organized as mutual associations. And the list of even less important forms goes on and on.

1

the organization require formal creation under state law? Does the organization have a legal personality separate from that of its owners? Do the organization's default decisionmaking rules separate ownership and control? Does the organizational form have freely alienable ownership interests? Does the organization have a potentially indefinite duration? Does the organization provide limited liability for its owners? Matching the answers to these questions to the needs of the client usually is the best place to start when choosing an organizational form.[2] Each of these attributes will be discussed in far greater detail during the course of this text, but an overview at the outset may prove helpful.

I.   The Agency Relationship

Agency is the most pervasive form of business relationship. Just as a sole proprietor and his single employee are in an agency relationship, so are a Fortune 500 company and its president. As a result, both the Wall Street lawyer working on mega-billion dollar deals and the small-town lawyer setting up a mom-and-pop operation routinely encounter problems of agency law. In this section, however, we focus on the familiar concept of an agency relationship within a simple sole proprietorship.[3]

An agency relationship comes into existence when there is a manifestation by the principal of consent that the agent act on his behalf and subject to his control, and the agent consents to so act.[4] The requisite manifestation of consent can be implied from the circumstances, which makes it possible for the parties to have formed a legally effective agency relationship without realizing they had done so. The purpose of the relationship need not be a business one; in theory, if you send a friend to the vending machine to get you a soda, you have retained an agent.

Formalities of Creation. At common law, there are no formalities associated with the creation of a sole proprietorship.[5] As a result, the sole proprietorship is one of the two default types of business organizations, in the sense that it can be created without any formal action and, in fact, can be created without the owner

---

[2] Despite the wide array of "off-the-rack" statutory choices now available to the transaction planner, the business lawyer still often must tailor the chosen form to more precisely fit the client's needs. Typically, this will require identifying some attribute of the chosen form that is a poor fit for the particular client and determining how that attribute can be modified by contract or otherwise. We shall frequently see examples of such tweaking as we go forward.

[3] A sole proprietorship is an unincorporated business owned by a single person. It may or may not have employee-agents. There are more sole proprietorships in the U.S. than any other form of business organization; indeed, there are almost 3 times as many sole proprietorships as all other forms of business firms combined.

[4] RESTATEMENT (SECOND) §1.

[5] ROSIN & CLOSEN at 4 ("Because there is no separate legal entity, there is no general statute which governs the formation and operation of a sole proprietorship.").

even being aware that he has done so.[6] (The other is the general partnership.)

Unity of Ownership and Control. As a legal matter, the proprietor both owns and controls the sole proprietorship. This is true even if the proprietor hires an agent to whom substantial responsibility is delegated. Recall that the very definition of the agency relationship requires the principal have the right to control the agent's conduct. Agency law supplements the proprietor's control over the agent's behavior by imposing fiduciary duties on the agent. Of course, in many cases, the principal simply fires a misbehaving agent, rather than suing the agent for a breach of one of these duties.

Legal Personality. A sole proprietorship has no legal existence or identity separate from that of its owner. Although the owner may maintain some degree of separation between his personal life and the business, as by maintaining separate accounts and records, there is no legal distinction between the owner's personal assets and the business' assets.

Duration. A sole proprietorship has an indefinite duration, but not a perpetual one. Unlike a corporation, whose legal existence can continue long after its founders die, a sole proprietorship's life is coterminous with that of its owner.

At common law, the agency relationship (in the absence of agreement to the contrary) was said to be "at will," which meant that either party was free to terminate the relationship at any time. The principal's right to unilaterally terminate the relationship by firing the agent has been limited recently by judicial and legislative developments giving some agents some rights to continued employment. Keeping clients up-to-date on new decisions or statutes that erode the "employment at will" doctrine is an important part of being a business lawyer.

Free Transferability. The sole proprietor is always free to sell the business to another party. If the proprietor has hired an agent, a sale may terminate the agency relationship, depending on the nature of the agreement of the parties, but the agent has no right to block the sale.

Unlimited Liability. As noted above, the sole proprietorship's lack of a separate legal personality results in unlimited personal

---

[6] In some states, however, the proprietor must register under a Fictitious Business Name statute in order to conduct business under a name other than the proprietor's own. In addition, if the proprietor hires an agent, some agency relationships are subject to additional statutory requirements, such as that the relationship be manifested by a writing. These requirements vary considerably from state to state and from occupation to occupation.

liability on the proprietor's part for the business' obligations. This rule becomes especially important when the proprietor hires an agent. Agency law imposes liability on a principal for certain torts committed by his agent and for certain contracts entered into by the agent on the principal's behalf.

II. The General Partnership

A partnership is an association of two or more persons to carry on as co-owners a business for profit. Modern partnership law is a mixture of common law decisions and statutory rules. Almost all states adopted the Uniform Partnership Act of 1914 (UPA), with only minor variations among them. Today, however, most states have adopted the Uniform Partnership Act of 1997. We shall typically refer to these statutes as the UPA (1914) and UPA (1997), respectively.

Formalities of Creation. Under both the UPA (1914) and UPA (1997), forming a partnership involves none of the formalities required in the corporate context. All that is required is an agreement, explicit or implicit, between two or more people to act as co-owners of a business for profit. Like the sole proprietorship, the general partnership thus is a default form of business organization that "exists as soon as two or more people start doing business together without choosing another form of business" organization.[7] Perhaps oddly, it is thus possible for two people to form a partnership without realizing they have done so. As with agency relationships, however, some partnerships may be subject to special statutory requirements.

Unity of Ownership and Control. All partners have an equal right to participate in the partnership's management on a one-person/one-vote basis, with most decisions being made by majority vote of the partners. In the small firm setting, this rule is probably appropriate; if three people form a partnership to run a music store, the one-partner, one-vote rule usually makes sense. In the large firm setting, however, democratic firm government can become unmanageable. Consider, for example, the case of a large national law firm with many offices in different parts of the country and perhaps several hundred partners. It would be unworkable for such a firm to try to make every decision, or even every important decision, by majority rule.

Fortunately, the law of partnership is perhaps the most flexible branch of organization law. Very few partnership rules are mandatory. Instead, most of partnership law consists of default

---

[7] Hynes at 6.

rules.[8] This allows the partners to agree to just about any governance system they want. Accordingly, we see a variety of decisionmaking structures ranging from partnerships run by a single more or less dictatorial managing partner, to partnerships that delegate substantial amounts of authority to one or more committees that make decisions by consensus among the committee members, to partnerships (even rather large ones) that retain the traditional one-partner/one-vote democratic model.

Quasi-Separate Legal Personality. A theoretical debate raged for many years over whether a partnership is an entity separate from the partners or merely an aggregation of the partners. The answer to that question has a number of practical consequences. For example, if the partnership is an entity, it can sue and be sued in its own name. If it is an aggregation of individuals, however, each and every partner must be joined to a lawsuit involving the partnership. Numerous other examples could be cited, such as the names in which partnership property must be registered on a deed or certificate of title. The UPA (1914) does not come down squarely on one side or the other of this debate. Instead, the statute treats the partnership as an entity for some purposes and as an aggregate for others.

Knowing the circumstances under which each approach would be taken by statute or a court (and the implications of that approach) used to be an important, if mundane, aspect of practicing this branch of organization law. Today, however, most states have adopted separate statutes treating the partnership as a separate legal entity in most situations in which the partnership's status matters. The UPA (1997) codifies this result by declaring the partnership to be a legal entity separate from its partners.

Duration. Under the UPA (1914), a partnership dissolves whenever one partner dies, resigns, or otherwise leaves the partnership. As a legal matter, a dissolution leads to a winding up of the firm. As such, the legal consequences of a dissolution can be a significant drawback to the partnership form of doing business. Consider our earlier example of a large national law firm: If the law firm dissolved every time a partner died, retired or jumped ship, operating as a partnership would be highly impractical. Here again, the flexibility of partnership law provides a solution; within certain limits the partners can agree that the firm will continue to function even when one member withdraws. The UPA (1997), moreover, adopts a complex regime under which partners may sometimes

---

[8] A mandatory rule is one that the parties cannot modify by private agreement (although they may be able to evade it by some stratagem). A default rule is one that applies only if the parties' agreement is silent on the question and, thus, is one the parties may freely modify by agreement among themselves.

disassociate themselves from the firm without triggering a dissolution.

Limited Transferability of Ownership Interests. No one can become a partner without the unanimous consent of all other partners. A partner thus is effectively barred from selling his membership in the firm. A partner may assign his interest in the partnership to another party, but that interest consists only of the right to receive his share of partnership profits and losses. As a result, the assignee does not become a partner of the firm and has no rights vis-à-vis the firm other than the right to receive whatever profits are owed to the assignor partner. These rules significantly impede transferability of a partner's rights in the business, although they do not wholly preclude transfers.

Unlimited Liability. Under the UPA (1914), each partner is jointly and severally liable for a tort or breach of trust committed by another partner if committed within the scope of the firm's business. In addition, each partner is jointly liable for all other partnership debts and obligations. The UPA (1997) rules are the same, except that partners are jointly and severally liable for both types of obligations.

Because the partnership can be held liable for the acts of its non-partner agents, so too can the individual partners. The resulting liability exposure is compounded by the fact that each and every partner is an agent of the partnership with respect to its business and thus can enter into contracts binding the entire partnership. The partners' liability exposure is unlimited, moreover, so that each partner could be forced to pay his share of a partnership obligation to the full extent of his personal assets. This rule may be the single most important deterrent to doing business in the partnership form.

All 50 states have now created a variant on the general partnership called the limited liability partnership (LLP).[9] Unlike the traditional limited partnership, a LLP essentially is a general partnership that provides limited liability for all partners (in many states for tort claims only, however). Unlike a standard general partnership, formation of a LLP requires filing an appropriate application with the requisite state official (usually the state's Secretary of State). In many states, such as California, only members of certain professions—typically law, accounting, medicine, and the like—can form a LLP.

---

[9] *See* ROSIN & CLOSEN at 6 ("Wyoming was the last American state to enact LLP legislation").

The Limited Partnership. In a general partnership, there is one type of investor: a general partner having full rights of management, control and profit-sharing. Limited partnerships have two classes of partners: one or more general partners, whose rights are largely the same as in a general partnership; and one or more limited partners, who have much less expansive rights, but whose obligations are correspondingly limited. In effect, management of the limited partnership is vested in the general partners.

Limited partnerships likely would have long since faded out of existence except for certain quirks of the federal tax laws, which made them a tax advantageous vehicle in some situations. Tax reforms during the last decade have largely eliminated these advantages and the limited partnership may gradually fade away.

III. The Limited Liability Company

The limited liability company is an unincorporated business organization providing its members with pass through tax treatment, limited liability, and the ability to actively participate in firm management. All 50 states now have LLC statutes. As a result of its increasingly widespread availability and the various advantages it possesses over other forms of business organizations, the LLC has exploded onto the scene in the last decade. (See Figure 1.1).

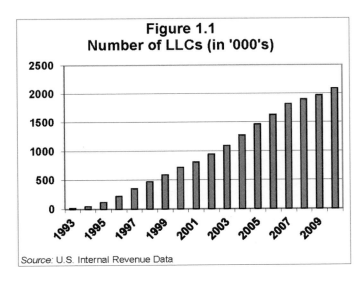

Figure 1.1
Number of LLCs (in '000's)

Source: U.S. Internal Revenue Data

Because it is a unique entity, differing in important ways from other types of business organizations, it is important to avoid thinking of the LLC as a partnership with limited liability. Granted, it is very useful to draw comparisons between LLCs and more familiar types of business organizations, but don't lose sight of the fact that the LLC is unique and should be treated as such.

Formalities of Creation. AN LLC requires formal creation, which is effected by filing articles of organization with the appropriate state official.[10] In addition, the LLC may adopt an operating agreement, which fulfills many of the same functions as a partnership agreement or corporate bylaws. Finally, the LLC must comply with various additional formalities, such as maintaining a registered office and keeping certain records.

Unity of Ownership and Control. Management of the LLC is vested in its members. Unlike the partnership's one-man/one-vote rule, the number of votes cast by each member of an LLC is determined by his proportional share in the book value of the membership interests.

The rules just discussed are both subject to any contrary provisions of the articles of organization and operating agreement. The LLC thus provides substantial flexibility in structuring the firm's decisionmaking processes. If the articles of organization so provide, the members may elect a manager to whom substantial authority may be delegated. Unless the articles provide to the contrary, the LLC's members lose control over areas delegated to the manager. Alternatively, one can have multiple managers, which allows committee management or even a corporate-like board of managers. The flexibility provided by the LLC statute is achieved at the cost of specificity. If the LLC's decisionmaking structure is to vary from the standard form contract, detailed contractual provisions are thus essential if later disputes are to be avoided.

Separate Legal Personality. AN LLC is a legal entity, with a personality separate from that of its members. Hence, the LLC may sue and be sued in its own name. The LLC also may own property in its own name. And so on.

Duration. The duration rules in most LLC statutes resemble those applicable to general partnerships, except that many LLC statutes formerly provided a maximum number of years during which the business may operate. The Delaware LLC statute, for example, formerly provided that the LLC must dissolve not later than 30 years after the LLC is formed. These provisions were designed to comply with old tax requirements discussed below. With the more recent liberalization of the tax laws applicable to LLCs, these requirements have fallen by the wayside.

---

[10] The articles of organization are comparable to corporate articles of incorporation and are treated as such by the statute with respect to such questions as amendment and filing.

Limited Transferability. The default rule is that admission of a new member requires the unanimous consent all members. The assignee of a member's interest receives only an entitlement to the assignor's share of profits. The rules restricting transferability are subject to any contrary agreement the members wish to make, but tax considerations and the practical limitations imposed by the absence of a secondary trading market often render transfer of LLC interests impractical.

Limited Liability. Members of an LLC, like shareholders of a corporation, are not personally liable for the firm's obligations. As we shall see, however, courts have routinely extended the corporate law doctrine of piercing the corporate veil to the LLC context. If such cases, the veil piercing remedy allows LLC members to be held personally liable for the firm's obligations.

IV. The Corporation

For the most part, the corporation lies outside the scope of this text. Yet, by most measures except sheer number of firms, the corporation is the predominant form of business organization in the United States. According to recent census data, U.S. business organizations include approximately 17 million unincorporated proprietorships, 1.7 million partnerships, and 4.6 million corporations. (See Figure 1.2.)

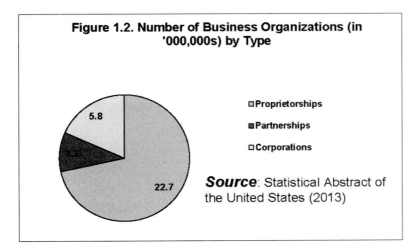

Figure 1.2. Number of Business Organizations (in '000,000s) by Type

□ Proprietorships
▣ Partnerships
□ Corporations

5.8
3.2
22.7

Source: Statistical Abstract of the United States (2013)

Although corporations thus account for only about one-fifth of all business organizations, they bring in almost 90% of all business receipts.[11] (See Figure 1.3.) In addition, many doctrines of unincorporated business association law can be understood only in

---

[11] U.S. Census Bureau, Statistical Abstract of the United States 545 (1999).

relation to their corporate law counterparts. Accordingly, a brief overview of the corporate form seems appropriate.[12]

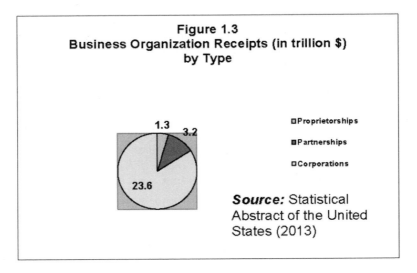

Figure 1.3
Business Organization Receipts (in trillion $)
by Type

1.3   3.2

☐Proprietorships

◼Partnerships

☐Corporations

23.6

Source: Statistical Abstract of the United States (2013)

Formalities of Creation. Someone creates a corporation by drafting articles of incorporation that comply with the statutory requirements of the state of incorporation.[13] The articles are then filed with the appropriate state agency, which in most states is the Secretary of State's office. In some states, the Secretary of State's office then issues a document called the certificate of incorporation. In other states, the Secretary of State will simply return a copy of the articles of incorporation along with a receipt to the incorporator. At this point, the corporation has come into existence. The initial board of directors thereupon holds an organizational meeting at which corporate bylaws are adopted,[14] officers are appointed, and other loose ends are tied up.

---

[12] For a more detailed treatment of the corporation, see Stephen M. Bainbridge, Corporate Law (2009).

[13] The articles of incorporation are the most important of the corporation's organic documents. The articles set out the corporation's essential basic rules of the road—the basic terms under which it will operate. Each state corporate statute sets forth the minimum provisions the articles must contain. Model Business Corporation Act § 2.02, for example, requires the articles to include the corporation's name, the number of shares the corporation is authorized to issue, the name and address of the corporation's registered agent, and the name and address of the incorporator. In addition, the comments to § 2.02 list numerous other provisions that must be included in the articles if the corporation wishes to avail itself of certain statutory options. Among the more important of these options are provisions relating to division of shares into classes and series and liability of directors.

[14] A corporation's bylaws are its internal operating rules. Other than certain provisions that must be contained in the articles of incorporation, most of the corporation's internal affairs will be governed by the bylaws. Virtually anything may be contained in the bylaws. Model Business Corporation Act § 2.06, for example, allows the bylaws to "contain any provision for managing the business and

Separation of Ownership and Control. Corporations differ from most other forms of business organizations in that ownership of the firm is formally separated from its control. Although shareholders nominally "own" the corporation, they have essentially no decisionmaking powers, other than the right to elect the firm's directors and to vote on certain very significant corporate actions.[15] Rather, management of the firm is vested by statute in the hands of the board of directors, who in turn delegate the day-to-day running of the firm to its officers, who in turn delegate some responsibilities to the company's employees.[16]

Legal Personality. As a legal matter, the corporation is an entity wholly separate from the people who own it and work for it. For most purposes the corporation is treated as though it were a legal person, having most of the rights and obligations of real people, and having an identity wholly apart from its constituents. Corporate law statutes, for example, typically give a corporation "the same powers as an individual to do all things necessary or convenient to carry out its business and affairs."[17]

Perpetual Duration. A corporation is said to have perpetual duration. A more accurate statement, however, is that the corporation has an indefinite legal existence that can be terminated only in rare circumstances. Among these are liquidation in bankruptcy, a vote of the shareholders to dissolve the company, an involuntary dissolution suit, or a merger or consolidation with another corporation.

---

regulating the affairs of the corporation that is not inconsistent with law or the articles of incorporation."

[15] The statutory separation of ownership and control applies to closely held corporations. Vesting formal decisionmaking power in the board of directors of a close corporation, however, is often unacceptable to the shareholders of such a firm. In this respect, a close corporation often closely resembles a partnership that for some business reason has been organized as a corporation. Under special statutory provisions, close corporations can be set up to give shareholders extensive management powers resembling those of partners.

[16] The corporation's senior employees are referred to as its managers (known collectively as the corporation's management). Officers are the most senior managers. A corporation's officers typically include its president (or chief executive officer), one or more vice-presidents, a treasurer or chief financial officer, and a secretary.

[17] MODEL BUS. CORP. ACT § 3.02 (1984). As a legal person, a corporation has most (but not all) of the constitutional rights possessed by natural persons. The constitutional rights possessed by corporations include: Freedom of speech, First Nat'l Bank of Boston v. Belloti, 435 U.S. 765, 784 (1978); Fourth Amendment protection against unreasonable searches and seizures, Hale v. Henkel, 201 U.S. 43, 76 (1906); equal protection of the law under the Fourteenth Amendment, Santa Clara County v. Southern Pacific Railroad Co., 118 U.S. 394, 416 (1886); and due process of law under the Fifth and Fourteenth Amendments, Minneapolis & St. Louis Railway Co. v. Beckwith, 129 U.S. 26, 28 (1888). Constitutional rights not possessed by corporations include: Fifth Amendment privilege against self-incrimination, Hale v. Henkel, 201 U.S. 43, 69–70 (1906); protection of the privileges and immunities clause of the Fourteenth Amendment or of the comity clause of Article IV, see Blake v. McClung, 172 U.S. 239 (1898) (comity clause).

Free Transferability of Shares. One of the great advantages of the corporate form is that shares of stock are freely transferable. Absent special contractual restrictions, shareholders are free to sell their stock to anybody at any price. A transfer of stock has no effect on the corporation, except that there is now a new voter of those shares. For public corporations, this process is greatly facilitated by the secondary trading markets.

Contractual exceptions to the rule of free transferability are often found in close corporations, which is one of the many ways in which such firms resemble partnerships more than other corporations. Although shares of stock in a closely held corporation are freely transferable in theory, the lack of a readily available secondary trading market for such shares means they seldom are easily transferable in practice. Moreover, investors in a closely held corporation often prefer to restrict transferability. Like any other personal relationship, the success or failure of a small business often depends upon maintaining a rather delicate balance between the owners. Free transferability of ownership interests threatens that balance. In closely held corporations, shareholders therefore often agree to special contractual restrictions on the alienability of shares.

Limited Liability. The limited liability doctrine holds that shareholders of a corporation are not personally liable for corporate obligations and thus put at risk only the amount of money that they invested in buying their shares. Suppose, for example, that an employee of Acme Co. commits a tort against Paula Plaintiff. Under the tort and agency law doctrine of vicarious liability, Acme is held liable to Plaintiff for $10 million in damages resulting from the employee's tortious conduct. Acme has only $1 million in assets. The limited liability rule bars Plaintiff from seeking to recover the unsatisfied $9 million remainder of her claim from Acme's shareholders. The shareholders' investment in Acme stock may be worthless if Acme becomes bankrupt as a result of Plaintiff's lawsuit, but the shareholders will have lost only that portion of their wealth they invested in Acme.

In rare circumstances, courts may invoke an equitable exception to the limited liability rule called "piercing the corporate veil." If invoked, the veil piercing remedy allows shareholders to be held personally liable for the corporation's obligations.[18] In the

---

[18] See generally Janet Cooper Alexander, Unlimited Shareholder Liability Through a Procedural Lens, 106 HARV. L. REV. 387 (1992); Stephen M. Bainbridge, Abolishing Veil Piercing, 26 J. CORP. L. 479 (2001); Richard A. Booth, Limited Liability and the Efficient Allocation of Resources, 89 NW. U. L. REV. 140 (1994); Franklin A. Gevurtz, Piercing Piercing: An Attempt to Lift the Veil of Confusion Surrounding the Doctrine of Piercing the Corporate Veil, 76 OR. L. REV. 853 (1997); Joseph A. Grundfest, The Limited Future of Unlimited Liability: A Capital Markets Perspective, 102 YALE L.J. 387 (1992); Robert W. Hamilton and Larry E. Ribstein,

immediately preceding example, if Paula Plaintiff successfully invokes the veil piercing doctrine, the court will allow her to recover the unsatisfied portion of her claim from Acme's shareholders.

V. Choice of Form

"One size fits all" is a lie. No one type of business organization is always appropriate. Rather, one of the business lawyer's most important jobs is considering the unique facts and circumstances of the particular client and providing advice as to which organizational form best serves that client's needs. This sort of advice requires a detailed knowledge of not only business organization law (i.e., corporate, agency, partnership, and LLC statutes and cases), but also tax, labor, and a host of other laws. In particular, tax considerations often play a key role in making the choice of form.

A. Tax Considerations

It is the rare client who is not concerned with minimizing his tax liability.[19] Accordingly, the tax treatment of the various types of business organizations often drives the choice of form.

Incorporating a business exposes its shareholders to double taxation. If a corporation is profitable, and the owners wish to pay a dividend, taxes will be paid both by the corporation and the shareholders. From the corporation's perspective, the dividends are not deductible because they are regarded as being paid from after-tax profits. From the shareholder's perspective, the dividends are regarded as ordinary income and are taxed as such.

In contrast, partnerships and LLCs can qualify for pass through taxation. They merely file an informational return,

---

Limited Liability and the Real World, 54 WASH. & LEE L. REV. 687 (1997); Henry Hansmann and Reinier Kraakman, Toward Unlimited Shareholder Liability for Corporate Torts, 100 YALE L.J. 1879 (1991); Robert W. Hillman, Limited Liability in Historical Perspective, 54 WASH. & LEE L. REV. 615 (1997); William A. Klein & Eric M. Zolt, Business Form, Limited Liability, and Tax Regimes: Lurching Toward a Coherent Outcome?, 66 U. COLO. L. REV. 1001 (1995); Stephen B. Presser, Thwarting the Killing of the Corporation: Limited Liability, Democracy, and Economics, 87 NW. U. L. REV. 148 (1992); Larry Ribstein, Limited Liability Unlimited, 24 DEL. J. CORP. L. 407 (1999); Larry E. Ribstein, Limited Liability and Theories of the Corporation, 50 MD. L. REV. 80 (1991); Robert B. Thompson, Piercing the Corporate Veil: An Empirical Study, 76 CORNELL L. REV. 1036 (1991).

[19] Entertainer Arthur Godfrey once remarked: "I'm proud to be paying taxes in the United States. The only thing is—I could be just as proud for half the money." In contrast, fellow entertainer Will Rogers thought few of us share Godfrey's pride: "The income tax has made more liars out of the American people than golf has." Judge Learned Hand confirmed one's entitlement to minimize one's tax burden, at least so long as one stops short of Will Roger's approach: "Any one may so arrange his affairs that his taxes shall be as low as possible; he is not bound to choose that pattern which will best pay the Treasury; there is not even a patriotic duty to increase one's taxes."

reporting any gain or loss. The firm's ordinary gains and losses are "passed through" to the owners as ordinary income or loss.

An example may be helpful. Alice Little and Bob Brown own a grocery store. The business operates on a calendar year basis. Last year the business brought in $300,000 in gross income and had $175,000 in deductible expenses, for total taxable income of $125,000. Under a long-standing agreement, Little and Brown divide profits equally at the end of each calendar year. Little and Brown are both single with no dependents; assume they have no exemptions or deductions.

Assuming the store is organized as a corporation, how much after-tax income will Little and Brown realize? Assuming an effective 25% corporate tax rate,[20] the corporation will pay $31,250 in federal income taxes, leaving $93,750 in after-tax earnings. Assuming all after-tax earnings are paid out as dividends to Little and Brown, they will each receive $46,875. Assuming an effective individual tax rate of 36%, Little and Brown will each pay taxes of $16,875, leaving them with $30,000 in after-tax income.

If the store is organized as a partnership (or LLC) qualifying for pass through taxation, Little and Brown will end up with much larger after-tax incomes. As a pass through entity, the partnership pays no taxes. Accordingly, Little and Brown will each receive $62,500 in pre-tax income (half of the business' entire $125,000 profit). Again assuming an effective individual tax rate of 36%, Little and Brown will each pay income tax of $22,500, leaving them with after-tax incomes of 40,000. All other things being equal, which of course they rarely are, Little and Brown obviously will prefer to organize their business as a pass through entity.

Under the so-called Kintner regulations, the Internal Revenue Service formerly considered six factors in determining whether an unincorporated association should be taxed as though it were a corporation: (1) associates; (2) a business purpose; (3) continuity of life; (4) centralization of management; (5) limited liability; and (6) free transferability of ownership. Because all partnerships and LLCs meet the first two requirements, they could be disregarded. If the entity in question met three or more of the remaining four criteria, it was treated as a corporation for tax purposes. Because LLCs possess limited liability it therefore used to be important that the transaction planner structure the entity so as to avoid at least two of the other three characteristics that distinguish partnerships from corporations for tax purposes; namely, free transferability of

---

[20] We are ignoring the complications caused by the progressive nature of our tax system, in which taxpayers (both corporate and individual) pay increasing marginal tax rates.

ownership, continuity of life, and centralized management. In 1996, however, the IRS adopted so-called "check the box" regulations that allow the partnership or LLC's members to elect between corporate and partnership tax treatment. The check the box regulations thus allow much greater organizational flexibility.

At first blush, the pass through treatment of partnerships and LLCs appears to be a substantial advantage for small businesses, because they allow one to avoid the double taxation of corporate profits. But it is easy to overstate the importance of tax treatment in choosing a business structure. Many small businesses qualify for treatment as an S corporation, which is taxed on a pass through basis. To be sure, an S corporation is subject to various restrictions that make it undesirable for some firms. But even so, there are many well-established methods by which non-S corporation closely held corporations can reduce the impact of double taxation to a *de minimis* level. Probably the most commonly used of these is distribution of profits in the form of salary rather than dividends. So long as the salary amounts are reasonable, the IRS will permit the corporation to deduct salary paid to shareholder-officers, which minimizes the effect of double taxation.

B.   The Import of Limited Liability

At first blush, limited liability appears to make the corporation or the LLC a far more attractive choice than the partnership. On closer examination, however, the advantage of limited liability is somewhat overstated. On the one hand, the limited liability doctrine often fails to provide complete protection. Many contract creditors, for example, insist that shareholders of a closely held corporation or members of an LLC guarantee the firm's debts. In addition, the common law doctrine of veil piercing enables courts to impose personal liability on shareholders (and presumably members of an LLC) in appropriate cases. On the other hand, adequate capital reserves and insurance can provide partners with substantial protection despite their nominally unlimited liability.

C.   Summary

It is worth reiterating that no one form of business is always appropriate in all settings for all clients. It is also worth reiterating that there are many additional relevant factors that are beyond the scope of this text. As a general rule of thumb, however, it is safe to say that the corporation is the most advantageous form for virtually all large businesses with widely dispersed investors and operations. Limited liability, free transferability of shares, and the separation of ownership and control make it possible to attract large sums of money from passive investors, which is precisely what such an enterprise requires. It also seems safe to assume that the LLC will emerge as the dominant form for small firms with a few investors who are actively involved in the operation of the business. Although the importance of pass through tax treatment and limited liability can be overstated, the LLC's combination of the two is a hard package to beat, as illustrated by the dramatic increase in LLCs reported in Figure 1.1 above.

Chapter 2

AGENCY

The ability of an agent to act on behalf of a principal is the key feature of the modern agency relationship. In most ancient legal systems, one could not act through an agent. Contracts had to be made in person, for example.[1] Medieval English common law, however, gradually developed the idea of an agent as a representative of the principal with power to bind the principal to a contract with some third party.[2] At first, the principal was bound only if he specifically instructed the agent to make the contract. The modern conception of an agent with general authority to make contracts binding on the principal without specific instructions came from the law merchant that governed trade fairs and caravans in medieval Europe. By the middle of the seventeenth century, the law merchant had been incorporated into English common law.[3] Among other things, this development led to the origin of our modern law of agency. By 1698, accordingly, Chief Justice Holt of the King's Bench was able to confidently opine that:

> For whoever employs another, is answerable for him, and undertakes for his care to all that make use of him. The act of a servant *is* the act of his master, where he acts by authority of the master.[4]

Here we find the central tenet of modern agency law; namely, the liability of the principal in both tort and contract by virtue of the agent's dealings with third parties.

Today we thus can speak of the "principal—agent—third-party" triangle (see Figure 2.1), which illustrates that the existence of (1) an agency relationship between the principal (P) and the agent (A) means that (2) words or conduct by the agent vis-à-vis the third party may create (3) a legal relationship between the principal and third party, who may never meet, imposing rights and duties on one or both of them.

---

[1] HYNES at 73.

[2] *See* GREGORY & HURST at 2.

[3] *See, e.g.,* Woodward v. Rowe, 87 Eng. Rep. 84 (K.B. 1666) (holding that the law of merchants was part of the law of the land).

[4] Jones v. Hart, 90 Eng. Rep. 1255 (K.B. 1698).

Figure 2.1

The Principal—Agent—Third-Party (PAT) Triangle

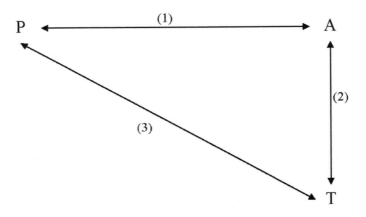

Of course, things are never quite this simple. Principals may be liable on an estoppel theory, for example, for the acts of persons who appear to be their agents but with whom they in fact have no agency relationship. The liability of principals for the tortuous conduct of their agents depends not merely on the existence of an agency relationship between them, but also on the type of agency relationship that exists. And so on.

The agency relationship is the most common form of business organization. Not only is the relationship between the sole proprietor and her employees an agency one, but so is the relationship between a Fortune 500 corporation and its officers. Agency relationships can be found in all sorts of commercial settings, including very complicated transactions, such as franchising, but also in very simple noncommercial settings, such as where one friend borrows another's car.

In most states, agency law is not codified by statute, as such, although some aspects of certain agency relationships are incidentally affected by statutes of general applicability.[5] Instead, agency law remains mainly a common law subject. In general, the single most influential source of legal rules in this area remains the American Law Institute's Restatement of Agency. The first Restatement of Agency was published in 1933. The Restatement

---

[5] For example, some types of agents must be licensed by the state in order to act on behalf of their principal. In seven states, agency law has been codified by statute: Alabama, California, Georgia, Louisiana, Montana, North Dakota, and South Dakota.

(Second) of Agency was published in 1958 and remains influential because of the considerable body of case law applying it. The current Restatement (Third) was published in 2006 and is now the most up-to-date authoritative exposition of agency law. As with all restatements, a so-called Reporter drafted the "black letter" law sections setting out the Reporter's understanding of the law, which are accompanied by explanatory comments, notes on legal sources, and illustrations.

I.   Who Is an Agent?

The Restatement (Third) defines the agency relationship as "the fiduciary relationship that arises when one person (a "principal") manifests assent to another person (an "agent") that the agent shall act on the principal's behalf and subject to the principal's control, and the agent manifests assent or otherwise consents so to act."[6] All of which is true, but perhaps not terribly enlightening. So let's break it down.

A.   Breaking Down the Restatement (Third) Definition

1.   "A person."

As used in the Restatement (Third), the word "person" includes not only natural persons but also legal persons. Accordingly, for example, a corporation can serve as either a principal or as an agent.[7]

2.   The Requisite "Manifestation" and Proof of Agency

The principal must manifest to the agent the principal's assent that the agent should act on the principal's behalf and subject to the principal's control.[8] The requisite manifestation need not be made

---

[6] RESTATEMENT (THIRD) § 1.01.

[7] *See* RESTATEMENT (THIRD) § 1.04(5) ("A person is (a) an individual; (b) an organization or association that has legal capacity to possess rights and incur obligations; (c) a government, political subdivision, or instrumentality or entity created by government; or (d) any other entity that has legal capacity to possess rights and incur obligations.").

[8] Suppose Pam's words or conducts reasonably lead Ted to believe that Ann was Pam's agent. A true agency relationship between Pam and Ann does not exist in this setting, because Pam did not communicate her assent to Ann. A so-called "apparent agency" may exist on these facts, however. *See, e.g.,* De Lage Landen Financial Services, Inc. v. Rasa Floors, LP, 792 F.Supp.2d 812, 841 (E.D.Pa. 2011) ("Apparent agency exists when a principal has not expressly granted the power to bind the principal but has led persons with whom [the] agent deals to believe that the power has been granted, for instance where the principal knowingly permits the agent to exercise such power or if the principal holds the agent out as possessing such power"; internal quotation marks omitted); Spurgeon v. Egger, 989 So.2d 901, 905 (Miss. App. 2007) ("An apparent or ostensible agent is one whom the principal has intentionally or by want of ordinary care induced third parties to believe is his agent, although no authority has been conferred on him either expressly or by implication.").

in writing or even orally, but may be implied from the parties' conduct.[9]

Conversely, the agent need not communicate its assent to so act to the principal. If Pam asks Ann to act on her half, and Ann does so, we may infer that Ann was Pam's agent, even absent any express communication by Ann to Pam.

If the existence of an agency relationship is contested in litigation, the burden of proof is on the party claiming an agency relationship exists.[10] While the existence of an agency relationship may be inferred from circumstantial evidence, the existence of an agency relationship may not be presumed.[11]

3. The Necessity of "Assent"

Restatement (Second) § 1(1) defined agency as "the fiduciary relation which results from the manifestation of consent by one person to another that the other shall act on his behalf and subject to his control, and consent by the other so to act." The drafters of the Restatement (Third) used the word "assent" rather than "consent." They explained that:

> In contrast to the formulation in Restatement Second, Agency § 1, the definition in this section refers to a principal's manifestation of "assent," not "consent." The different terminology is intended to emphasize that unexpressed reservations or limitations harbored by the principal do not restrict the principal's expression of consent to the agent. . . . A principal's manifestation of assent to an agency relationship may be informal, implicit, and nonspecific. . . .

> As to the agent, a relationship of agency as defined in this section requires that the agent "manifests assent or otherwise consents so to act," in contrast to the requirement in

---

[9] *See, e.g.,* M.D. & Assoc., Inc. v. Sears, Roebuck and Co., 749 S.W.2d 454, 456 (Mo. App. 1988) ("The existence of agency and the authority of an agent can be implied by proof of facts, circumstances, words, acts, and the conduct of the party to be charged with the agency. The prior conduct of the parties is a factor to be taken into account if such conduct is a part of the circumstances surrounding the transaction."; citations omitted); *see also* Carrier v. McLLarky, 693 A.2d 76, 78 (N.H. 1997); A. Gay Jenson Farms Co. v. Cargill, 309 N.W.2d 285, 290 (Minn. 1981).

[10] *See, e.g.,* B.J. McAdams, Inc. v. Best Refrigerated Express, Inc., 579 S.W.2d 608, 610 (Ala. 1979); Norton v. Martin, 703 S.W.2d 267, 272 (Tex. App. 1985); State Farm Mutual Auto. Ins. Co. v. Weisman, 441 S.E.2d 16, 19 (Va. 1994). The agency relationship must be proved by a preponderance of the evidence. Barbara Oil Co. v. Kansas Gas Supply Corp., 827 P.2d 24, 32 (Kan. 1992).

[11] *See* Trans Union Leasing Corp. v. Hamilton, 600 P.2d 256, 258 (N.M. 1979); Smith v. Leber, 209 P.2d 297, 301 (Wash. 1949); Pavlic v. Woodrum, 486 N.W.2d 533, 535 (Wis.Ct. App. 1992). The common law prohibition against presumptions of an agency relationship's existence has been overruled by statute in a few areas. *See, e.g.,* Schimmelpfennig v. Cutler, 783 A.2d 1033 (Conn. App. 2001) (discussing a statutory presumption that that the operator of motor vehicle is the agent of the vehicle's owner).

Restatement Second, Agency § 1 that the agent "consent." The formulation in this section, consistent with Restatement Second, recognizes that it is not necessary to the formation of a relationship of agency that the agent manifest assent to the principal, as when the agent performs the service requested by the principal following the principal's manifestation, or when the agent agrees to perform the service but does not so inform the principal and does not perform.[12]

The Restatement (Third) thus continues the longstanding rule that there must be an agreement between the principal and agent in order for an agency relationship to come into existence, but there need not be a contract between the parties.[13] This formulation, distinguishing between the necessary agreement and the unnecessary contract, reflects several basic principles of agency. First, while all agency relationships necessarily imply some agreement between the parties, the agreement need not be supported by legal consideration. Indeed, the agreement can be purely gratuitous.[14] Second, there typically does not need to be a formal or written agreement between the parties, because, at common law, there are no formalities associated with the creation of an agency relationship.[15] Finally, the capacity required to form an agency relationship differs from the capacity necessary to make a binding contract. A natural person has capacity to act as principal—i.e., to have a legally consequential act performed by an agent—if he has the capacity to do the act in person.[16] For example, suppose Pam is a minor who under applicable state contract law lacks capacity to make a binding contract. Because Pam would not

---

[12] Restatement (Third) § 1.01 cmt. d.

[13] A. Gay Jenson Farms Co. v. Cargill, 309 N.W.2d 285, 290 (Minn. 1981) ("In order to create an agency there must be an agreement, but not necessarily a contract between the parties.").

[14] *See* RESTATEMENT (THIRD) § 1.04(3) ("A gratuitous agent acts without a right to compensation."); *see, e.g.,* Maurillo v. Park Slope U-Haul, 606 N.Y.S.2d 243, 211 (App. Div. 1993) (holding that "members of a family may enter into a gratuitous agency relationship where there is no evidence of any payment incident to the agency relationship").

[15] The drafters of the Restatement (Third), however, explain that:

Creating actual authority . . . does not require a writing or other formality. However, legislation in many states imposes what is often termed an "equal dignity" requirement for the creation of authority or agency applicable to specific types of agreements. As with the Statute of Frauds more generally, the purpose is to prevent fraud and perjury by safeguarding the principal against agreements made by an agent who lacks authority. Under an equal-dignity rule, if a transaction is unenforceable unless the party to be charged has agreed in writing to be bound, an agent's authority to enter into such a transaction on behalf of a principal must likewise be in writing. Such rules also apply to ratification. If an agent acted with apparent authority . . . but no writing or record evidences the agent's authority, the principal is not bound to contracts or other transactions to which an equal-dignity rule applies.

RESTATEMENT (THIRD) § 3.02 cmt. b (citations omitted).

[16] RESTATEMENT (THIRD) § 3.04 cmt. b.

have the capacity to make a contract in person, Pam lacks capacity to retain an agent to do so on her behalf. Conversely, however, any person with the physical or mental ability to take action that affects the principal's legal relations has the capacity to be an agent.[17] Even though Pam is a minor who lacks capacity to make binding contracts on her own behalf, Pam nevertheless has capacity to act as Paula's agent and any contracts Pam makes on Paula's behalf will bind Paula.

The requisite consent may exist even where the parties are unaware that their relationship constitutes an agency relationship and did not intend for their relationship to carry with it the legal consequences of creating an agency relationship.[18] To be sure, there is no such thing as an "unwitting agent," in the sense that every agency relationship requires knowing consent by both parties.[19] What then is it to which the parties must "consent"? The principal must consent that the agent shall act on the principal's behalf and subject to the principal's control. The agent must consent to so act. If they do so, they have an agency relationship, even if they did not "consent" to the legal consequences that follow.

4. *"On Behalf of" the Principal*

The agent must be acting primarily for the principal's benefit, not for the agent's own benefit or that of another party.[20] The agent need not produce an actual benefit for the principal, so long as there was an expectation at the outset that the agent would strive to do so.[21] Hence, an agent who loses money in the management of the principal's business is still an agent.

A principal may retain an agent to perform almost any act.[22] Where a statute or contract requires the principal to perform personally, however, the principal may not assign these "nondelegable acts" to an agent.[23] If LeBron James contracts to play

---

[17] RESTATEMENT (THIRD) § 3.05 cmt. b.

[18] See, e.g., A. Gay Jenson Farms Co. v. Cargill, 309 N.W.2d 285, 290 (Minn. 1981) ("An agreement may result in the creation of an agency relationship although the parties did not call it an agency and did not intend the legal consequences of the relation to follow.").

[19] State v. Luster, 295 S.E.2d 421 (N.C. 1982) ("We find the phrase 'unwitting agent' to be a contradiction in terms. . . . An agency relationship must be created by mutual agreement.").

[20] The fact that an agent is compensated is irrelevant. Because the agent is being compensated for trying to be of service to the principal, the paid agent is still considered to be acting on the principal's behalf. HYNES at 16–17. In limited circumstances, an agent may act on behalf of two principals simultaneously. Such an agent is known as a "dual agent." *Id.* at 56–57.

[21] RIBSTEIN & LIPSHAW at 12.

[22] See Henson v. Henson, 268 S.W. 378, 381 (Tenn. 1925) ("What a party can lawfully do himself he can do through an agent.").§

[23] RESTATEMENT (THIRD) § 3.04(3) ("If performance of an act is not delegable, its performance by an agent does not constitute performance by the principal.").

basketball for the Los Angeles Lakers, he cannot delegate that duty to an agent. Instead, James has a so-called "nondelegable duty" to perform in person. A principal also may not validly delegate power to an agent to perform an act that is "criminal, tortious, or otherwise opposed to public policy."[24]

The so-called "dual agency rule" provides that an agent may not act on behalf of an adverse party to a transaction connected to the agency relationship without the consent of the principal.[25] If the agent does so, both of the parties for whom he acts are deemed principals. If neither of the principals was aware of the agent's dual capacity, any transaction between them is voidable by either party.[26] The agent may be held liable to the principals for any resulting loss on grounds of fraud and breach of fiduciary duty.[27] If one of the principals had secretly retained the agent to deal with the second without disclosure, the defrauded principal can rescind the contract and/or sue either the principal or agent for damages.[28]

5.   *"Control" by the Principal*

It does not take much on the way of control by the principal in order for an agency relationship to exist. A "principal need not exercise physical control over the actions of its agent" so long as the principal may direct "the result or ultimate objectives of the agent relationship."[29] Hence, the requisite level of control may be found so long as the principal is able to specify the task the agent is to perform, even if the principal is unable to ensure that the agent carries out that task:

> Control is a concept that embraces a wide spectrum of meanings, but within any relationship of agency the principal initially states what the agent shall and shall not do, in specific or general terms. Additionally, a principal has the right to give interim instructions or directions to the agent once their relationship is established. . . .

---

[24] RESTATEMENT (SECOND) § 19.

[25] HYNES at 56.

[26] Reed v. Smith Steel, Inc., 78 S.W.3d 118, 124 (Ark. App. 2002) ("an agent may represent both parties to a transaction with their knowledge and consent; however, without such knowledge and consent, an agent's contracts relating to the transaction between his principals are voidable at the instance of either who may feel aggrieved, even though the principals are not in fact injured or the agent intends no wrong, or the other party acts in good faith").

[27] *See, e.g.,* Brown v. FSR Brokerage, Inc., 72 Cal. Rptr.2d 828 (Cal. App. 1998); Egan v. Burkhart, 657 N.E.2d 401 (Ind.Ct. App. 1995); Bazal v. Rhines, 600 N.W.2d 327 (Iowa Ct. App. 1999).

[28] HYNES at 57.

[29] Green v. H & R Block, Inc., 735 A.2d 1039, 1050 (Md. 1999).

A principal's control over an agent will as a practical matter be incomplete because no agent is an automaton who mindlessly but perfectly executes commands. . . .

The power to give interim instructions distinguishes principals in agency relationships from those who contract to receive services provided by persons who are not agents.[30]

6. Alternative Formulations

Although the Restatement is the gold standard of agency definitions, one occasionally encounters other definitions in the case law. In *Green v. H & R Block, Inc.,*[31] for example, the court identified three factors to be considered in determining whether a relationship is one of agency: "(1) the principal's right of control over the agent, (2) the agent's duty to act primarily for the benefit of the principal, and (3) the agent's power to alter the legal relations of the principal." This definition is problematic in at least two respects. First, as the court acknowledged, it fails adequately to emphasize the consensual nature of the agency relationship. Second, and more important, this test assumes its own conclusion. The "agent's power to alter the legal relations of the principal" is a consequence of the agency relationship. Including this factor in the definition thus puts the cart before the horse—one only decides whether the agent could affect the principal's legal relations after one has already decided that the agent is in fact an agent.[32]

7. Undisclosed or Partially Disclosed Principals

A principal is undisclosed when the third party is unaware that the agent is acting on behalf of a principal.[33] Put another way, an undisclosed principal is one "whose existence and identity is not revealed to a third party who is transacting business with the

---

[30] RESTATEMENT (THIRD) § 1.01 cmt. f. *See also* Demming v. Underwood, 943 N.E.2d 878 (Ind. App. 2011) ("To satisfy the control element, '[i]t is necessary that the agent be subject to the control of the principal with respect to the details of the work.' However, the principal need not exercise complete control over every aspect of the agent's activities within the scope of the agency.").

[31] 735 A.2d 1039 (Md. 1999).

[32] *See also* MJ & Partners Restaurant Limited Partnership v. Zadikoff, 10 F. Supp.2d 922 (N.D. Ill. 1998), in which the court stated: "To determine whether an agency relationship exists the court must consider two factors: (1) whether the principal has the right to control the manner and method in which agent performs his services, and (2) whether the agent has the power to subject the principal to personal liability." *Id.* at 931. The same objection lodged in the text against *Green* applies to the second prong of the *Zadikoff* standard.

[33] *See* Kavanaugh v. Ealy, 364 S.W.3d 759, 764 (Mo. App. 2012) ("An agent for another who enters into a contract without disclosing the fact of his or her agency, or who discloses his or her agency status without disclosing the identity of the principal, is considered an agent for an undisclosed principal."); Oil Supply Co., Inc. v. Hires Parts Service, Inc., 726 N.E.2d 246, 248–49 (Ind. 2000) ("If a party to a transaction has no notice that the agent is acting for a principal, the party for whom he acts is called an undisclosed principal, and the relationship between the agent and the principal is called an undisclosed agency.").

undisclosed principal's agent."[34] Where the third party knows or is on notice that the agent is for a principal but does not know the identity of the principal, the principal is "partially disclosed."[35] The comments to Restatement (Second) § 4 offer these illustrations:

> 1. A contracts with T in his own name, T reasonably believing that A is acting for himself. After the execution of the contract, A reveals to T that he was acting as agent for P. P is an undisclosed principal.

> 2. A, acting as agent for P and so stating to T, executes a memorandum of the contract which he signs with his own name. P is a disclosed principal. . . .

> 5. A, a factor, sells goods sometimes on his own account but usually on account of consignors, as T knows. A contracts in his own name, as is his usage whether or not selling for consignors, to sell to T goods consigned to A for sale on account of P. T does not inquire whether A is acting for himself or another. P is a partially disclosed principal.

Where the third party if reasonably should have known that the person with whom he was dealing was acting as an agent on behalf of a principal, he will be deemed to have knowledge of the principal's existence but will not be charged with knowledge of principal's identity, thereby creating a partially disclosed principal situation.

B. Illustrations and Applications

1. *The Gratuitous Act of Kindness*

The Soda Springs (Idaho) High School football team was preparing for a trip to Paris (Idaho, not France) to play its arch-rival. The team planned to travel in private cars rather than by bus. School teacher Doty subsequently related a conversation she had with team Coach Garst, as follows: "I asked him if he had all the cars necessary for his trip to Paris the next day. He said he needed one more. I said that he might use mine if he drove it. That was the extent of it." Garst thereafter in fact borrowed and drove Doty's car. On the way home from the game, Garst caused an accident in which Richard Gorton, one of his passengers/players, was injured. Gorton sued.

Gorton did not sue the coach, who had died in the accident. Gorton did not sue the school, presumably because the school at that time (1937) could have invoked some form of sovereign

---

[34] Old Republic Ins. Co. v. Hansa World Cargo Service, Inc., 51 F.Supp.2d 457, 471 (S.D.N.Y. 1999).

[35] *Id.*

immunity defense. Instead, Gorton sued Doty, who must have been very surprised indeed. Doty must have been even more surprised, however, when a trial court held (and the Idaho supreme court affirmed) that Garst was her agent and that she was liable for his negligence.[36]

The court inferred that Doty manifested her consent that Garst act on her behalf from the fact that, instead of driving the car herself, she volunteered the use of her car subject to the requirement that Garst be the driver. This is a puzzling holding. What benefit did Doty anticipate from allowing Garst to use her car? The record discloses none. Doty was not compensated for the use of her car nor was there any evidence of any other benefit. Indeed, if anybody benefited, it was the school, which avoided having to pay for a bus.

As the dissenting judge complained, moreover, the most plausible reading of the facts is that Doty simply made "a kindly gesture." In the dissenter's view, you do not become an agent simply by offering to help out a friend or doing them a favor.[37] As we saw above, however, the agency relationship in fact can be purely gratuitous. The Restatement (Second) offers the following example: "when one . . . asks a friend to do a slight service for him, such as to return for credit goods recently purchased from a store," an agency relationship exists even though no compensation or other consideration was contemplated.[38] Did Doty's conduct rise to the relatively low level contemplated by the Restatement? It seems doubtful, as it hard to see what service the coach rendered Doty. In the event, however, none of these difficulties prevented the majority from finding an agency relationship.

The majority next concluded that Coach Garst was to be subject to Doty's control from the mere fact that she set a condition precedent on the use of the car; namely, that he be the driver of the car. In my experience, students often find this holding to be the most outrageous aspect of the case. In fact, however, the court was on reasonably solid ground here. As we have seen, it doesn't take much control to satisfy the Restatement (Second) standard. Indeed, it suffices that the principal have the power to control the end result of the agent's actions, which power "may be exercised by

---

[36] Gorton v. Doty, 69 P.2d 136 (Idaho 1937).

[37] *See, e.g.,* Sandrock v. Taylor, 174 N.W.2d 186 (Neb. 1970) (holding that transportation provided as "a friendly and neighborly favor" did not give rise to an agency relationship between driver and passenger); *see also* Edwards v. Freeman, 212 P.2d 883, 884 (Cal. 1949); Violette v. Shoup, 20 Cal.Rptr.2d 358, 363 (Cal. App. 1993).

[38] RESTATEMENT (SECOND) § 1(1) cmt. b.

prescribing the agent's obligations before or after the agent acts, or both."[39]

Finally, the court assumed that the coach agreed to act on her behalf and subject to her control based on the simple fact that he indeed used the car and was driving it at the time of the accident. Here, again, the court was on reasonably solid ground. Remember that the agent need not communicate the agent's consent to the principal.

Despite the plausible basis for the court's holding on the latter issues, many students are outraged by this result (or, at least, as outraged as one gets in business classes). Granted, the court's analysis is awfully thin. Granted also, the result seems counterintuitive. Should I be exposed to potentially significant liability just for doing a favor for a friend? The decision becomes easier to understand (and maybe accept), however, when one realizes that the opinion was a results-driven one intended to effect public policy.

Consider the *ex post* planning implications of the result in *Gorton v. Doty*: Suppose that you are Ms. Doty's attorney. A few months after the decision was handed down, she stops by your office. She tells you that the new football coach wants to use her car to take some players to another game. She asks for your advice as to how she could avoid liability in the event of an accident. What do you tell her?

First, it won't help to expressly state that the coach is not her agent, or even to put that in writing. The issue is not how the parties describe their relationship, but rather whether the Restatement (Second) standard is satisfied under all of the circumstances. Second, while it would help to avoid requiring the coach to drive her car, she may want to impose such a requirement rather than letting some teenage football player drive her car. Under the circumstances, the best advice you can give is to tell Doty to make sure that her auto insurance policy covers accidents caused by people who use her car with her permission.

This analysis should tip you off as to the policy goal the court was trying to effect. But here's another clue: During his closing argument, counsel for plaintiff Gorton stated to the jury that "you have a right to draw on your experience as business men in determining the facts in this case, and that you know from your experience as business men that prudent automobile owners usually protect themselves against just such contingencies as are involved in this case." Counsel for defendant Doty objected, and moved for a mistrial, on grounds that it was improperly prejudicial

---

[39] Green v. H & R Block, Inc., 735 A.2d 1039, 1051 (Md. 1999).

to encourage the jury to assume that the defendant had an insurance policy that would cover any damages. Both the trial court and the supreme court majority rejected that objection.

So what was going on here? The court used (and arguably bent) agency law principles to effect what it regarded as sound public policy. The owner of a car is clearly the person best able to insure against these sort of losses. By using agency law to impose liability on car owners, the courts thus create an incentive for owners to insure. This explanation of the *Gorton v. Doty* majority's motivation is supported by the fact that state motor vehicle statutes now uniformly create a presumption that the driver of a vehicle is the agent of the vehicle's owner.

2.   *The Creditor and its Debtor*

Defendant Warren Seed & Grain Co. was a grain elevator operator based in Warren, Minnesota, a farming community of approximately 2,000 persons in the rural northwest part of the state. Warren functioned as a middleman between big agricultural corporations and local farmers. It bought seed from the big firms, which it then sold to farmers. At harvest, Warren bought grain from the farmers, which it then sold to the corporations.

In 1964, Warren obtained what appears to be a revolving line of credit from Cargill, Inc., secured by its grain inventory.[40] The loan maximum initially was $175,000, but this maximum was gradually increased to $1.25 million. Warren paid its expenses by issuing drafts, which were imprinted with both names, drawn on Cargill. Proceeds from Warren's sales were deposited with Cargill and credited to Warren's account. Cargill also was given a right of first refusal on Warren's market grain. From 1964 to 1977, the relationship continued to develop, with increasingly close contacts between the parties.

In 1977, Warren collapsed as a result of financial misconduct by some its executives. At that point, Warren owed Cargill $3.6 million. Warren also owed 86 local farmers a total of $2 million. The farmers sued Cargill, alleging that Cargill was jointly liable for Warren's indebtedness on grounds that Cargill was Warren's principal. Plaintiffs prevailed, albeit in a jury trial held in the town of Warren, and Cargill appealed. The major issue before the court was whether an agency relationship existed between Cargill and Warren.

---

[40] A revolving line of credit is a type of loan in which the borrower is allowed to draw up to a specified amount as needed from time to time. The borrower pays interest only on the amount actually borrowed at any given time, rather than on the maximum value of the loan. In some sense, the familiar credit card is a line of credit.

Applying the Restatement (Second) standard, the Minnesota supreme court held that an agency relationship did exist between Cargill and Warren.[41] First the court concluded that Warren acted on Cargill's behalf by procuring grain, over which Cargill had a right of first refusal, in operations totally financed by Cargill's line of credit. Second, the court concluded that Cargill had the requisite control over Warren, as evidenced by Cargill's frequent recommendations as to how Warren's business should be conducted. Cargill had informed Warren that "since Cargill money was being used, Warren should realize that Cargill had the right to make some critical decisions regarding the use of the funds." Cargill's regional manager met with Warren both at monthly planning meetings and on a day-to-day basis. The loan agreement also gave Cargill various other rights, as discussed below. Finally, the court ignored the issue of whether Warren agreed to act on Cargill's behalf and subject to its control. Presumably, the court inferred Warren's consent from Warren's course of conduct, but a decent regard for the reader would have obliged the court to mention it.

Cargill argued that its relationship with Warren was not one of principal and agent, but rather one of creditor and debtor. Under Restatement (Second) § 14O, a creditor becomes the debtor's principal when the creditor assumes *de facto* control over the conduct of the debtor, regardless of the terms of the formal contract between them. In response, the court noted nine factors tending to indicate Cargill controlled Warren. If one looks closely at these factors, they tend to fall into three categories: (1) Those factors relating to communications between Cargill and Warren. Cargill frequently made recommendations to Warren by telephone. Cargill's correspondence with Warren criticized Warren's finances, officers' salaries, and inventory practices. (2) Those factors giving Cargill, in effect, a veto power over certain actions by Warren. Warren was unable to enter into mortgages, to repurchase its own stock, or to pay dividends without Cargill's approval. Cargill financed all Warren's purchases of grain and operating expenses and had the power to discontinue its financing of Warren's operations on short notice. (3) Other factors. Cargill had a right of first refusal on grain. Cargill had a right of entry onto Warren's premises to carry out periodic checks and audits of Warren's books and records. Cargill provided drafts and forms to Warren upon which Cargill's name was imprinted. At trial, correspondence was introduced in which Cargill's regional manager stated that Warren needed "strong paternal guidance," which is precisely the sort of sound-bite a plaintiff's lawyer would love. Taken together, the court

---

[41] A. Gay Jenson Farms Co. v. Cargill, Inc., 309 N.W.2d 285 (Minn. 1981).

held, these indicia of control indicated the existence of an agency rather than a mere creditor-debtor relationship.

Should the result in *Cargill* worry banks and other financial institutions? A banking group in fact filed an amicus curiae brief in *Cargill,* arguing against imposing liability on Cargill and expressing concern that the decision would expose creditors to substantially greater risk of liability for misconduct by debtors. The court tried to reassure creditors, opining that: "We deal here with a business enterprise markedly different from an ordinary bank financing, since Cargill was an active participant in Warren's operations rather than simply a financier." Cargill also was a supplier and customer of Warren and, as such, was using its control for purposes broader than merely protecting its loan. In fact, however, many creditors possess at least as much control over their debtors as did Cargill. Where a bank issues a revolving line of credit to a small business, which is the debtor's main source of financing, the loan agreement will often give the lender most of the rights that Cargill possessed. As a result, these so-called controlling creditor cases are becoming more and more common and courts are increasingly willing to find an agency relationship in creditor-debtor relationships.[42]

The court also rejected Cargill's alternative contention that it should be regarded as a supplier and buyer, rather than a principal. Restatement (Second) § 14 K provides: "One who contracts to acquire property from a third person and convey it to another is the agent of the other only if it is agreed that he is to act primarily for the benefit of the other and not for himself." The comments to that section further explain: "Factors indicating that one is a supplier, rather than an agent, are: (1) That he is to receive a fixed price for the property irrespective of price paid by him. This is the most important. (2) That he acts in his own name and receives the title to the property which he thereafter is to transfer. (3) That he has an independent business in buying and selling similar property." Citing these provisions, the court thereupon held that "it must be shown that the supplier has an independent business before it can be concluded that he is not an agent." Holding that Warren had no independence, because of Cargill's total financing of Warren and its almost total purchases of Warren's market grain, the court rejected Cargill's argument that it was a mere buyer. The court's reading of the Restatement, however, was quite disingenuous. When a legal standard speaks of "elements," each element must be present in

---

[42] *See, e.g.,* Jeffrey John Hass, Comment, *Insights into Lender Liability: An Argument for Treating Controlling Creditors as Controlling Shareholders,* 135 U. PA. L. REV. 1321 (1987); J. Dennis Hynes, *Lender Liability: The Dilemma of the Controlling Creditor,* 58 TENN. L. REV. 635 (1991).

order for the standard to be satisfied. When a legal standard speaks only of "factors," however, no one prong of the test dominates and not all need be present. Instead, factors are simply items to be considered and weighed against each other. The Restatement (Second) thus merely says that courts should consider whether the debtor has an independent business as one factor among several, and not even the one deserving the greatest weight.

As with *Gorton v. Doty,* can we explain the result in *Cargill* by pointing to some policy goal the court might have been trying to implement? The Cargill court clearly felt that Cargill had all of the economic indicia of ownership over Warren and, in effect, treated Warren as though it were part of Cargill's operation. Perhaps the court believed that Cargill had set up a system under which it got all of the benefits of controlling Warren, while seeking to evade the legal obligations that accompany control.[43] If so, the Court seemingly concluded that if Cargill was to get the benefits of ownership, it should also suffer the obligations of ownership; namely, legal status and corresponding liability as a principal of its agent.[44]

As a policy matter, why should economic control result in legal obligations? After all, Warren cheated Cargill too. Indeed, Warren apparently had been lying to Cargill for quite some time. Whatever degree of control Cargill had, clearly was not enough. Why then should Cargill's control over Warren result in Cargill's being held liable?

There is a strong cultural sense in our society that responsibility comes with authority. This cultural imperative has a rational economic basis: Those with authority may shirk—i.e., they may use their authority irresponsibly. They do this because they reap all the benefits of shirking, but only part (maybe even none) of the costs. In effect, those who shirk are able to externalize part of the cost of their shirking, while internalizing all of the benefits.[45]

---

[43] *But see* RIBSTEIN & LIPSHAW at 19 (arguing that because "Cargill did not share the *profits* from Warren's business" Cargill was forced to "bear the costs but not the rewards of ownership"). This analysis, however, overlooks the local monopoly typically enjoyed by grain elevators. Cargill's relationship with Warren gave it the benefit of Warren's local monopoly—i.e., sole access to the grain harvested in the area.

[44] The other possibility is that farmers always win commercial law cases. Famed contracts scholar Grant Gilmore supposedly observed that commercial law, as applied to farming, could be boiled down to just two sections: (1) "It shall be against the law to refuse to lend money to a farmer." (2) "It shall be against the law to collect a debt from a farmer." *See* KLEIN ET AL. at 18 (noting that the case was tried to a local jury in Warren's home town, a village of some 2,000 persons located in a rural county with a population of 15,000).

[45] Externalities are a very important concept in welfare economics. Suppose Acme built a factory that spewed toxic fumes into the air. If those fumes injured the health and property of Acme's neighbors, the damage they suffered would be an externality—a cost that Acme's actions had imposed upon its neighbors without their

By imposing liability on Cargill, the court forces Cargill to internalize the costs associated with running its business, such as those entailed in monitoring the grain elevator operators Cargill uses to buy grain from farmers.

Finally, what are the planning implications of this decision? Suppose you were Cargill's lawyer. After this decision was handed down, the head of Cargill's lending operation asked for your advice as to how Cargill should structure its business? What advice would you offer? Most importantly, Cargill should consider whether it wants or needs a high degree of control. If so, it should accept the fact that it may be deemed to be a principal, assume a high level of control, and use its control to try to prevent its agents from harming others.

3.   *The Manufacturer and Its Dealers*

Hunter Mining Laboratories, Inc. ("Hunter") purchased computer equipment and software manufactured by Management Assistance, Inc. and M.A.I. Application Software Corporation ("MAI companies") from Hubco Data Products. Hubco Data Products and The Data Doctors, both licensed dealers of MAI computer products, were then hired to install and program the equipment. After both dealers failed to complete the agreed upon installation, Hunter brought a breach of contract action against the MAI companies, whose liability, plaintiff claimed, stemmed from an agency relationship between Hubco and Data Doctors, the contract signatories, and the MAI companies.[46]

A jury found the MAI companies liable for breach of contract, but the judge granted a motion for judgment notwithstanding the verdict. The Supreme Court of Nevada upheld the judgment n.o.v. In doing so, the court concluded that no evidence supported the jury's verdicts against the MAI companies given missing elements of an agency relationship.

First, relying on Restatement (Second) of Agency § 14, the court noted that for an agency relationship to exist, the principal must possess the right to control the agent's conduct. In this context, an agency relationship arises when a manufacturer controls the day-to-day details of a dealer's business. The court

---

consent. Where one reaps the full benefits of an activity, but only internalizes part of the costs, one is likely to engage in more of the activity than is socially desirable. Assume Acme's profit from running the factory is $80 per month, while the costs borne by its neighbors are $100 per month. Acme will keep operating the factory because it is making a profit, even though from a societal perspective it would be better if the factory shut down.

[46] Hunter Mining Labs., Inc. v. Management Assistance, Inc., 763 P.2d 350, 351 (Nev. 1988).

found that MAI had no power to control operative details such as the dealers' business expenditures, customer rates, employee relations or installation procedures. The court conceded that some degree of control existed, such as reporting of sales and monitoring of advertisements, to "protect MAI's goodwill and the integrity" of the product line. These types of controls, however, are typical in manufacturer/dealer agreements to and did not create an agency relationship.

Second, the court held that an essential element of the agency relationship is a fiduciary obligation on the part of the agent to act primarily for the benefit of the principal.[47] Technically, this is a consequence of an agency relationship coming into existence rather than a condition for the creation of such a relationship. The relevant facts, however, tended to further show that the purported agents were not subject to control by the MAI Companies. Hubco and Data Doctors paid a set price for and received title to the MAI equipment. The dealers were then free to set their own price at which they resold the products and had no duty to account to MAI for any profit made. Furthermore, the dealers acted independently and in their own names. Thus, the court correctly held that, as a matter of law, the relationship between the MAI and the dealers was that of seller and buyer rather than principal and agent.

4.   *Baseball and its Commissioner*

In the gambling dispute that has kept him out of the Hall of Fame, baseball player Pete Rose sought a temporary restraining order and preliminary injunction in state court against baseball commissioner A. Bartlett Giamatti, Major League Baseball, and the Cincinnati Reds. Giamatti moved to remove the case to United States district court, with the consent of the other defendants. Rose objected to the removal, asserting a lack of compete diversity of citizenship between himself and the defendants.[48] In order to resolve that procedural dispute, the court had to decide whether the Commissioner of Baseball is an agent of Major League Baseball.

That the Cincinnati Reds Baseball Club was a citizen of Ohio is not in dispute. Treating Major League Baseball as an unincorporated association formed by the twenty-six baseball clubs

---

[47] The comments to Restatement (Second) § 14J list a number of indications that the parties have an agreement that the buyer/distributor does not have a fiduciary obligation to and is not to act as agent of the seller: dealer gets legal title and possession of the goods; dealer is responsible for paying an agreed price; dealer has right to fix the price at which it will sell to third parties without a duty to account to seller for any profit; dealer obtains incomplete or unfinished goods to be completed by dealer before sale to third parties; dealer bears risk of loss; dealer has right to deal in goods of persons other than seller; dealer deals in its own name with no duty to disclose that goods are those of seller.

[48] Rose v. Giamatti, 721 F. Supp. 906 (S. D. Ohio 1989).

joined under the Major League Agreement, the court noted that, for purposes of determining citizenship, an unincorporated association has no citizenship of its own, but is a citizen of every state in which its constituent members is a citizen. Because the Cincinnati Reds Baseball Club was one of the members of Major League Baseball, the court found Major League Baseball to be a citizen of Ohio for diversity purposes. Hence, complete diversity of citizenship did not exist between Rose and each of the defendants. However, the court then determined that Major League Baseball and the Cincinnati Reds were merely nominal parties who had not been properly joined, so their citizenship could be ignored for purposes of the removal issue.

With respect to Major League Baseball, the court held that Rose's dispute was not with the unincorporated association, but with the Commissioner of Baseball over his alleged failure to follow his own investigative procedures. Rejecting Rose's argument that Major League Baseball was a proper party because it could be held liable for the Commissioner's actions on a principal-agent theory, the court noted that a party cannot be held liable for conduct of a person over whom it has no control. Examining the unique history of Major League Baseball, the court determined that it cannot be equated with a typical unincorporated association with control over all of its agents' activities. The constituent clubs agreed to allow a completely independent commissioner to govern disciplinary matters. Since the Major League Agreement and the terms of Rose's own employment contract vest absolute power to police activities "not in the best interests" of baseball in the Commissioner, the court concluded that Giamatti was not acting as an agent for Major League Baseball with regard to such disciplinary functions.

5. Corporate Officers and Directors

Corporate employees, especially officers, are agents of the corporation.[49] Curiously, however, neither an individual director nor even the board as a whole is regarded as agents of the corporation.[50] An individual director, as such, "has no power of his own to act on the corporation's behalf, but only as one of the body of directors acting as a board."[51] As for the board, when it acts

---

[49] RESTATEMENT (SECOND) § 14 C cmt. a. A subsidiary of a corporation will not be deemed the agent of the parent corporation even though the latter has the power to control the former. A parent corporation thus cannot be held liable for the acts of its subsidiary on a principal-agent basis; instead, a plaintiff seeking to hold the parent liable must pierce the corporate veil of the subsidiary. Bunch v. Centeon, L.L.C., 2000 WL 1741905 (N.D. Ill. 2000).

[50] RESTATEMENT (SECOND) § 14 C.

[51] RESTATEMENT (SECOND) § 14 C cmt. b. Directors thus are a type of non-agent fiduciary, as are "trustees, ... executors, guardians, ..., partners and joint adventurers, and attorneys. . . ." Chisholm v. Western Reserves Oil Co., 655 F.2d 94, 97 (6th Cir. 1981). See Young v. Colgate-Palmolive Co., 790 F.2d 567 (7th Cir. 1986)

collectively, the board functions as a principal rather than as agent. Unless shareholder approval is required, after all, the act of the board is the act of the corporation. Consequently, the board can be said to personify the corporate principal.

C. General v. Special Agents

The Restatement (Second) defines a general agent as one who is "authorized to conduct a series of transactions involving a continuity of service."[52] A special agent is one who is only "authorized to conduct a single transaction or a series of transactions not involving continuity of service."[53] The distinction is significant because a general agent has much broader authority to act on the principal's behalf. A general agent has full power to bind the principal with respect to "all matters coming within the usual and ordinary scope and character" of the business entrusted to the agent, while a special agent has the power to "act for the principal only in a particular transaction, or in a particular way."[54]

II. Liability of Principal to Third Parties in Contract

An agent may have actual, apparent, or inherent authority to enter into contracts on behalf of the principal. In addition, the principal also can be bound to a contract made by its agent on grounds of estoppel or ratification.

Determining whether an agent had the requisite authority in any given situation can be challenging. The differences between the various categories of authority are complex and subtle. In addition, many of the categories overlap. In fact, it is not at all uncommon for more than one type of authority to be present in a single transaction. Finally, the courts are not always precise when using labels. For example, estoppel and inherent authority are often called apparent authority. For our purposes, however, it is critical for you to understand that the legal consequences of an agent's actions do not depend on the type of authority at hand. For purposes of determining whether or not the corporate principal is

---

(holding that "the directors are not acting as agents in their management of the corporation, but as fiduciaries"); U.S. v. Griswold, 124 F.2d 599 (1st Cir. 1941) ("The directors of a corporation for profit are 'fiduciaries' having power to affect its relations, but they are not agents of the shareholders since they have no duty to respond to the will of the shareholders as to the details of management."); Arnold v. Soc'y for Sav. Bancorp, 678 A.2d 533, 539–40 (Del.1996) ("Directors, in the ordinary course of their service as directors, do not act as agents of the corporation. . . . A board of directors, in fulfilling its fiduciary duty, controls the corporation, not vice versa.").

[52] RESTATEMENT (SECOND) § 3(1).

[53] RESTATEMENT (SECOND) § 3(2).

[54] Washington Nat'l Ins. Co. v. Strickland, 491 So.2d 872, 874 (Ala. 1985).

bound by the contract vis-à-vis the third party to the transaction, authority is authority and the different types of authority are essentially irrelevant.[55]

Why then does the law distinguish between different categories of authority? A former student of mine claimed that it was a deliberate attempt to confuse people, which called to mind the old joke: "Just because you're paranoid doesn't mean you aren't being followed." As Justice Holmes once observed, albeit in a different context, "common sense is opposed to the fundamental theory of agency."[56]

It will be helpful to focus for a moment on the two basic types of authority: "actual authority" and "apparent authority." Consider the following hypothetical: Pam owns Whiteacre. Alan is her real estate broker and, indisputably, her agent. Ted is an outsider who claims that Alan entered into a contract on Pam's behalf to sell Whiteacre. Suppose Ted seeks to prove the existence of authority by evidence relating to communications between Pam and Alan, such as a letter from Pam to Allen in which Pam directed Alan to sell Whiteacre. In this instance, Ted is attempting to establish the existence of actual authority. (See Figure 2.2.)

Figure 2.2
Authority (a.k.a. Actual Authority)

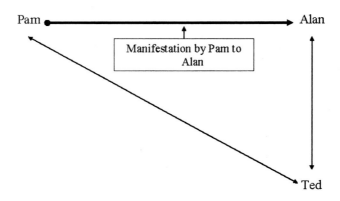

[55] In addition to determining whether a contract is binding on the principal, authority is also relevant to determining whether the principal is on notice of facts known to the agent. If the agent has actual or apparent authority to receive notifications on the principal's behalf, notice to the agent is the same as notice to the principal. RESTATEMENT (SECOND) § 268(1).

[56] Oliver Wendell Holmes, Jr., *Agency II*, 5 HARV. L. REV. 1, 14 (1891).

In contrast, suppose Ted seeks to establish authority by evidence relating to communications from Pam to Ted. Suppose Pam sent Ted a letter in which she said that she had ordered Alan to sell Whiteacre. In this case, Ted is trying to establish apparent authority. (See Figure 2.3.)

Figure 2.3
Apparent Authority

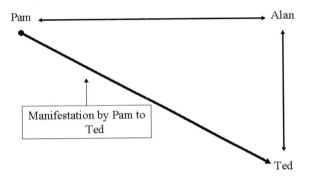

Importantly, the contract will be no less binding if Ted proves apparent authority rather than actual. The difference between actual and apparent authority thus arises out of the way in which Ted seeks to prove that Alan was authorized to enter into the contract. In other words, the different categories of authority really are ways of classifying the proof the plaintiff must offer to bind the principal to the contract.

A.   Actual Authority

Actual authority exists when the agent reasonably believes the principal has consented to a particular course of conduct.[57] Actual authority can be express, as where the principal instructs the agent to "sell Whiteacre on my behalf." Actual authority can also be implied, however, if the principal's acts or conduct are such the agent can reasonably infer the requisite consent. Notice that in cases of actual authority we are looking solely at what the agent believes about the scope of its authority. What the third party believes is irrelevant to actual authority.

---

[57] RESTATEMENT (SECOND) §§ 7 & 26. Confusingly, the Restatement (Second) refers to this type of authority simply as "authority." To help keep the various categories straight, we will use the term actual authority to refer to the authority that exists because the agent reasonably believed the principal had consented to the action.

1. Express Actual Authority

Express actual authority is most clearly created when a principal gives an agent a written instrument setting forth the agent's powers.[58] In most cases, however, it suffices if the agent is told orally that he has the power in question. Some Statutes of Frauds, however, as well as other statutes governing the formation of agency relationships, impose what is known as an equal dignity requirement pursuant to which a transaction required to be evidenced in writing is not enforceable unless the agent's grant of authority also was in writing.[59] Many courts recognize an exception to equal dignity requirements where a corporate officer acts on behalf of the corporate principal without written authorization.[60] Restatement (Third) § 3.02 provides an additional exception for cases in which the third party "has been induced to make a detrimental change in position by the reasonable belief that an agent has authority to bind the principal that is traceable to a manifestation made by the principal."

Express authority can exist even where the principal did not intend to confer the authority but did so mistakenly. For example, if Mary wants to buy Blackacre but mistakenly tells Paul to buy Whiteacre on her behalf, Paul has actual express authority to buy Whiteacre and no authority to buy Blackacre.

When interpreting a grant of express authority, the courts will usually limit application of broad grants of authority to what appears to be the business actually intended by the parties and specific language in the grant of authority will prevail over general statements. In *King v. Bankerd*,[61] for example, the principal executed a power of attorney authorizing the agent to "convey, grant, bargain, and/or sell" a plot of real property.[62] The agent

---

[58] In the corporate context, express actual authority is usually vested in officers by a resolution of the board and/or a description of the officer's duties set forth in the bylaws. *Compare* Musulin v. Woodtek, Inc., 491 P.2d 1173 (Or. 1971) (unless authorized by the bylaws or board resolution, corporate officers lacked authority to execute a promissory note on the corporation's behalf); Daniel Webster Council, Inc. v. St. James Ass'n, Inc., 533 A.2d 329 (N.H. 1987) (officers have only such actual authority as provided in the bylaws or board resolutions) *with* King World Prod., Inc. v. Financial News Network, Inc., 660 F. Supp. 1381 (S.D.N.Y. 1987) (corporate officer had actual authority to execute a lease based, *inter alia*, on the job description in his employee contract).

[59] *See, e.g.,* Travel Centre Ltd. v. Starr-Matthews Agency, Inc., 333 S.E.2d 26 (Ga. 1985) (holding that a lease required to be in writing was invalid because the agent's grant of authority was not in writing).

[60] GREGORY & HURST at 234.

[61] 492 A.2d 608 (Md. 1985).

[62] "A power of attorney authorizes another to act as one's agent. An agent holding a power of attorney is termed an "attorney in fact" as distinguished from an attorney at law. Under a durable power of attorney, the authority of an attorney in fact survives the principal's subsequent disability or incapacity." First Colony Life Ins. Co. v. Gerdes, 676 N.W.2d 58, 63 (Neb. 2004). A springing power of attorney is one "that becomes effective only when needed, at some future date or upon some

subsequently made a gift of the property to a third party, presenting the issue of whether the power of attorney authorized the agent to make a gratuitous disposition of the property. The court concluded that it did not. Instead, such a power exists only if it "(1) is expressly conferred, (2) arises as a necessary implication from the conferred powers, or (3) is clearly intended by the parties, as evidenced by the surrounding facts and circumstances."

In *Von Wedel v. McGrath,*[63] the court took the principle of strictly construing powers of attorney to a remarkable extreme. Shortly before the United States entered World War II, a German national residing in the United States executed a power of attorney giving his agent the power "to do any and all acts which I could do if personally present." The power of attorney also set forth a nonexclusive list of specific powers, including the power to "sell, transfer, or do any other acts concerning any stocks or bonds" owned by the principal. The principal then left the United States, leaving behind his U.S. national wife. After the war broke out, Congress began work on a statute that would seize and forfeit to the U.S. government all U.S. property of German nationals. To avoid the seizure of the principal's property, the agent transferred it to the principal's wife. The government nevertheless seized the property. The court concluded that the power of attorney only gave the agent authority with respect to "ordinary business affairs," which did not include the power to make a gratuitous transfer of the principal's power.[64] The concurring judge described the majority's analysis as "incongruous":

> A man has said, in effect, that he gives another the power to do everything for him. Then he enumerates certain specific things which the other may do, carefully saying, however, that the does not mean to alter the general power by stating specific powers. Then he ends up by saying that he means his language to be as broad as he stated it. Yet the rule seems to be that he is held to mean something much less than indicated by the language he used. Perhaps the law cannot quite say that white is black. But in this instance it certainly can make white look a pretty dark grey.[65]

In fact, the result is best understood as an overly rigorous enforcement of a wartime statute aimed at enemy aliens. In other

---

future occurrence, usually upon the principal's incapacity." Black's Law Dictionary 1210 (8th ed. 2004).

[63] 180 F.2d 716 (3d Cir. 1950).

[64] *See* HYNES at 287–88; ROSIN & CLOSEN at 207.

[65] Von Wedel v. McGrath, 180 F.2d 716, 718 (3d Cir. 1950) (Goodrich, J., concurring).

words, the case should be regarded as a sport motivated by lingering post-war anti-German animus. Its continuing precedential value is minimal, at best.

2. *Implied Actual Authority*

Implied actual authority incorporates several different concepts. As the comments to Restatement (Third) § 2.01 explain, for example:

> The term "implied authority" has more than one meaning. "Implied authority" is often used to mean actual authority either (1) to do what is necessary, usual, and proper to accomplish or perform an agent's express responsibilities or (2) to act in a manner in which an agent believes the principal wishes the agent to act based on the agent's reasonable interpretation of the principal's manifestation in light of the principal's objectives and other facts known to the agent. These meanings are not mutually exclusive. Both fall within the definition of actual authority.

The key question in all implied authority cases is determining what the agent reasonably believed about the scope of his or her authority.

Perhaps the most common form of implied actual authority is the concept of incidental authority, under which the agent (absent clear contrary instructions from the principal) has the authority to use all means reasonably necessary to carry out a particular result expressly mandated by the principal.[66] For example, if Paul hires Ann to manage his apartment building, Ann likely would be deemed to have incidental authority to employ a janitor, purchase heating fuel, arrange for routine repairs and engage in any similar transaction that Paul had not forbidden. Ann's authority to carry out such acts, while not expressly granted, is implied by law because such acts are necessarily incidental to the proper management of the building.

Implied authority can also arise from custom. If it is customary in the trade or community for a certain type of agent to have certain powers, then the agent has implied actual authority to exercise such powers unless the principal directs otherwise.[67] Similarly, implied authority can arise from a pattern of conduct between the particular principal and agent in question. If the principal knows that the agent has engaged in a pattern of behavior and the principal fails to object to the continuance of that behavior, the

---

[66] *See* RESTATEMENT (SECOND) § 35.

[67] *See* RESTATEMENT (SECOND) § 36.

agent has implied actual authority to continue to engage in that type of transaction.[68]

Whether an agent has implied authority to hire another agent has generated a substantial amount of case law.[69] In *Mill Street Church of Christ v. Hogan*,[70] the Church hired Bill Hogan, a church member, to paint the church building. In the past, when the Church had hired Bill for similar jobs, he had been allowed to hire his brother Sam Hogan as a helper. Sam was no longer a church member, however, and the Church Elders had decided that another church member, one Gary Petty, should be hired if a second painter was needed. Although the possibility of hiring Petty was communicated to Bill, no one told him that he was obliged to do so. When Bill decided that he needed a helper, he hired his brother Sam rather than Petty. After a half hour on the job, Sam was injured when a ladder broke. Sam sought worker's compensation, the availability of which turned on whether he was an employee, which turned on whether Bill had authority to hire him.

The court held for Sam. First, Bill had incidental actual authority to hire a helper, because the job required two men. Second, Bill had implied actual authority to hire Sam based on the Church's acquiescence in his past practice. In order to eliminate that authority, the Church needed to specifically instruct Bill not to hire Sam and to hire only Petty.[71]

Other cases take a more restrictive view, however. In *White v. Consumers Fin. Serv., Inc.*,[72] the court held that an agency relationship may be created only by the consent of the principal. Accordingly, absent express authority,[73] one agent may not engage a second except "in case of emergency, where he is unable to perform the work alone." This result is inconsistent with the Restatement (Second), which authorizes an agent to delegate "the performance of incidental mechanical and ministerial acts" but not acts that "involve discretion or the agent's special skill."[74] In *White*, the issue was whether a lender's agent charged with repossessing a car could delegate the task of driving the car back to the lender's lot. Because driving a car seems unlikely to require either

---

[68] *See* RESTATEMENT (SECOND) § 43(2).

[69] *See* HYNES at 289–90.

[70] 785 S.W.2d 263 (Ky. 1990).

[71] Bill also had apparent authority based on Sam's past experience in having been hired to work with Bill.

[72] 15 A.2d 142 (Pa. 1940).

[73] RESTATEMENT (SECOND) § 77 provides that "authority to appoint agents, subagents, or servants of the principal can be conferred in the same manner as authority to do other acts for the principal. . . ."

[74] RESTATEMENT (SECOND) § 78.

discretion or special skills, the Restatement (Second) likely would authorize the delegation at issue in *White*.

Another frequently litigated issue is whether an attorney has implied authority to settle a case on a client's behalf. Typically, upon employment, an attorney's general powers to manage the procedural aspects of a client's case include implied actual authority to engage in settlement negotiations with opposing counsel.[75] The attorney's authority to open settlement negotiations, however, does not extend to reaching an actual settlement. The client retains legal control over the subject matter of litigation and important decisions affecting the client's substantial rights. Thus, the employment relationship alone does not provide an attorney with implied authority to settle a case on behalf of the client.[76]

Sometimes a client, even one that may not intend for an attorney to settle a claim, may imply to the attorney an intention to confer settlement authority. Such implied actual authority results from the client's conduct toward the attorney, which causes the attorney to reasonably believe the client wants the attorney to act on the client's behalf.[77] Implied actual authority is determined by a reasonableness standard looking at the totality of the relationship between the client and attorney.[78]

In *Pohl v. United Airlines*,[79] for example, the court found the attorney had implied authority to settle based on objective evidence of communications between the attorney and client supporting the attorney's testimony that the client was informed of and approved each aspect of the settlement. Evidence presented showed a number of phone calls the attorney placed to the client, each one of which was preceded or followed by a call placed to opposing counsel. Furthermore, the client did not object when the attorney sent the

---

[75] RESTATEMENT (THIRD) OF THE LAW GOVERNING LAWYERS § 21 (2000); New England Educ. Training Serv., Inc. v. Silver Street Partnership, 528 A.2d 1117, 1120 (Vt. 1987).

[76] Leffler v. Bi-State Dev. Agency, 612 S.W.2d 835, 837 (Mo. Ct. App. 1981) (holding that no implied authority to bind client in a settlement arises from mere fact attorney was hired); Khan v. Hospital Laundry Services, 2002 U.S.Dist. LEXIS 13169, *10–11 (N.D.Ill. 2002) (" '[A]n attorney's general authority to represent the client in litigation does not extend so far as to permit the attorney to waive the rights of the client.' "). Some states presume express authority has been given when the attorney represents that he has such authority and then reaches a settlement with opposing counsel. This presumption that settlement power was expressly authorized is rebuttable, but the burden is on the party disputing the attorney's authority, i.e. the client. Leffler v. Bi-State Dev. Agency, 612 S.W.2d 835, 837 (Mo. Ct. App. 1981).

[77] Tieran v. Devoe, 923 F.2d 1024, 1034 (3d Cir. 1991); *see also* Federal Land of Omaha v. Sullivan, 430 N.W.2d 700 (S.D. 1988) (holding the client acquiesced in its attorney's actions, allowing the attorney to believe he possessed actual authority to settle the case).

[78] Edwards v. Born, Inc., 792 F.2d 387, 391 (3d Cir. 1986); *see also* RESTATEMENT (THIRD) OF THE LAW GOVERNING LAWYERS § 22 cmt. c. (authorization can be "fairly implied from the dealings of lawyer and client.").

[79] 213 F.3d 336 (7th Cir. 2000).

client a letter confirming the settlement; rather, the client's reaction was "okay, great, they settled it." The court found such a reaction to be incompatible with one a client would have had he not given his attorney authority to settle the case.[80]

An interesting variation on this problem was presented in *In re Drier*,[81] which presented "the question whether a client is bound when his attorney forges the client's signature to a settlement he never authorized." Paul Gardi is an investment manager who runs a fund specializing in identifying undervalued technology. Gardi entered into an investment agreement with JANA, a hedge fund, which Gardi later claimed Jana breached. In the subsequent litigation between Gardi and JANA, attorney Marc Drier represented Gardi. Drier negotiated a settlement agreement with JANA, which Gardi refused to sign. Drier then forged Gardi's signature on the settlement agreement. JANA gave Drier a check for $6.3 million in accordance with the purported settlement, which Drier then proceeded to steal to invest in a Ponzi scheme he was running on the side. When he learned of Drier's misconduct, Gardi argued that the purported settlement with JANA was unenforceable and, as a result, his claims against JANA remained viable. If the court had accepted that argument, JANA would have borne the loss caused by Drier's theft. The Court rejected that argument:

> Dreier duped both parties, and the well-settled rule of agency law dictates that as between two innocent parties, "the risk of loss from the unauthorized acts of a dishonest agent falls on the principal that selected the agent." . . .

> Here, the Gardi Parties must bear the loss. The Gardi Parties retained Dreier and authorized him to negotiate a resolution with JANA. Dreier served as the conduit for all of the communications between his clients and JANA; there is no

---

[80] A lawyer may also have apparent authority to settle a case. As discussed in the next section, apparent authority to bind a principal also stems from the principal's conduct. Apparent authority occurs when the conduct or manifestation of authority placed upon the attorney by the client causes a third party, such as opposing counsel, to believe the client intends for the attorney to have authority. The conduct must be that of the client and the reliance by the third party must be reasonable. In some cases, the requisite client conduct can take the form of inaction. Section 27 of Restatement (Third) of The Law Governing Lawyers offers the following illustration of another situation that may give rise to an attorney having apparent authority to settle: The opposing party observes that the client is present as the judge orders the attorney to attend a settlement conference either with authority to settle or with a person who has such authority. The client leaves the conference without commenting on the attorney's authority. In such a case, it may be reasonable for the opposing party to believe from the client's actions that the client has conferred settlement authority upon the attorney. If the opposing party relies on such a belief in settling the case, the client is bound by the settlement. *See* RESTATEMENT (THIRD) OF THE LAW GOVERNING LAWYERS § 27 cmt. d, illus. 4 (2000).

[81] 450 B.R. 452 (S.D.N.Y. 2011).

evidence that Gardi dealt directly with JANA. JANA was justified in believing that the JANA Version that Dreier sent contained Gardi's signature. As a result of Dreier's fraud, JANA paid over $6.3 million, and should not be compelled to pay a second time. As between the Gardi Parties and JANA, the injury caused by Dreier's fraud must be allocated to the Gardi Parties, Dreier's principals.

3.　*A Note on Co-Agents versus Sub-Agents*

Where one agent has authority to retain a second, they are usually treated as co-agents. In such cases, both agents are deemed to be agents of the principal and both have power to affect the principal's legal relations. In some cases, however, the principal and agent may agree that the agent may delegate some responsibilities to other persons for whose conduct the agent agrees to be primarily responsible. Such a person is a subagent of the principal.[82] The distinction is important because an agent generally has no liability to either principal or third parties for the acts of a co-agent,[83] but an agent does have such liability with respect to the acts of a subagent.

B.　Apparent Authority

Apparent authority looks to what the third party reasonably believes about the relationship between the principal and the agent.[84] The basic rule is that apparent authority exists only when two criteria are satisfied. First, the principal must in some way hold out the agent as possessing certain authority. Second, the third party must reasonably rely on the agent having such authority.[85]

Apparent authority can be created in several ways. The most straightforward is some direct communication by the principal to the third party, such that we can identify words or conduct of the principal that led the third to reasonably believe the agent has

---

[82] RESTATEMENT (SECOND) § 5(1).

[83] The appointing agent may be liable for a co-agent's misconduct if the appointing agent was negligent in selecting the co-agent. RESTATEMENT (SECOND) § 405(2).

[84] *See* RESTATEMENT (SECOND) § 8 ("Apparent authority is the power to affect the legal relations of another person by transactions with third persons, professedly as agent for the other, arising from and in accordance with the other's manifestations to such third persons."); *see also* RESTATEMENT (THIRD) § 2.03 cmt. c ("Apparent authority holds a principal accountable for the results of third-party beliefs about an actor's authority to act as an agent when the belief is reasonable and is traceable to a manifestation of the principal.").

[85] *See* RESTATEMENT (SECOND) § 27 ("apparent authority to do an act is created as to a third person by written or spoken words or any other conduct of the principal which, reasonably interpreted, causes the third person to believe that the principal consents to have the act done on his behalf by the person purporting to act for him"); *see also id.* § 8 cmt. c ("Apparent authority exists only to the extent that it is reasonable for the third person dealing with the agent to believe that the agent is authorized."). Restatement (Third) §2.03 adopts the same rule.

authority. The simplest example of this scenario is the one we used earlier, in which the principal sends the third party a letter stating that the agent has authority to perform some act.

Apparent authority also can result from inaction by the principal. For example, suppose that in Pam's presence Al tells Ted that he is Pam's agent and can act on her behalf. If Pam does not speak up to deny that assertion, Al has apparent authority by virtue of her inaction.

In the real world, of course, things rarely are this cut and dried.[86] Consider, for example, *Three-Seventy Leasing Corp. v. Ampex Corp.*[87] John Joyce was a lessor of computer equipment, doing business through his one-man corporation 370 Leasing. Joyce negotiated a deal with Ampex, a computer equipment manufacturer, to purchase six "core memory units" for $150,000 each, which Joyce would then lease to Electronic Data Systems. The terms were $150,000 cash and the remaining $450,000 on credit payable over five years. The deal was negotiated on Amex's behalf by Thomas Kays, who was a sales representative employed by Ampex. Kays' superior at Ampex was one Mueller. At Mueller's direction, Kays sent a draft agreement to Joyce memorializing the contract. Joyce executed the document on November 6, 1972, but it was never signed by anyone at Ampex. On November 9, Mueller issued an intra-office memorandum announcing the agreement. Mueller's memorandum also announced that, at Joyce's request, all communications between Ampex and 370 Leasing were to be made by Kays. On November 17, Kays sent Joyce a letter confirming the delivery dates and instructions for the equipment. Ampex later refused to perform and Joyce sued. The court concluded that Kays had apparent authority to make a binding contract, *inter alia*, by virtue of Ampex's inaction. First, Ampex had never notified Joyce that Kays lacked authority to make this contract. Second, by virtue of Mueller's intra-office memo, Ampex had acquiesced in Joyce's request that all communications be channeled through Kays. As a result, "Joyce could reasonably expect that Kays would speak for the company." Hence, the draft agreement Kays sent Joyce was deemed an offer that, when Joyce accepted it by signing, created a binding contract.

A recurrent question presented by this case is the extent to which an agent can create its own authority. In *Three Seventy Leasing*, for example, Joyce's only contacts with Ampex were his dealings with Kay (and, perhaps, Mueller). How then did Ampex

---

[86] *See* RIBSTEIN & LIPSHAW at 29 ("Apparent authority is a messy concept, particularly in a complex world.").

[87] 528 F.2d 993 (5th Cir. 1976).

make the requisite manifestation? Where the agent's position carries with it certain customary powers, the act of placing the agent in such a position, if known by the third party, constitutes the requisite manifestation. Alternatively, and potentially more problematically, the requisite manifestation can be made where the principal authorizes the agent to state that he is authorized. If Pam tells Al, "go tell Ted you are my agent for purposes of selling Blackacre," and Al does so, she has made the requisite manifestation.[88] But what if Al fails to fully disclose the scope of his authority? Suppose Pam told Al that Blackacre should be sold "as is," without any warranty of habitability. Al fails to disclose that fact to Ted and the sales contract negotiated by Al includes a warranty of habitability. Some courts would say that Al lacked apparent authority in this situation, although most such courts would find Al had inherent authority. The modern trend is to say that Al had apparent authority, despite the incomplete statement of authority.

Apparent authority may be implied from a course of conduct. If the principal allows its agents to carry out a series of transactions over an extended period of time, such that a third party would reasonably believe that the most recent transaction also was authorized, apparent authority exists.[89] In *Essco Geometric v. Harvard Industries*,[90] for example, the defendant for over 20 years had allowed its purchasing manager to negotiate contracts on its behalf. During that period, plaintiff had entered into many contracts with the defendant. Following a change in management, the purchasing manager's authority was reduced, but nobody told the plaintiff. Based on the prior course of conduct, the court concluded that the defendant's purchasing manager still had

---

[88] *See, e.g.,* Taylor v. Ramsay–Gerding Construction Co., 196 P.3d 532, 536 (Or. 2007) ("An agent's actions, standing alone and without some action by the principal, cannot create authority to bind the principal. . . . [But] the third party need not receive information respecting either the nature or the extent of that conduct directly from the principal. . . . Thus, information that has been channeled through other sources can be used to support apparent authority, as long as that information can be traced back to the principal."); Badger v. Paulson Investment Co., Inc., 803 P.2d 1178, 1184 n.9 (Or. 1991) (quoting RESTATEMENT (SECOND) § 27 cmt. a, which states that "[t]he information received by the third person may come directly from the principal by letter or word of mouth, from authorized statements of the agent, from documents or other indicia of authority given by the principal to the agent, or from third persons who have heard of the agent's authority through authorized or permitted channels of communication.").

[89] Note that prior acts of the principal can also create implied actual authority if the agent reasonably believed, on the basis of the prior course of conduct, that the transaction was authorized. *See* RESTATEMENT (SECOND) § 43(2). If the principal had given the agent express instructions to the contrary, however, the agent could no longer reasonably believe he had authority and no implied actual authority could exist. Implied apparent authority could still exist, however, if the third party were aware of the prior course of conduct and had no notice of the principal's instructions to the agent.

[90] 46 F.3d 718 (8th Cir. 1995).

apparent authority to enter into a contract on defendant's behalf with the plaintiff.

Finally, apparent authority may also be created by custom. In *Hamilton Hauling, Inc. v. GAF Corp.*,[91] the court explained that: "apparent authority can be created by appointing a person to a position, such as that of manager or treasurer, which carries with it generally recognized duties; to those who know of the appointment there is apparent authority to do the things ordinarily entrusted to one occupying such a position, regardless of unknown limitations which are imposed on the particular agent." As the court's analysis suggests, for apparent authority to arise by virtue of custom, two conditions must be satisfied. First, the third party must know that the principal has placed the agent in a certain position. Second, it must be customary for an agent in that position to have authority to enter into the type of agreement in question.[92] In the *Essco Geometric* case, for example, several witnesses testified that "the industry custom presumed, without question, that the purchasing manager possessed authority to bind the company."[93] Accordingly, even though the terms of the specific contract in question were somewhat unusual, the principal was nevertheless bound.

In sum, the requisite manifestation by the principal can take many forms.

> These include explicit statements that a principal makes directly to a third party, as well as statements made by others concerning an actor's authority that reach the third party and are traceable to the principal. For example, a principal may make a manifestation about an agent's authority by directing that the agent's name and affiliation with the principal be included in a listing of representatives that is provided to a third party. The principal may make a manifestation by directing an agent to make statements to third parties or directing or designating an agent to perform acts or conduct negotiations, placing an agent in a position within an

---

[91] 719 S.W.2d 841 (Mo. App. 1986).

[92] Restatement (Third) § 2.03 cmt. c takes the position that the party must be aware of the custom in question when the contract is made. Restatement (Second) § 27 cmt. d, in contrast, took the position that apparent authority by virtue of custom existed as to those persons who know the agent has been placed in a position carrying customary powers even if they do not know what those powers are. The Restatement (Third) approach is preferable, as it comports with the requirement that the third party reasonable believe the agent was authorized to act. If the third party is unaware of the customary powers of someone in the agent's position, after all, how could the third party reasonably believe anything about the agent's authority?

[93] Essco Geometric v. Harvard Industries, 46 F.3d 718, 727 (8th Cir. 1995).

organization, or placing the agent in charge of a transaction or situation.[94]

Regardless of which form the principal's manifestation takes, apparent authority also requires that the third party must reasonably believe that the agent was authorized to act. A third party on notice that the principal has restricted the agent's authority, such as where the principal has instructed the agent not to exercise powers customarily associated with the agent's position, cannot satisfy the reasonable belief requirement. Does a third party lacking such notice have any affirmative duty to inquire into the scope of the agent's authority, however? Some cases hold that the third party does have a duty of exercising "reasonable diligence" to "verify an agent's authority to enter contracts on behalf of its principal."[95] Other cases, however, hold that the duty of inquiry extends only to actual authority. In *Herbert Construction Co. v. Continental Insurance Co.*,[96] for example, the Second Circuit opined that New York law required a third party relying on a claim of actual authority to have made inquiry into the scope of the agent's authority. The court further opined that New York law did "not impose a duty of inquiry as a prerequisite to asserting a cause of action under apparent authority," except where the circumstances put the third party on notice of the need to inquire, the transaction is extraordinary, or the "novelty" of the transaction suggests the possibility of fraud. If this is a correct statement of New York law, the New York approach gets it exactly backwards. Actual authority has nothing to with the third party's knowledge, state of mind, or what have you. Actual authority is determined solely by reference to what the agent believed about the scope of its authority. Hence, actual authority can exist without regard to any action by the third party. If due diligence is to be required at all, it would seem more appropriate with respect to apparent authority, because it is that form of authority that rests on what the third party reasonably believes.

As to whether due diligence should be required, the better view takes into account the totality of the circumstances.[97] Third parties receive many signals from many sources, including acts of the principal, authorized and unauthorized representations by the agent, course of conduct, industry custom, and so on. The court

---

[94] RESTATEMENT (THIRD) § 2.03 cmt. c.

[95] Progress Printing Corp. v. Jane Byrne Political Comm., 601 N.E.2d (Ill. 1992).

[96] Herbert Construction Co. v. Continental Insurance Co., 931 F.2d 989 (2d Cir. 1990).

[97] *See* RESTATEMENT (THIRD) § 2.03 cmt. d ("Absent circumstances that should raise questions in the mind of a reasonable third party, as a general matter there is no requirement that the third party inquire into the scope of an agent's authority.").

therefore should ask whether, given the totality of the circumstances, it was reasonable for the third party to believe the agent had authority without making any inquiry into the scope of the agent's authority. In doing so, the court should recognize the requiring the third party to make a detailed inquiry into the exact scope of the agent's authority is inconsistent with the rationale of the apparent authority doctrine. As Judge Learned Hand explained: "The very purpose of delegated authority is to avoid constant recourse by third persons to the principal, which would be a corollary of denying the agent any latitude beyond his exact instructions. Once a third person has assured himself widely of the character of the agent's mandate, the very purpose of the relation demands the possibility of the principal's being bound through the agent's minor deviations."[98]

A somewhat related question is whether the third party must reasonably rely on the agent's authority. In particular, must the third party have made a detrimental change in position in reliance on the agent having authority? Although there are some cases to the contrary, the commentary to both Restatement (Second) § 8 and Restatement (Third) § 2.03 makes clear that reliance is not required. Although the Restatement view is the better one, note that a third party's lack of reliance could be used as evidence that third party did not believe the agent was authorized to act.

Students (and judges and juries) often seem to think there is something unfair about apparent authority. Recall our hypothetical in which Paul hires Ann to manage an apartment building. Local custom gives apartment managers the power to hire janitorial services to clean their buildings, but Paul specifically instructs Ann not to hire a janitorial service to clean the building she manages. Ann nevertheless hires a service. Did Ann have authority? She would not have actual authority. An agent will not have incidental authority if the principal has given the agent clear instructions not to use some particular means of accomplishing the task. But she likely would have apparent authority by virtue of custom. Why should the liability be placed on Paul in this case? Ann is the one who was at fault: she violated her instructions. What did Paul do wrong?

Paul did nothing wrong, of course, but it is still appropriate that he bear the loss. Most rules of agency law are default principles—i.e., a set of off-the-rack rules provided by the law so that parties will not have to incur bargaining costs drafting their own detailed set of rules. In general, the law should reflect the so-called majoritarian default—i.e., the rule most parties would

---

[98] Kidd v. Thomas A. Edison, Inc., 239 Fed. 405, 408 (S.D.N.Y. 1917).

bargain for if they could do so costlessly. Providing the majoritarian default minimizes transaction costs, because most parties will simply adopt it off-the-rack, while idiosyncratic parties who want a different rule are free to modify it by agreement.

If principals and third parties could costlessly bargain over the question of apparent authority, what would be the majority rule? Almost certainly, they would not adopt either of the all-or-nothing rules.[99] If only contracts made with actual authority were binding on the principal, such that third parties always bore the risk of loss associated with unauthorized transactions, third parties would be reluctant to deal with agents. At the very least, third parties would be unwilling to transact with agents absent very clear evidence of the agent's actual authority. On the other hand, however, if principals were liable for all unauthorized transactions, they would be less willing to act through agents. Because the ability of a principal to transact business through an agent considerably reduces transaction costs, neither all-or-nothing rule will be acceptable.

As a middle ground, principals and third parties likely would settle on a rule based on the cheaper cost avoider concept (a.k.a. least cost avoider).[100] Where an activity generates losses, society wants to reduce the size of those losses in the cheapest possible way. It makes no sense, after all, to expend two dollars on precautions against a loss if doing so only reduces those losses by one dollar. Thus, in many situations, it makes sense to impose liability on the cheapest cost avoider (i.e., the party who could have most cheaply taken precautions against the loss). Doing so gives that party an incentive to take precautions, while minimizing the cost of those precautions. The principal often will be the cheaper cost avoider. In our hypothetical, because most apartment owners let their managers hire janitors, Paul's position is idiosyncratic. It will be cheaper for the few idiosyncratic owners to take precautions, such as posting notices in the place of business, then to require all potential third parties to take precautions. In addition, if Ann goes ahead and signs a contract for Paul without calling him, then Paul is bound by the contract, but Ann has breached her fiduciary duty to Paul and Paul can sue her for damages. In contrast, where the third party could not reasonably have believed that the agent had actual authority, it likely will be cheaper to insist that the third party take the precaution of making an inquiry into the scope of the agent's authority.[101]

---

[99] RIBSTEIN & LIPSHAW at 34.

[100] KLEIN ET AL. at 37; RIBSTEIN & LIPSHAW at 34.

[101] *See* John Armour & Michael J. Whincop, *An Economic Analysis of Shared Property in Partnership and Close Corporations Law*, 26 J. CORP. L. 983, 996 (2001)

C.   Inherent Authority

Inherent authority—a.k.a. inherent agency power—is a difficult concept around which to get one's hands. The authors of the Restatement created it to solve a problem. The drafter's job is to "restate" the law. They had one set of cases that fit nicely into actual authority. They had another set that fit well into apparent authority. Those sets were the genesis of Restatement (Second) §§ 7 and 8. But they also had a handful of other cases, in which the contract was deemed binding, but there was neither actual nor apparent authority. Some of those cases closely resembled the equity doctrine of estoppel or could be explained as an *ex post* ratification, both of which were categorized in the Restatement (Second) as §§ 8B and 82, respectively. After all that, however, the drafters still had a small set of cases that didn't fit well into any of those categories. All of these were cases in which the contract was deemed binding, because the agent was deemed to have some sort of authority, but none of the recognized forms of authority appeared to be present. Hence, we may assume, the drafters decided to solve the problem by creating a new category—i.e., Restatement (Second) § 8A's inherent authority provision:

> Inherent agency power is a term used in the Restatement of this subject to indicate the power of an agent which is derived not from authority, apparent authority or estoppel, but solely from the agency relation and exists for the protection of persons harmed by or dealing with a servant or other agent.

As the otherwise almost unintelligible phrasing of this provision may suggest, § 8A was intended as a catch-all to capture cases in which our educated intuition tells us that the principal ought to be bound, but we can't fit the case into any of the other categories. Some examples will therefore be helpful.

1.   Unauthorized Acts of a General Agent of an Undisclosed Principal

Watteau v. Fenwick[102] is one of the great cases of agency law. It is also a classic case on inherent authority—arguably, *the* classic case. Watteau and the other defendants owned the Victoria Hotel, a

---

(positing "a least-cost-avoider standard to determine the allocation of loss for unauthorized transactions as between the firm and an outsider"); James L. Burns, Note, *Pruning the Judicial Oak: Developing a Coherent Application of Common Law Agency and Controlling Person Liability in Securities Cases*, 93 COLUM. L. REV. 1185, 1221 (1993) ("Assuming that the client was aware of the firm's regulations precluding personal transactions with brokers, the client is the least-cost avoider, and therefore, should bear the loss.").

[102] [1893] 1 Queens Bench 346 (1892).

pub. The defendants kept the fact of their ownership a secret.[103] In any event, the prior owner, Humble, appeared to be the owner. Humble's name was above the door as proprietor.

Defendants told Humble he was to buy everything he needed from them, with the exception of bottled ales and mineral waters. Humble violated this agreement by buying cigars and Bovril from the plaintiffs. Apparently Humble thereafter flew the coop or was fired. In any event, plaintiffs sued the defendants for payment for the cigars and Bovril.[104]

Where the agent of an undisclosed principal has actual authority to make the contract in question, the contract is binding as a matter of agency law on both the principal and the third party. As to the principal, Restatement (Second) § 186 provides that:

> An undisclosed principal is bound by contracts and conveyances made on his account by an agent acting within his authority, except that the principal is not bound by a contract which is under seal or which is negotiable, or upon a contract which excludes him.

As to the third party, § 302 provides that:

> A person who makes a contract with an agent of an undisclosed principal, intended by the agent to be on account of his principal and within the power of such agent to bind his principal, is liable to the principal as if the principal himself had made the contract with him, unless he is excluded by the form or terms of the contract, unless his existence is fraudulently concealed or unless there is set-off or a similar defense against the agent.

As comment a to Restatement (Second) § 186 observes, these rules "appear to violate one of the basic theories of contracts," namely the need for a meeting of the minds between the parties to the contract, but the comment goes on to explain that:

> The relation between the principal and a person with whom the agent has made an authorized contract is spoken of as

---

[103] I am told by Professor Kevin Outterson that the defendants were a firm of brewers, seeking to control the outlet for their product. Accordingly, the defendants wanted to control the sale of keg beers and ales, but were not as concerned with the incidentals. They presumably concealed their identity because there was some controversy at the time in England because "free houses" (pubs not owned by a brewer) were increasingly being purchased by brewers.

[104] Bovril is a liquefied beef extract dating from the 1870s. Sold in jars as a thick paste, it is used to make broths, soups and drinks, and occasionally spread on toast like Marmite. It is currently banned from importation into the US due to mad cow disease fears. Bovril was originally named "Johnston's Fluid Beef" by its inventor, John Lawson Johnston, who later renamed it Bovril by combining "bo" from the Latin word for cow—"bos"—and a neologism—"vril"—which had appeared in a science fiction novel of the time as the name of "an electric fluid."

contractual, although by definition there has been no manifestation of consent by the third person to the principal or by the principal to him. In fact, the contract, in the common law sense, is between the agent and the third person. In spite of this, the law of agency finds it expedient to create rights and liabilities between the other party to the transaction and the principal as if the latter were a contracting party. It may be said that the principal becomes a party to the contract by operation of law, without the will of the third party and, in some cases, contrary to the will of the principal.

The same rules apply to cases in which the agent of a partially disclosed principal acts within the scope of the agent's actual authority.[105]

In *Watteau*, however, Humble lacked actual authority to buy cigars and Bovril from plaintiffs. Recall that actual authority looks to the communications between the principal and the agent: What could the agent have reasonably believed the scope of his authority to be? In the face of explicit instructions not to do something, an agent has no actual authority to do it.

Humble also lacked apparent authority, because there was no holding out by the principal. Plaintiff didn't even know that the principals existed. If you don't know that there is a principal, how can there be a holding out?

Yet, the court held the defendants liable, explaining:

[O]nce it is established that the defendant was the real principal, the ordinary doctrine as to principal and agent applies—that the principal is liable for all the acts of the agent which are within the authority usually confided to an agent of that character, notwithstanding limitations, as between the principal and the agent, put upon that authority. It is said that it is only so where there has been a holding out of authority— which cannot be said of a case where the person supplying the goods knew nothing of the existence of a principal. But I do not think so. Otherwise, in every case of undisclosed principal, or at least in every case where the fact of there being a principal was undisclosed, the secret limitation of authority would prevail and defeat the action of the person dealing with the agent and then discovering that he was an agent and had a principal.

---

[105] *See, e.g.,* Old Republic Ins. Co. v. Hansa World Cargo Service, Inc., 51 F.Supp.2d 457 (S.D.N.Y. 1999) ("A partially disclosed principal is also responsible for the actions of his agent taken within the agent's authority."); Badger State Bank v. Taylor, 688 N.W.2d 439 (Wis. 2004) ("An undisclosed or partially disclosed principal . . . becomes a party to a transaction between the agent . . . and the third party . . . even if the third party . . . is unaware of the name or existence of the principal.").

Note how, as with apparent authority, the rationale for the rule is grounded in the cheaper cost avoider concept. The defendants' position was idiosyncratic, because most pub owners let their managers buy cigars. It will be cheaper for the few idiosyncratic owners to take precautions, than to require all cigar sellers to take precautions.[106] Indeed, how could the dealer take precautions when he doesn't even know the defendants exist? Because the undisclosed principal is in the best position to avoid the loss, we let the loss fall on the principal rather than the innocent third party.

Students (not to mention judges and practicing lawyers) often have difficulty distinguishing inherent authority from apparent authority by virtue of custom. As *Watteau* suggests, the two concepts are most clearly different in cases where there is an undisclosed principal. Where there is a disclosed or partially disclosed principal—i.e., where the third party knows that the principal exists and has placed the agent in a position carrying certain customary powers—the requisite manifestation by the principal exists to create apparent authority. Where there is an undisclosed principal, however, by definition there has been no communication—let alone a manifestation of authority—between principal and third party.

Inherent authority therefore comes into play in the undisclosed principal setting precisely because it does not require any holding out. Restatement § 195 explains: "An undisclosed principal who entrusts an agent with the management of his business is subject to liability to third persons with whom the agent enters into transactions usual in such businesses and on the principal's account, although contrary to the directions of the principal."[107] In an inherent authority case, the third party thus is saying: "It is customary for people in this position to have power to make this contract. I reasonably believed that this person had such authority. I did not know, nor did I have any reason to believe, that this person had no such authority." So long as the agent's acts are "usual in such businesses," inherent authority exists.

---

[106] Whether this is true, of course, needs to be evaluated on a case-by-case basis. As Ribstein and Lisphaw observe, in some cases "the principal's disclosure costs may not be trivial." RIBSTEIN & LIPSHAW at 43. Where the third party is the least cost avoider, the policy rationale for inherent authority—which many regard as thin to begin with—evaporates.

[107] Note the requirement that the acts be done on the principal's account. (The same requirement is found in RESTATEMENT (SECOND) § 161, which applies to general agents of disclosed or partially disclosed principals (*see infra*).) This requirement suggests a potentially significant wrinkle on the *Watteau* case. Why did Humble violate his principals' instructions? If Humble was cheating by selling the cigars and Bovril for his own profit, one could argue that he was not acting on the principals' account. If so, the case would turn on whether the defendants have any liability for fraud committed by their agent.

2. *Unauthorized Acts of a General Agent of an Disclosed Principal*

Restatement (Second) § 161 provides that: "A general agent for a disclosed or partially disclosed principal subjects his principal to liability for acts done on his account which usually accompany or are incidental to transactions which the agent is authorized to conduct if, although they are forbidden by the principal, the other party reasonably believes that the agent is authorized to do them and has no notice that he is not so authorized." It is almost impossible to see what § 161 adds to the concept of apparent authority by virtue of custom. Consider, for example, the leading case of *Kidd v. Thomas A. Edison, Inc.*[108] In the years following his invention of the phonograph, Edison developed a marketing scheme in which live singers would give recitals at which their record albums also would be played. The idea was to demonstrate how accurately the albums and phonograph reproduced music. (Older readers will recall the advertising slogan—"Is it live or is it Memorex"—used in a comparable advertising campaign for blank cassette tapes.)

An Edison employee named Maxwell engaged an agent named Fuller to engage the singers. According to Edison, the singers were to be paid by the dealers at whose stores the recitals. According to the plaintiff, one of the hired singers, Fuller promised her an extended singing tour with her fees to be paid by Edison. In his opinion, Judge Learned Hand ranged widely across such doctrines as estoppel, implied actual authority, and apparent authority.

On the stated facts, *Kidd* seems like an easy case for applying the principle of apparent authority by virtue of custom. Plaintiff proved that Fuller offered her a singing tour. Plaintiff also proved that it is a "common thing to engage singers for [musical] recitals," even though the precise purpose of these recitals was novel. Further, the court found that "the customary implication would seem to have been that his authority was without limitation of the kind here imposed, which was unheard of in the circumstances." What need is there for inherent authority on such facts?

What about the fact that plaintiff Kidd dealt solely with Fuller, however? Fuller's statements to Kidd were the only basis she had for knowing that he was Edison's agent. Apparent authority by virtue of custom finds the requisite manifestation by the principal where the third party knows the principal placed the agent in a position customarily carrying certain powers. Here, Kidd's knowledge comes from the agent's own statements. This is not a

---

[108] 239 F. 405 (S.D.N.Y.), *aff'd*, 242 F.2d 923 (2d Cir. 1917).

problem, however. Recall that the requisite manifestation is present when the principal authorizes "the agent to state that he is authorized."[109] Fuller was so authorized, so he could create apparent authority through his own statements to the plaintiff.

Section 161 therefore ends up being relevant only in a very few cases, almost all of which will involve relatively unusual facts. Section 161, for example, comes into play where the third party is unaware of the usual powers of agents. Section 161 also comes into play where the principal did not authorize the agent to hold himself out as having authority to make the contract. Outside of these situations, however, § 161 is swallowed up by apparent authority.

3. Rethinking Inherent Authority

Although it has been around for almost half-a-century, inherent authority remains highly controversial. Judge Frank Easterbrook, for example, once referred to the "new brand of 'inherent' authority" as a form of "bootstrapping."[110]

The Restatement (Third) drops the phrase "inherent agency power." Instead, it offers a revised and broader version of apparent authority, making clear that conduct such as placing an agent in a position of authority can create apparent authority to do what is customary. This new refinement will adequately address cases like *Kidd*. To deal with cases like *Watteau*, the Restatement adopts a new concept called "estoppel of an undisclosed principal." The rule is essentially the same as old Restatement (Second) § 195.

4. A Final Thought

Restatement (Second) § 161 suggests that the issue with respect to inherent authority is whether the third party reasonably believes that the agent had authority to make the contract and whether such contracts usually are incidental to the sorts of conduct the agent has authority to do. Restatement (Third) § 2.03 continues that line of inquiry. Accordingly, the issue of whether the agent's acts were of the sort that "usually accompany or are incidental to transactions which the agent is authorized to conduct" is to be analyzed from the third party's perspective rather than that of the principal.[111] Even if it is not customary in the industry in question for agents to exercise the power in question, inherent authority thus can still exist if the third person reasonably believes it is customary for agents of this sort to commit such acts.

---

[109] RESTATEMENT (SECOND) § 8 cmt. b.

[110] Cange v. Stotler & Co., 826 F.2d 581, 598 (7th Cir. 1987).

[111] Crosiant v. Watrud, 432 P.2d 799 (Ore. 1967).

It would make more sense to ask whether the agent's deviation was reasonably foreseeable by the principal.[112] In other words, we should focus on the question of whether it was reasonably foreseeable by the principal—rather than the third party—that the agent would enter into such contracts even despite instructions to the contrary. This approach makes for an appealing symmetry: actual authority depends on what the agent reasonably believes; apparent authority depends on what the third party reasonably believes; and inherent authority depends on what the principal believes. The main justification for this approach, however, is (again) based on the cheaper cost avoider principle. If we assume that the agent's misconduct was reasonably foreseeable to the principal, we might reasonably assume that the principal is in a better position to control the agent's conduct than is some third party.[113]

D. Estoppel

Hoddeson v. Koos Brothers remains the classic example of a situation in which a "principal" may be estopped to deny the existence of an agency relationship and the authority of the purported agent.[114] In the "forenoon of August 22, 1956," Joan Hoddeson and family "Happily journeyed" to the Koos Brothers furniture store to purchase some bedroom furniture "she ardently desired." As the court's lighthearted opinion observes, what happened next "will be informative and perhaps admonitory to the unwary shopper." While shopping on the business' premises, Hoddeson was assisted by "a tall man with dark hair frosted at the temples and clad in a gray suit." He accepted her order and her $168.50 in cash. When the furniture was not delivered, she sued. As you will have guessed by now, the tall man with dark frosted hair turned out to be an imposter who had absconded with Hoddeson's funds.

It seems obvious why Hoddeson sued. She was a poor woman with four children who had been able to buy the furniture only as a result of a gift of $165 from her mother. It is less obvious why Koos Brothers litigated the case so vigorously. The court opined: "Obviously, the endeavor of the defendant is to elicit from us a precedential opinion concerning a merchant's liability in the exceptional circumstances disclosed by the evidence to which we

---

[112] *See* EISENBERG & COX at 15 (advocating this approach).

[113] *Cf.* Gandy v. Cole, 193 N.W.2d 58 (Mich. App. 1971) (O'Hara, J., dissenting) ("When, as in this case, a principal permits an agent to present to potential customers a business card proclaiming to all and sundry that he, the principal, is a 'business counselor' and that the card bearer is his representative, the principal had better make it his business to know what 'counseling' is done, particularly when the counseling results in doing a customer of the principal out of some $15,000.")

[114] 135 A.2d 702 (N.J. App.Div. 1957).

have already alluded, and by the supplementary evidence to which we shall presently refer." Yet, while a precedent is useful, it is something of a public good. All merchants would benefit from a successful precedent, but only Koos Brothers is bearing the legal costs to generate a precedent. In economic terms, all other merchants are free riding on Koos Brothers. Why then would Koos Brothers do it? Does this sort of thing happen often enough to Koos Brothers to justify the expense of setting a precedent? If so, it likely would have been be simpler to tighten up floor security. So it remains a puzzle.

In any case, the trial court's instructions to the jury were based solely on the theory that the tall man with dark frosted hair was an employee of the store with apparent authority. The appeals court reversed, holding that there was no evidence to support this view. Koos' failure to police its sales floor could not constitute the requisite manifestation to establish apparent agency. "A manifestation is conduct by a person, observable by others, that expresses meaning."[115] Koos' failure to police its sales floor simply does not rise to the level of expressive conduct necessary for apparent agency (and, hence, apparent authority) to be put in issue.

The appeals court, however, remanded the case for a new trial so that Hoddeson could be given a chance to prove her case on a theory of estoppel. In pure estoppel cases, like *Hoddeson,* the court recognizes that the purported agent had no actual or apparent authority to engage in the transaction at hand; indeed, the purported agent may be an imposter. Due to some fault of the principal, however, the court will hold that the principal is bound. As the *Hoddeson* court explained, estoppel operates "to preclude a defendant's denial of liability. It matters little whether for immediate purposes we entitle or characterize the principle of law in such cases as 'agency by estoppel' or 'a tortious dereliction of duty owed to an invited customer.'" Under either rubric, "where a proprietor of a place of business by his dereliction of duty enables one who is not his agent conspicuously to act as such and ostensibly to transact the proprietor's business with a patron in the establishment, the appearances being of such a character as to lead a person of ordinary prudence and circumspection to believe that the impostor was in truth the proprietor's agent, in such circumstances the law will not permit the proprietor defensively to avail himself of the impostor's lack of authority and thus escape liability for the consequential loss thereby sustained by the

---

[115] RESTATEMENT (THIRD) § 1.03 cmt. b.

customer."[116] Hence, where the doctrine is applicable, the principal is estopped from raising the lack of authority as a defense to a breach of contract suit by the third party.

The distinction between estoppel and apparent authority sometimes can be quite subtle. Courts, in fact, routinely get the two bollixed up. In many cases, moreover, both will be present. A critical distinction between estoppel and apparent authority, however, is the need for a change in position by the third party. If the plaintiff in *Hoddeson* had not paid the imposter, but instead had merely entered into a contract to buy the furniture, then there would have been no change of position to justify estoppel. Proof of estoppel, after all, requires showing "(1) the principal's intentional or negligent acts, including acts of omission, created an appearance of authority in the agent, (2) on which a third party reasonably and in good faith relied, and (3) such reliance resulted in a detrimental change in position on the part of the third party."[117] In the absence of such proof, the issue would have been whether the imposter was an apparent agent, which would require some manifestation from the principal to the third party, as opposed to estoppel's possibility of a mere "failure to take reasonable steps" to protect the plaintiff.[118] Since Hoddeson could show detrimental reliance, however, by having paid cash which was then lost, she could prevail on a theory of estoppel without the need to show any holding out by Koos Brothers. As Restatement (Third) § 2.05 explains: "A person who *has not made a manifestation* that an actor has authority as an agent and *who is not otherwise liable* as a party to a transaction purportedly done by the actor on that person's account is liable to a third party who justifiably is induced to make a detrimental change in position because the transaction is believed to be on the person's account, if (1) the person intentionally or carelessly caused such belief, or (2) having notice of such belief and that it might induce others to change their positions, the person did not take reasonable steps to notify them of the facts."[119]

E. Ratification

One surprisingly often encounters situations in which one person, A, purports to act on behalf of another, P, without any type of authority to do so. It may be that A exceeded A's authority or it

---

[116] Hoddeson v. Koos Bros., 135 A.2d 702, 707 (N.J. App.Div. 1957). Where the place of business is not open to the general public, courts have declined to find estoppel. *See, e.g.*, Raclaw v. Fay, Conmy & Co., 688 N.E.2d 114, 118 (Ill. App. 1996).

[117] Minskoff v. American Express Travel Related Services Co., 98 F.3d 703, 708 (2d Cir. 1996) (citations omitted).

[118] *Compare* RESTATEMENT (SECOND) § 8 (apparent authority), *with* RESTATEMENT (SECOND) § 8B(1)(b) (estoppel).

[119] RESTATEMENT (THIRD) § 2.05 (emphasis supplied.)

may simply be that there was no prior agency relationship between P and A. In either situation, P may still be bound by A's act if P subsequently ratifies the action. If ratified, a transaction will be treated as though it had been authorized when entered into in the first instance. In a sense, ratification is an *ex post facto* authorization which relates back to the time the agreement was made. Consequently, once there has been an effective ratification, both principal and third party are bound by the contract.

In order for an effective ratification to occur, the principal must affirm the contract.[120] Obviously, one can expressly affirm a contract; P could say something like, "Gosh, what a wonderful deal; I'll go forward with it," and P would thus affirm the contract. Express affirmations are rarely litigated, of course. Rather, litigation tends to involve some form of implied affirmation.

1. Ratification by Accepting Benefits of Transaction

Suppose Pam is a writer. Her husband Alex enters into a contract with ABC Book Publishers under which Pam's next book is to go to ABC. Pam gets a check from ABC, representing the advance on the contract, which she cashes. She then spends the proceeds on a new computer for her office. Some months later Pam tries to sell her new book to another publisher. ABC claims the book. Pam correctly points out that Alan had no authority to act as her agent.[121] But ABC responds by saying that she had ratified the contract. Who wins? Probably ABC. This would be an implied affirmation through acceptance of the benefits of the transaction.[122]

Suppose Pam argues that she thought the check was for royalties on one of her previous books, which ABC had published. She asserts that she neither knew nor had reason to know that it was an advance on her next book. In order for there to be a valid ratification, at the time of the alleged affirmation the principal must know or have reason to know the material facts relating to the transaction.[123] Whether the principal "had reason to know" the material facts was the issue in *Outboard Marine Center v. Little Glasses Corp.*[124] There it was alleged that the principal implicitly ratified a transaction through retention of its benefits. The court held that the principal was on notice of material facts relating to the alleged ratification that could have been discovered by

---

[120] RESTATEMENT (SECOND) § 82.

[121] A marital relationship does not by itself establish that one spouse is the agent of another. Botticello v. Stefanovicz, 411 A.2d 16, 26 (Conn. 1979).

[122] RESTATEMENT (SECOND) § 98.

[123] Ratification requires "acceptance of the results of the act with an intent to ratify, and with full knowledge of all the material circumstances." Ansonia v. Cooper, 30 A. 760, 762 (Conn. 1894).

[124] 338 P.2d 1101 (Okla. 1959).

inspection of records in the principal's possession. Accordingly, there was an effective affirmation.

Let's change the facts of our working hypothetical slightly. Alan is a fan of Pam's books, who, unfortunately, is slightly off his rocker. He goes to a local landscaping company. Pretending to be Pam's butler, he asks the company to cut Pam's grass.[125] Pam arrives home just after the men finished up. Pam thanks them and goes inside. The company sues her for refusing to pay. Pam correctly points out that Alan had no authority to enter into this contract. The company claims she ratified the contract by accepting and retaining its benefits. Who wins? On the ratification issue, probably Pam. The alleged affirmation must come at a time when it is possible to decline to accept such benefits. Pam cannot be held responsible if Pam never had an opportunity to turn down the benefits given by the third party. Of course, Pam might be liable on some other theory, such as quasi-contract.

Now let's make a major change in the facts of our working hypothetical. Suppose Paula is an investor. She opens an account at a local brokerage. She instructs Al, her broker, only to purchase U.S. treasury bonds for the account. Al disregards those instructions and buys stock in a new very risky high-tech company. Paula does not learn about this until her first monthly statement arrives. She decides to take a wait and see attitude. When her next monthly statement arrives she notices that the stock's price has dropped rather drastically. She calls Al up and demands that he close the account and reimburse her for the money she lost. She correctly claims he had no authority to buy the stock. Al closes the account, but refuses to make Paula's losses good. Al claims Paula ratified the purchase by waiting. Who's right: Paula or Al? Al. This is an instance of implied affirmation through silence or inaction. A principal can't wait forever before repudiating an unauthorized transaction.

But what if Paula had insisted that Al close the account when she first learned of the unauthorized trade. Would that change the result? Yes. All the principal is required to do is to promptly disavow the transaction as soon as the principal either knew of the transaction or had reason to know of it.

---

[125] The putative agent must at least purport to be acting on the supposed principal's behalf. Botticello v. Stefanovicz, 411 A.2d 16, 29 (Conn. 1979). "Thus if the original transaction was not purported to be done on account of the principal, the fact that the principal receives its proceeds does not make him a party to it." RESTATEMENT (SECOND) § 98.

2. *Ratification by Litigation*

Suppose Paula hires Alan to sell her used boat. Alan sells the boat to Ted. Alan gives Ted an express warranty that the boat is seaworthy. First time out the boat sinks. Ted refuses to pay for the boat. Paula sues for breach of contract. Ted defends by saying that the boat didn't live up to the warranty. Paula correctly says Alan had no authority to give the warranty. But Ted says that by suing on the contract, Paula has ratified Alan's conduct and is bound by the warranty. Who is right? Probably Ted. This would be implied affirmation through bringing a lawsuit to enforce the contract.[126] Paula cannot selectively ratify only part of the contract; if the deal is ratified, she will be bound by the entire deal, including the unauthorized warranty.

The prospect of ratifying an unauthorized contract by bring suit for breach of that contract makes it very important for the lawyer to carefully craft the lawsuit. Paula could have sued Alan or Ted for conversion of her property. Alternatively, Paula could sue Alan for breach of duty. But if her lawyer is not careful and brings the suit as one on the contract, ratification will result.

3. *When Attempted Ratification Will Be Unavailing*

In some cases, an attempt by P to ratify the transaction will be unavailing. Generally this is done where necessary to protect the rights of an innocent third party.[127] Suppose that in our last hypothetical, Ted had withdrawn from the contract before the boat was delivered. Paula then attempts to ratify by bringing suit on the contract. Who wins? Ted. To make an effective ratification the principal must ratify before the third party withdraws.

What about a change of circumstance? Suppose Paula owns Whiteacre. Alan, having no authority to do so, enters into a sale contract with Ted by which Ted is to purchase Whiteacre. The next day the house burns to the ground. Paula then expressly affirms the contract. Ted says she's too late. Who wins? Ted. Since ratification is a way for Paula to get the benefits of an unauthorized bargain, ratification will not be effective in settings where it would prejudice the rights of an innocent third-party.

In these settings, the third party can chose whether or not to be bound to the contract; the principal cannot enforce the

---

[126] *See, e.g.,* Navrides v. Zurich Ins. Co., 488 P.2d 637 (Cal. 1971). What if Paula said something like this in her complaint: "By bringing this action I am merely affirming the sale, I hereby disavow any intention to affirm or ratify Alan's giving of a warranty of seaworthiness to Ted." Would that change the result? No. Ratification is an all-or-nothing proposition. The principal must ratify the entire transaction or repudiate it entirely. *See* RESTATEMENT (THIRD) § 4.07.

[127] RESTATEMENT (THIRD) § 4.05.

agreement unless the third party elects to be bound. Generally these situations arise where there has been some material change in the circumstances between the time of the transaction and the time of the purported ratification.

    4. Distinguishing Ratification from Authority by Acquiescence

    Be careful to distinguish problems of ratification from those in which authority is created by acquiescence of the principal in unauthorized actions of the agent. "Acquiescence by the principal in a series of acts by the agent indicates authorization to perform similar acts in the future."[128] In other words, unless disavowed by the principal, acquiescence as to past unauthorized conduct can create actual or apparent authority as to future transactions.

    The harder question is whether acquiescence by the principal can be used as evidence that the act was authorized. If so, the act is binding on the principal without any need for it to be ratified. Restatement (Second) § 43(1) explains: "Acquiescence by the principal in conduct of an agent whose previously conferred authorization reasonably might include it, indicates that the conduct was authorized; if clearly not included in the authorization, acquiescence in it indicates affirmance." In other words, if the unauthorized conduct in which the principal acquiesced was closely related to the agent's actual authority, the principal's acquiescence may be used as evidence that the agent had actual or apparent authority. If not, the transaction must be ratified.

F. Agent's Liability on the Contract

    Whether a third party can hold an agent liable where the principal fails to perform on a contract entered into by the agent on the principal's behalf depends mainly on whether the principal was disclosed, partially disclosed, or undisclosed. Where an agent acts on behalf of a disclosed principal, the agent generally has no liability to third parties but may incur such liability in two limited situations. First, if the clear intent of the parties is that the agent, as well as the principal, is to be a party to the contract, then the agent is bound under ordinary contract principles.[129] The tough issue in these cases is usually figuring out precisely what the parties intended. In general it will be presumed that the intent was

---

    [128] RESTATEMENT (SECOND) § 43(2).

    [129] RESTATEMENT (SECOND) § 323. This is true even if the agent had only apparent authority. *See, e.g.,* Joe & Dan Int'l Corp. v. U.S. Fidelity & Guaranty Co., 533 N.E.2d 912, 916 (Ill. App. 1988).

only to bind the principal,[130] but the agent is obviously safer if the contract says so explicitly.

Second, there are situations in which the agent had no authority to bind the principal and the principal refuses to ratify the contract. Can the third party get compensation for all or part of its loss from the agent? In the vast majority of jurisdictions the answer is yes, although the theories used often differ. A few old decisions let the third party sue the agent for breach of the contract.[131] Restatement (Second) § 328 rejects this approach, however. A few jurisdictions hold that the third party can sue the agent in tort for deceit.[132] Restatement (Second) § 330 accepts this approach, but relegates liability to tort law. Most jurisdictions hold that there is an implied warranty of authority—the agent implicitly warrants to the third party that he or she has the authority to enter into the contract.[133] Restatement (Second) § 329 adopts this approach.

A potential problem with the latter two approaches is that the court may permit the third party to recover only its actual damages—not damages for breach of contract. The comments to Restatement (Second) § 329 split the baby. The agent is not made a party to the contract, but the third party is entitled to "the amount by which he would have benefited had the authority existed."

As for partially disclosed or undisclosed principals, both the agent and the principal are liable for contracts entered into by an authorized agent on behalf of a partially disclosed or undisclosed principal.[134] More precisely, the agent is liable as though he were a party to the contract. Under the law prior to the Restatement (Third), the third party could not get a judgment against both the principal and agent, although in most states he could sue both of them in the same action.[135] Once the third party elected which of the two parties he would obtain a judgment against, however, the could not go back and obtain a judgment against the other party if

---

[130] *See, e.g.,* Golf Digest/Tennis, Inc. v. Diode, Inc., 849 S.W.2d 617, 618 (Mo. App. 1993).

[131] HYNES at 431.

[132] *See, e.g.,* Mendelsohn v. Holton, 149 N.E. 38 (Mass. 1925).

[133] *See, e.g.,* Yoakum v. Tarver, 64 Cal. Rptr. 7, 11 (Cal. App. 1967); McKnight v. Hialeah Race Course, Inc., 242 So.2d 478, 480–81 (Fla. App. 1970); Ware v. Christenberry, 637 P.2d 452, 456 (Kan. App. 1981); Husky Industries Inc. v. Craig Industries, Inc., 618 S.W.2d 458, 461 (Mo. App. 1981); Glendale Realty, Inc. v. Johnson, 495 P.2d 1375 (Wash. App. 1972).

[134] *See, e.g.,* Jensen v. Alaska Valuation Service, 688 P.2d 161 (Ala. 1984); Atlantic Salmon A/S v. Curran, 591 N.E.2d 206 (Mass. App. 1992).

[135] *See, e.g.,* Owen v. King, 84 S.W.2d 743, 750 (Tex.Civ.App.1935) (following "the rule that the [third party] may sue both the agent and the undisclosed principal, and at his option may, before judgment, elect to hold the undisclosed principal liable by taking a nonsuit as against the agent").

the third party was unable to obtain satisfaction on the original judgment.[136]

Restatement (Third) § 6.09 rejects this so-called "election" rule:

> When an agent has made a contract with a third party on behalf of a principal, unless the contract provides otherwise, (1) the liability, if any, of the principal or the agent to the third party is not discharged if the third party obtains a judgment against the other; and (2) the liability, if any, of the principal or the agent to the third party is discharged to the extent a judgment against the other is satisfied.

The drafters assert that this new "satisfaction" rule "is consistent with the contemporary view that a judgment against one person who is liable for a loss does not terminate the claim that the injured party may have against another party who may also be liable for the loss."[137] The drafters also pointed out that the election rule operated asymmetrically to the disadvantage of the third party. Payment by the third party to the agent does not discharge the third party's obligation to the principal, unless the agent had actual authority not only to make the contract but also to collect payment.[138]

G.   Authority of Corporate Officers

Most of the case law on the apparent authority of corporate officers relates to the powers of presidents. Corporate presidents are regarded as general agents of the corporation vested with considerable managerial powers. Accordingly, contracts that are executed by the president on the corporation's behalf and arise out of the ordinary course of business matters are binding on the corporation.[139]

---

[136] Amortibanc Inv. Co. v. Rappaport Assoc. Mgmt, Inc., 627 P.2d 389, 394 (Kan. App. 1981); Morris Oil Co., Inc. v. Rainbow Oilfield Trucking, Inc., 741 P.2d 840, 844 (N.M. 1987).

[137] RESTATEMENT (THIRD) § 6.09 cmt. c.

[138] *See generally* Grinder v. Bryans Road Bldg. & Supply Co., Inc., 432 A.2d 453, 461 (Md. 1981) (arguing that the election rule is "unjust, since as a result the principal who ordinarily profits from the transaction and who has not met his obligations is relieved by the mistake of the other party in believing that the agent has sufficient assets to pay the debt, since in all cases where the matter is of importance, the agent is insolvent"). The court in that case further noted that academic "commentators appear to be nearly unanimous in their support of the minority, i. e., satisfaction, rule." *Id.* at 462.

[139] *See, e.g.,* Buxton v. Diversified Res. Corp., 634 F.2d 1313 (10th Cir. 1980) (president had authority to sign audit statements in the ordinary course of his job); Evanston Bank v. Conticommodity Servs., Inc., 623 F. Supp. 1014 (N.D.Ill. 1985) (president's inherent authority extended only to ordinary matters); Belcher v. Birmingham Trust Nat'l Bank, 348 F. Supp. 61 (N.D.Ala. 1968) (president has power to bind corporation in ordinary course of business); Custer Channel Wing Corp. v. Frazer, 181 F. Supp. 197 (S.D.N.Y. 1959) (president had authority to bring suit on the corporation's behalf because doing so was incidental to the ordinary business of the firm); Western Am. Life Ins. Co. v. Hicks, 217 S.E.2d 323 (Ga. App. 1975)

Cases dealing with the authority of subordinate officers are much rarer. As to vice presidents, a number of (mostly older) cases hold they have little or no implied or apparent authority to bind the corporation. Accordingly, they have only such authority as is expressly conferred on them in the bylaws or by board resolution.[140] The corporate secretary—a statutory officer appointed by the board of directors—is assumed to be the custodian of the corporation's books and records. Accordingly, the secretary has actual authority to certify those records. Otherwise, however, the secretary has no authority other than that conferred on him by the bylaws or board resolutions.[141]

An important line of cases limits the implied and apparent authority of corporate officers to matters arising in the ordinary course of business. In the leading decision of *Lee v. Jenkins Bros.,* the Second Circuit held:

> The rule most widely cited is that the president only has authority to bind his company by acts arising in the usual and regular course of business but not for contracts of an "extraordinary" nature. . . .
>
> Apparent authority is essentially a question of fact. It depends not only on the nature of the contract involved, but the officer negotiating it, the corporation's usual manner of conducting business, the size of the corporation and the number of its stockholders, the circumstances that give rise to the contract, the reasonableness of the contract, the amounts involved, and who the contracting third party is, to list a few but not all of the relevant factors. In certain instances a given contract may be so important to the welfare of the corporation that outsiders would naturally suppose that only the board of directors (or even the shareholders) could properly handle it. It

---

(president has power to act in ordinary course of business); Quigley v. W. N. Macqueen & Co., 151 N.E. 487 (Ill. 1926) (by virtue of his office, president has power to bind the corporation to contracts made in the ordinary course of business).

[140] *See, e.g.,* Interstate Nat'l Bank v. Koster, 292 P. 805 (Kan. 1930); James F. Monaghan, Inc. v. M. Lowenstein & Sons, 195 N.E. 101 (Mass. 1935); Musulin v. Woodtek, 491 P.2d 1173 (Or. 1971).

[141] *See, e.g.,* In re Drive-In Development Corp., 371 F.2d 215 (7th Cir. 1966) (corporation estopped to deny validity of board resolutions certified by corporate secretary); Meyer v. Glenmoor Homes, Inc., 54 Cal.Rptr. 786 (Cal. App. 1966) (secretary had power to affix corporate seal to documents but no authority re contracts of indebtedness); Blair v. Brownstone Oil & Refining Co., 120 P. 41 (Cal. App. 1911) (no authority to execute release); Ideal Foods, Inc. v. Action Leasing Corp., 413 So.2d 416 (Fla. App. 1982) (secretary is a ministerial position with no authority to conduct business); Shunga Plaza, Inc. v. American Employer's Ins. Co., 465 P.2d 987 (Kan. 1970) (corporate secretary has no power to bind the corporation unless the board has entrusted him with management of the business); Easter Oil Corp. v. Strauss, 52 S.W.2d 336 (Tex.Civ. App. 1932) (secretary had no authority to execute promissory note).

is in this light that the "ordinary course of business" rule should be given its content.[142]

As *Lee* suggests, there is no bright line between ordinary and extraordinary acts. It seems reasonable to assume, however, that acts consigned by statute to the board of directors will be deemed extraordinary.[143] Consequently, for example, extraordinary acts doubtless include the various acts specified in MBCA § 8.25(e) that a board of directors may not delegate to a committee.[144] (Of course, once the board has made its decision with respect to an extraordinary matter, implementation of that decision can be delegated to officers.)

In general, when one must decide a particular action is ordinary or extraordinary, the following factors seem especially pertinent:[145] How much of the firm's assets or earnings are involved? Suppose a corporation running a video tape rental store has $10,000 in cash available. A decision to spend $50 to buy a new tape would be ordinary, a decision to spend $5,000 to establish a line of compact discs for rent probably would be regarded as extraordinary. How much risk is involved? A decision to buy one tape is not very risky and would be an ordinary action, while a decision to open a new store might be very risky and therefore extraordinary. A decision to buy tapes on installment where the purchase price is paid off in three months probably would be seen as ordinary. A decision to take out a thirty year loan probably would be seen as extraordinary. How long will the action have an effect on the corporation? How much would it cost to reverse the decision? A decision to open a new store might be very expensive to reverse, as the corporation might not be able to get out of the lease if things went bad. Such a decision thus would be extraordinary.

As to most matters falling in the gray area between ordinary and extraordinary, a small host of decisions could be cited on either side.[146] There is relatively little consistency of outcome in this area.

---

[142] 268 F.2d 357, 365 n70 (2d Cir.), *cert. denied*, 361 U.S. 913 (1959). *See also* In re Mulco Products, Inc., 123 A.2d 95 (Del.Super.Ct. 1956); Lucey v. Hero Int'l Corp., 281 N.E.2d 266 (Mass. 1972).

[143] See, e.g., Plant v. White River Lumber Co., 76 F.2d 155 (8th Cir. 1935) (sale of all or substantially all corporate assets).

[144] The Model Business Corporation Act provides that the following decisions may not be delegated to a committee of the board, but rather must be made by the board as a whole: (1) Authorize dividends or other distributions, except according to a formula or method, or within limits, prescribed by the board of directors. (2) Approve or propose to shareholders action that the statute requires be approved by shareholders. (3) Fill vacancies on the board of directors or, in general, on any of its committees. (4) Adopt, amend, or repeal bylaws. MODEL BUS. CORP. ACT ANN. § 8.25(e) (2003).

[145] AMERICAN LAW INSTITUTE, PRINCIPLES OF CORPORATE GOVERNANCE: ANALYSIS AND RECOMMENDATIONS § 3.01 rptr. note (1994).

[146] For cases holding particular acts to be "ordinary," see, e.g., Lee v. Jenkins Bros., 268 F.2d 357 (2d Cir.), cert. denied, 361 U.S. 913 (1959) (hiring or firing

Courts are divided, for example, as to whether such basic matters as filing a lawsuit[147] or executing a guarantee of another corporation's debts are ordinary or extraordinary.[148] One is tempted to remind the courts that Emerson's famous dictum against a fetish for consistency holds only that a "foolish consistency is the hobgoblin of little minds."

How should cases falling between the extremes be resolved? In general, the authority of corporate officers should be regarded as virtually plenary. Only matters expressly reserved to the board by statute, the articles of incorporation, or the bylaws should be deemed "extraordinary" and, consequently, beyond the scope of senior officers' authority.

One rationale for this position is suggested by simple statutory interpretation. Both the Model Business Corporation Act and Delaware law provide that the business of the corporation "shall be managed by or under the direction of a board of directors."[149] The use of the disjunctive prior to the phrase "under the direction of" suggests that the statute's drafters anticipated that the corporation

---

employees and fixing their compensation and benefits); United Producers and Consumers Co op. v. Held, 225 F.2d 615 (9th Cir. 1955) (same); Custer Channel Wing Corp. v. Frazer, 181 F. Supp. 197 (S.D.N.Y. 1959) (initiating lawsuit); Memorial Hosp. Ass'n of Stanislaus County v. Pacific Grape Products Co., 290 P.2d 481 (Cal. 1955) (making charitable pledge); In re Mulco Products, Inc., 123 A.2d 95 (Del.Super.Ct. 1956) (executing promissory note); Quigley v. W. N. Macqueen & Co., 151 N.E. 487 (Ill. 1926) (corporation would repurchase stock from shareholder at latter's option); Sperti Products, Inc. v. Container Corp., 481 S.W.2d 43 (Ky. App. 1972) (executing guarantee of another firm's debts); Emperee v. Meyers, 269 A.2d 731 (Pa. 1970) (executing note for benefit of prospective employee).

For cases holding particular acts to be extraordinary, see, e.g., In re Lee Ready Mix & Supply Co., 437 F.2d 497 (6th Cir. 1971) (mortgaging assets); Maple Island Farm, Inc. v. Bitterling, 209 F.2d 867 (8th Cir. 1954) (lifetime employment contract); Abraham Lincoln Life Ins. Co. v. Hopwood, 81 F.2d 284 (6th Cir. 1936); (contract to effectuate a merger); Computer Maint. Corp. v. Tilley, 322 S.E.2d 533 (Ga. App. 1984) (shareholder buy sell agreement); First Nat'l Bank v. Cement Products Co., 227 N.W. 908 (Iowa 1929) (guaranteeing debt of another firm); Ney v. Eastern Iowa Tel. Co., 144 N.W. 383 (Iowa 1913) (initiating a lawsuit against the corporation's largest shareholder); Chesapeake & Potomac Tel. Co. v. Murray, 84 A.2d 870 (Md. 1951) (lifetime employment contract); Daniel Webster Council, Inc. v. St. James Ass'n, Inc., 533 A.2d 329 (N.H. 1987) (land sales contract); Myrtle Ave. Corp. v. Mt. Prospect Bldg. & Loan Ass'n, 169 A. 707 (N.J. 1934) (postponing mortgage foreclosure); Burlington Indus., Inc. v. Foil, 202 S.E.2d 591 (N.C. 1974) (guaranteeing another firm's debts); Brown v. Grayson Enter., Inc., 401 S.W.2d 653 (Tex.Civ. App. 1966) (making lifetime employment contract); Lloydona Peters Enterprises, Inc. v. Dorius, 658 P.2d 1209 (Utah 1983) (initiating litigation).

[147] *Compare* Custer Channel Wing Corp. v. Frazer, 181 F. Supp. 197 (S.D.N.Y. 1959) (president had authority to do so) *with* Lloydona Peters Enter., Inc. v. Dorius, 658 P.2d 1209 (Utah 1983) (no authority to do so); Ney v. Eastern Iowa Tel. Co., 144 N.W. 383 (Iowa 1913) (no authority to do so with respect to the corporation's largest shareholder).

[148] *Compare* Sperti Products, Inc. v. Container Corp. of Am., 481 S.W.2d 43 (Ky. App. 1972) (president had authority) *with* First Nat'l Bank v. Cement Products Co., 227 N.W. 908 (Iowa 1929) (no authority to do so); Burlington Indus., Inc. v. Foil, 202 S.E.2d 591 (N.C. 1974) (president lacked authority, *inter alia*, because making such guarantees was not part of the corporations' ordinary business).

[149] DEL. CODE. ANN. tit. 8, § 141(a) (2001); MODEL BUS. CORP. ACT § 8.01 (1984).

would be managed by its officers with the board mainly exercising oversight authority. Unless a decision is expressly reserved to the board, the statutory language thus contemplates that a corporation may act through its officers subject to review by the board.

This reading of the statute comports with modern board practice. The *de facto* role of the board in most large public corporations consists of providing informal advice to senior management (especially the CEO) and episodic oversight. An extensive definition of extraordinary acts thus seems a needless formality. An alternative justification for the proposed rule rests on the costs the existing rule imposes on third parties. Persons who do business with a corporation do so at some peril of discovering that their transaction will be deemed to implicate an extraordinary act and, accordingly, required express board action. An expansive definition of extraordinary matters increases this risk. Transaction costs thus increase in several respects. An expansive variant of the rule creates uncertainty, obliging third parties to take costly precautions. They may insist, for example, on seeing an express authorization from the board. Uncertainty about the outer perimeters of the rule also encourages opportunism by the corporation. If contracts dealing with extraordinary matters are voidable, the corporation effectively has a put with respect to the transaction. Uncertainty as to the enforceability of a contract gives the board leverage to extract a favorable settlement of the third party's claims.

III. Liability of Principal to Third Parties in Tort

One fine fall day in 1975, the Baltimore Orioles visited Fenway Park to play a baseball game against their divisional rival the Boston Red Sox. Ross Grimsley, a pitcher for the Orioles, was warming in the bullpen when a group of Red Sox fans, including one Manning, the plaintiff, began heckling him. The heckling apparently got to Grimsley, who fired a fastball at his tormenters. Although a wire fence separated the bullpen from the stands, it failed to stop the ball, and Manning was hit and injured. Manning sued Grimsley and the Orioles for negligence and battery.

How do the Orioles come into it? As Grimsley's principal, the Orioles were vicariously liable for the tortious conduct of its agent.[150] Restatement (Second) § 219(1) explains: "A master is subject to liability for the torts of his servants committed while acting in the scope of their employment."

A principal's vicarious liability in tort depends not only on whether an agency relationship existed between the tortfeasor and

---

[150] Manning v. Grimsley, 643 F.2d 20 (1st Cir. 1981).

the principal, but also on the kind of agency relationship that is involved. A principal is only liable for the acts of his agent if the agent is deemed the principal's "servant." (In which case the principal is known as a "master.") If the agent is deemed to be the principal's "independent contractor," the principal is not liable for torts committed by the agent. As we shall see, it is not always easy to tell into which category a particular relationship falls. Moreover, we will also see a variety of exceptions to the general rule. Having said that, however, the distinction between a servant and an independent contractor still forms the starting point from which analysis must proceed.

A.   Servant versus Independent Contractor

Restatement (Second) § 2(2) defines a servant as "an agent employed by a master to perform service in his affairs whose physical conduct in the performance of the service is controlled or is subject to the right to control by the master." By way of contrast, § 2(3) defines an independent contractor as "a person who contracts with another to do something for him but who is not controlled by the other nor subject to the other's right to control with respect to his physical conduct in the performance of the undertaking." In order for a master-servant relationship to be found, the master does not have to actually control the agent's physical performance of the assigned task. The master merely must have the right to exercise such control. In contrast, where a principal sets forth the desired result but does not have the right to tell the agent how to achieve that result, the agent is an independent contractor.

A potential source of confusion must be addressed at the outset. All servants are agents, but not all independent contractors are agents. If Pam hires Al to build a house for her at a stipulated price and Pam reserves no power of direction over the conduct of the work, Al is an independent contractor but not an agent (typically referred to as a nonagent independent contractor).[151] Al has no fiduciary duties to Pam and has no power to affect Pam's legal relations. Hence, for example, no contracts entered into by Al purporting to be on Pam's behalf will be biding on Pam as a matter of agency law. We are concerned here only with those independent contractors who are also agents (referred to by some as agent-type independent contractors and by others as nonservant agents).

---

[151] *See, e.g.,* Kemether v. Pennsylvania Interscholastic Athletic Ass'n, Inc., 15 F. Supp.2d 740, 748 (E.D.Pa. 1998) ("Where prerequisites of agency, such as control, are not satisfied, a non-agent independent contractor relationship may exist: A person who contracts to accomplish something for another or to deliver something to another, but who is not acting as a fiduciary for the other is a non-agent contractor. . . . The term is used colloquially to describe builders and others who have contracted to accomplish physical results not under the supervision of the one who has employed them to produce the results.").

1. General Principles

In some cases, of course, it is relatively clear which type of relationship is involved. For example, lawyers, real estate brokers and stock brokers are usually deemed to be independent contractors, rather than servants of their clients, because the clients have little, if any, control over the day-to-day conduct of their lawyer or broker. In contrast, a legal assistant typically would be viewed as the lawyer's servant, because the lawyer is likely to have a great deal of control over the assistant's work.[152]

Unfortunately, these simple examples are polar extremes on a spectrum of types of relationships and many arrangements fall into the vast grey area in the middle. As an aid to categorizing ambiguous relationships, Restatement (Second) § 220(2) identifies the following nonexclusive list of factors to be considered:

(a) the extent of control which, by the agreement, the master may exercise over the details of the work;

(b) whether or not the one employed is engaged in a distinct occupation or business;

(c) the kind of occupation, with reference to whether, in the locality, the work is usually done under the direction of the employer or by a specialist without supervision;

(d) the skill required in the particular occupation;

(e) whether the employer or the workman supplies the instrumentalities, tools, and the place of work for the person doing the work;

(f) the length of time for which the person is employed;

(g) the method of payment, whether by the time or by the job;

(h) whether or not the work is a part of the regular business of the employer;

(i) whether or not the parties believe they are creating the relation of master and servant; and

(j) whether the principal is or is not in business.

The commentary to § 220 suggests that the two most important factors, which together have "almost conclusive weight," are the customs of the locality with respect to the degree of control

---

[152] Senior corporate executives are usually deemed servants, because they are subject to supervision by the board of directors. *See* RESTATEMENT (SECOND) § 220 cmt. a (referring to "managers of great corporations" as "superior servants").

exercised by the principal and the amount of skill required by the agent's occupation.

Although several of the § 220(2) factors refer to employment, consideration is not required. Per Restatement § 225, a person serving gratuitously nevertheless may be deemed a servant. On the other hand, many courts stress that merely doing someone a favor does not make you their servant.[153] Instead, the gratuitous actor's performance of the task must be subject to the physical control of the master and the master must have consented to the relationship.

2.   Illustrations and Applications

The delivery driver. Frank Frausto was a delivery driver for the Arizona Republic newspaper. Frausto's car collided with a motorcycle driven by plaintiff William Santiago, who then sued the newspaper. The newspaper defended by claiming that Frausto was an independent contractor. The trial court agreed, granting the newspaper summary judgment on the issue as a matter of law. Applying an 8 factor test tracking Restatement (Second) § 220(2), the Arizona supreme court reversed and remanded for trial.[154]

First, as to control by the alleged master, the court noted that the newspaper exercised little actual supervision, but was able to give Frausto specific instructions with the expectation that they would be followed. Pointing out that the power to fire is regarded as "one of the most effective methods of control," the court noted that Frausto could be terminated without cause on 28 days notice and, moreover, could be terminated for unsatisfactory service without any notice. Second, the court noted that Frausto had no independent delivery business. He worked only for the newspaper, payments went to the newspaper and not the carrier, and accounts were serviced by the newspaper. This distinguished the case at bar from other newspaper carrier cases in which the delivery firm bought the newspapers from the publisher and resold them to delivery customers at a profit. Third, the court noted that being a newspaper carrier required little specialized or skilled training, which suggests that Frausto was a servant. Fourth, while the newspaper did not provide all of the necessary supplies, it did supply the newspapers and designated the route to be covered. Fifth, the court observed that the relationship was of indefinite duration, which points towards finding that Frausto was a servant. Sixth, Frausto was paid a regular weekly salary. Seventh,

---

[153] *See, e.g.,* Joseph v. Dickerson, 754 So.2d 912, 917 (La. 2000); Sandrock v. Taylor, 174 N.W.2d 186 (Neb. 1970).

[154] Santiago v. Phoenix Newspapers, Inc., 794 P.2d 138 (Ariz. 1990). *But see* LaFleur v. LaFleur, 452 N.W.2d 406 (Iowa 1990) (newspaper carrier was an independent contractor as a matter of law).

newspaper delivery was a core part of the publisher's business. Finally, Frausto stated that he regarded himself as an employee. In sum, on all of the § 220 factors there was at least some support for treating Frausto as a servant and summary judgment was inappropriate.

The construction contractor. In *Reith v. General Telephone Co. of Illinois,*[155] the defendant hired a construction company to install an underground cable. The construction company failed to place warnings or barriers around the installation ditch. The plaintiff fell into the ditch and sought compensation for his injuries. The trial court granted summary judgment for defendant, finding as a matter of law that the construction company was an independent contractor and that the defendant therefore could not be held vicariously liable for its conduct. The intermediate Illinois appellate court reversed, finding that there was a triable issue of fact as to whether the construction company was the telephone company's servant.

The appeals court concluded that the agreement between the parties gave the telephone company "a great deal of control . . . over the work to be performed." Perhaps most importantly, the contract gave the defendant the right to control the number of men in each crew and the number of crews to be employed. Second, the telephone company had a right to audit the contractors' books, which were to be kept in a manner satisfactory to the defendant. Third, the construction company had to submit detailed daily work reports on the progress of the construction.

You might fairly ask why the latter two factors get much weight. In short, they should not. A principal may undertake to ensure that its independent contractor is carrying out the assigned task according to the terms of their agreement and/or is operating in a safe manner without thereby converting the contractor into a servant.[156] In other words, it is probably permissible for a principal to set the general policies and scope of the undertaking, but once the principal starts meddling in the minutiae of the performance of the undertaking, the principal runs the risk of finding that the agent is no longer an independent contractor but rather is a servant.

Suppose that on remand the following additional facts were brought out *Reith*: (1) some of the phone company's employees do this type of work; (2) about two-thirds of the phone company's cables are laid by its own employees; (3) the contract terminated

---

[155] 317 N.E.2d 369 (Ill. App. 1974).

[156] *See, e.g.,* Eden v. Spaulding, 359 N.W.2d 758, 762 (Ned. 1984); Noonan v. Texaco, Inc., 713 P.2d 160, 167 (Wyo. 1986).

when this job was completed; (4) the actual digging was done by use of heavy equipment supplied by the construction company and manned by its trained employees; (5) the phone company had someone periodically visit the site to inspect the work and visit the construction company's office to inspect the records; and (6) the construction company was paid a set fee for laying the cable, regardless of how long the job takes. How would the multi-factor test provided by Restatement (Second) § 220(2) apply to *Reith* on those facts? (a) The extent of control: Defendant can limit the number of men and number of crews, but has little other control over the physical performance of the task. The more such control, of course, the more likely it is that the construction company was the defendant's servant. (b) A distinct business? The construction company has an independent, distinct business, which suggests independent contractor status. (c) The degree of supervision is substantial, albeit not with respect to the physical performance of the task. This factor may lean slightly towards servant status. (d) Skill required: We may assume that a fair amount of skill it required to use the heavy machinery in question, which suggests independent contractor status. (e) Who supplies the equipment? here it was the construction company, which suggests independent contractor status. (f) The length of time employed? It was a one-job contract, which suggests independent contractor status. (g) The method of payment was by the job, which suggests independent contractor status. (h) was the task part of the employer's regular business? Arguably, which suggests servant status. (i) The parties' belief: They probably thought the construction company was an independent contractor. (j) The principal is in business, which suggests servant status.

This discussion should illustrate that the Restatement does not completely solve the problem of distinguishing between servants and independent contractors. In many cases, not all of the factors will point to the same result. Rather, the courts are often faced with situations in which some factors point one way and others point another. In those situations, courts applying the Restatement approach must try to balance the competing factors. On balance, and assuming the additional facts we gave before, how would you vote in this case and why? It is a close case, perhaps leaning towards independent contractor status. In your own evaluation, be sure to emphasize the extent to which the telephone company actually has the right to control the construction company's performance of the assigned task.

Franchises. Domino's Pizza, Inc., does not own most local Domino's Pizza stores. Instead, Domino's is a franchisor who licenses local franchisees to use the Domino's name, trademarks, and so on. When a local franchisee injures someone, what responsibility does a franchisor like Domino's have?

The Parker family was injured when a driver employed by a J & B Enterprises, the local Domino's franchisee, negligently caused an auto accident. The driver doubtless was J &B Enterprises' servant, as suggested by the *Santiago* case described above. The issue litigated by the Parkers, however, was whether J & B Enterprises in turn was Domino's servant so that Domino's itself could be held liable.[157]

The franchise agreement between Domino's and J & B Enterprises expressly stated that the latter was an independent contractor. Although Restatement (Second) § 220(2)(j) treats the parties' belief as a factor, the court held that the contractual characterization was not dispositive. The court further held that the extent to which Domino's actually exercised control over J & B Enterprises also was not dispositive, as what matters is "the right to control." The court then parsed the franchising agreement and the operating manual. The former contained at least 24 provisions giving Domino's control over various aspects of the franchisee's business, including several provisions by which Domino's set standards governing the delivery process. The latter was "a veritable bible for overseeing a Domino's operation," including standards for how all aspects of the business should be run. The court held that these documents alone created a triable issue of fact as to whether J & B Enterprises was Domino's servant.

Franchising as a way of organizing economic activity arose after the servant/independent contractor dichotomy was well-established. In many ways, the franchisor-franchisee relationship is a hybrid having attributes of both servant and independent contractor status. Accordingly, case outcomes often appear inconsistent and even arbitrary.

Consider two older cases involving service station franchises. Today, of course, most service stations operate as mini-marts—miniature grocery stores that happen to sell gasoline as well as beef jerky and soda. Back in the day, however, service stations serviced automobiles rather than their drivers' stomachs. Service stations pumped the gas (there were no self-serve pumps), sold auto parts, and did basic auto repair. In both of the following cases, negligence by employees of the service station operator injured some third party who then sought to hold the oil company franchisor liable.

---

[157] Parker v. Domino's Pizza, 629 So.2d 1026 (Fla. App. 1993).

In *Humble Oil & Refining Co. v. Martin*,[158] Humble Oil owned a service station that it leased to a local operator named Schneider. A customer left her car at the station for repairs, but failed to set the hand brake. The car rolled off the station's lot and struck plaintiff Martin and his children. The attendant at the time was a fellow named Manis, who apparently was negligent in failing to ensure that the parking brake was set. The court found that Schneider was Humble Oil's servant. Humble closely supervised and controlled the way in which Schneider acted. Among other indicia of control, Humble set the hours of operation. Humble held title to auto supplies that Schneider sold on consignment. Humble paid a substantial percentage of Schneider's operating costs. Schneider's only real power was to hire and fire workers.

In *Hoover v. Sun Oil Co.*,[159] the service station operator was found to be an independent contractor of the oil company. Yet, the facts of the two cases look an awful lot alike. Sun Oil owned the service station, which was leased to local operator Barone. When an employee of the station dropped his cigarette while filling the plaintiff's gas tank, causing an explosion and fire, the plaintiff sought to hold Sun Oil liable.

A review of the relevant facts suggests relatively little that distinguishes the two cases. Humble Oil could require reports from Schneider, while Barone made no written reports to Sun Oil. Sun Oil did not set the hours of operation, but so what? In both cases, the local operator hired, paid, and supervised the station's employees. Schneider's contract was terminable at will, while Barone was entitled to 30 days' notice. In both cases, the service station and even the employee's uniforms displayed the oil company name and logo. Schneider, under the contract, was required to "perform other duties in connection with the operation of said station that may be required of him from time to time by." Barone was under no obligation to follow the advice he received from Sun Oil's sales representative. But while it may appear that Humble thus had more control, Sun Oil's power to terminate the contract on relatively short notice is a strong indicator of master-like control. (On the other hand, while Barone probably listens to Sun Oil's recommendations, termination is a drastic action, which Sun Oil may be loath to use.)

The really significant difference between the two cases lies in the financial arrangements. Both nominally involved leases, but Barone bore considerably greater financial risk than did Schneider. Humble Oil charged rent based on the amount of Humble products

---

[158] 222 S.W.2d 995 (Tex. 1949).
[159] 212 A.2d 214 (Del. 1965).

sold. Sun Oil charged Barone a rent "partially determined by the volume of gasoline purchased but there was also a minimum and a maximum." As a result, Barone had "overall risk of profit and loss." If we assume that the party bearing the ultimate risk of financial loss will both insist on and possess control, which seems plausible, we might infer that Sun Oil likely had less control than did Humble. But it is an awfully fine distinction.

How should these franchise cases come out? In general, franchisors should be liable for acts of their franchisees. A franchisor, such as Domino's Pizza, typically is a national or regional company that has expended considerable efforts in establishing brand identity and loyalty, persuading customers that the company's local stores offer a good service or product. The franchisor makes a return on its investment by selling to local operators the right to use its name in providing that good or service. If a local operator performs poorly, there will be an immediate loss of revenue in that area. More importantly, given the nature of our mobile society, poor service in one locality may have an impact on all of the other franchises. If you have a bad experience with one Domino's Pizza, you may only eat at Pizza Huts in the future, no matter in which locality you happen to be at the moment. Most franchisors therefore set a high level of standards up to which all franchisees are required to perform. The franchisor strives to create look-alike businesses, providing uniform levels of service at all stores. Think about McDonalds restaurants. From the inside, are there really significant differences between the stores' food and atmosphere?

From an agency law perspective, however, this poses a problem for the franchisor. The amount of control it needs to exercise over a local franchise in order to uphold standards will often be so great that the franchisor in effect has most of the practical indicia of ownership. In the Domino's Pizza case, the franchising agreement and operating manual left local operators little room for creativity and diversion from the corporate norms. Hence, courts will often ignore the form of a relationship and impose the legal obligations of ownership in cases where the economic benefits of ownership are present. The franchisor thus often should be held vicariously liable for the torts of its local operator.

Should the franchisor care? Would we advise the franchisor to reduce the amount of control it exercises? No. The risk of being held liable for the torts of the local operator is just a cost of doing business and a worthwhile cost at that. Of course, franchisors rarely concede that the local operator is a servant; to the contrary, they often litigate the issue rather strongly; my point, however, is only that losing such cases is a risk necessary to carrying out their economic goals. Changing the relationship to avoid this risk, by giving up control over the franchisee, would pose more business problems than it would solve.

What then do we advise the franchisor to do? Simple. The franchisor should carry adequate insurance. It should require the local operator to carry adequate insurance. It might put a clause in the agreement requiring the local operator to indemnify (reimburse) the franchisor for any loss of this type. It should retain the right to terminate local operators who fail to take adequate steps to prevent this type of loss (even though the power to terminate is a factor indicating that the agent is a servant).

3.   Some Concluding Thoughts on Terminology

There is a growing tendency towards using the terminology of employer and employee rather than master and servant. The Restatement (Third), for example, does away with all three of the classic terms—master, servant, and independent contractor—and replacing them with employer, employee, and nonemployee agent. The old distinction between nonservant agents and nonagent independent contractors also was abolished in favor of the terms nonemployee agent and nonagent service provider.

Admittedly, the terms master and servant are archaic and politically incorrect. The implication of menial service, moreover, is usually erroneous. Yet, it is not clear that employer and employee are an improvement. In particular, both common usage and many legal regimes treat some agents as employees even though they would not be deemed servants under the Restatement (Second) definition. If vicarious liability is grounded in the principal's ability to control the agent's physical performance of a task, however, as it has been traditionally, it would seem that something beyond mere fulltime employment must be shown. A growing number of courts, however, seem willing to infer the requisite level of control from the mere fact of fulltime employment. Some courts have even abandoned the control requirement: "Thus in this case where it is agreed that a regular employee is sent upon a specific errand, using his own car with the knowledge and permission of the employer, and it is agreed he was acting within the scope of his employment at the time of the accident, the employer is liable for his acts whether it had control of his detailed operation of the motor vehicle or not."[160] These courts have gone full circle back to the days of *Jones v. Hart*. The distinction between independent contractors and servants did not exist until the 1840s, prior to which time a principal was held vicariously liable for the torts of his agents of

---

[160] Hunter v. R.G. Watkins & Son, Inc., 265 A.2d 15, 17 (N.H. 1970).

either type.[161] The distinction arose, however, precisely because it makes sense to impose vicarious liability only where the principal may exercise its control so as to prevent accidents. By eviscerating the terminological distinction between servants and independent contractors, the Restatement thus may contribute towards this unfortunate trend of treating principals as insurers of their agents.[162]

B.   Tort Liability and Apparent Agency

In the franchise cases discussed in the preceding section, casual customers of the establishments in question probably are unaware that they are dealing with a local franchisee rather than the big national company whose name and logo is plastered all over the facility, the employee uniforms, and the products being sold. In some such cases, courts have relied on principles of apparent authority to hold the principal liable.[163] The use of authority concepts here makes no sense, of course. In the *Domino's Pizza* case, for example, the Parkers could not have reasonably believed that Domino's Pizza authorized the local store's employee to negligently cause an accident. To the contrary, it is generally assumed that a principal will never authorize their agents to be negligent.[164] Instead, the correct question in this context is whether a principal should be held liable on a theory of apparent agency. In other words, if the principal's manifestations reasonably lead the third party to believe that the tortfeasor was the principal's servant, the principal should be liable even if there is no actual agency relationship between them.

It should not be enough that the third party believes the tortfeasor to be the purported principal's agent, however, whether reasonably or not. Otherwise, virtually all franchise cases would be decided against the franchisor on an apparent agency theory. Restatement (Second) § 267 thus provides that: "One who

---

[161] Stockwell v. Morris, 22 P.2d 189 (Wyo. 1933).

[162] In any event, while it is not always easy to distinguish between servants and independent contractors, it may not prove any easier to distinguish between employee and nonemployee agents.

[163] *See, e.g.,* Gizzi v. Texaco, 437 F.2d 308 (3d Cir. 1981); Billops v. Magness Construction Co., 391 A.2d 196 (Del.Sup. 1978).

[164] W. EDWARD SELL, SELL ON AGENCY 89 (1975). Having said that, however, we should note two situations in which authority issues come into play with respect to tort liability. Where the principal both authorized and intended the tortious conduct, the principal may be held liable, but that liability is grounded in tort rather than agency law. RESTATEMENT (SECOND) § 212 cmt. a. Where the principal "unintentionally authorizes conduct of a servant or other agent which constitutes a tort to a third person" the principal may be held liable without regard to whether the agent was a servant or not. *Id.* § 215. The commentary to § 215 limits the rule to torts involving "trespasses to the person, chattels and land, to conversions, and to interferences with pecuniary interests and reputation, as by defamation, deceit, and acts causing harm to contractual and business relations." *Id.* cmt. c.

represents that another is his servant or other agent and thereby causes a third person justifiably to rely upon the care or skill of such apparent agent is subject to liability to the third person for harm caused by the lack of care or skill of the one appearing to be a servant or other agent as if he were such." In other words, the third party must have relied on a manifestation by the apparent principal and it must have been that reliance which exposed the third party to harm. Courts, however, not infrequently ignore this nicety.

Restatement (Third) § 7.08 provides that:

> A principal is subject to vicarious liability for a tort committed by an agent in dealing or communicating with a third party on or purportedly on behalf of the principal when actions taken by the agent with apparent authority constitute the tort or enable the agent to conceal its commission.

The drafters offer several illustrations of this principle at work, including:

> 1. P Numismatics Company urges its customers to seek investment advice from its retail salespeople, including A. T, who wishes to invest in gold coins, seeks A's advice at an office of P Numismatics Company. A encourages T to purchase a particular set of gold coins, falsely representing material facts relevant to their value. T, reasonably relying on A's representations, purchases the set of coins. P is subject to liability to T. . . .

> 3. O, who owns an office building, retains P, a construction firm, to renovate the building. T, a prospective tenant, visits the building. T asks P's site manager, A, whether it will be safe for T to inspect a particular group of offices. A tells T to ask G, a security guard in the building, saying "G's our point person for safety." G tells T that the offices in question are safe to visit although G does not know whether this is so. Unbeknownst to T, G is an employee of Guards, Inc., not P. P and Guards, Inc., have instructed A and G never to direct prospective tenants within the building, but T neither knows nor has reason to know this. T reasonably believes that G, to whom A directs T, has authority to answer questions from prospective tenants. T is injured when T falls through the weakened flooring in one of the offices. P is subject to liability to T.

C. Scope of Employment

A master is not liable for the torts of a servant unless the tort occurred within what is called "the scope of the employment." In other words, the tortious conduct must somehow be connected with the employment in order for the principal to be liable.

1. Scope of the Employment in the Restatements

The Restatement (Second) contains a veritable plethora of provisions dealing with the minutiae of this issue. Restatement (Second) § 228(2), however, boils all the relevant learning down to three basic issues: (1) Was the conduct of the same general nature as, or incidental to, the task that the servant was employed to perform? (2) Was the conduct substantially removed from the authorized time and space limits of the employment? Where the servant takes off on a so-called "frolic and detour," the servant no longer is acting within the scope of the employment. (3) Was the conduct motivated at least in part by a purpose to serve the master?

The Restatement (Third) provides in § 7.07(2) that:

> An employee acts within the scope of employment when performing work assigned by the employer or engaging in a course of conduct subject to the employer's control. An employee's act is not within the scope of employment when it occurs within an independent course of conduct not intended by the employee to serve any purpose of the employer.

The drafters note that the Restatement (Third) phrases the standard in "more general terms" than did the Restatement (Second),[165] which is quite an understatement. The further explain that:

> Under Restatement Second, Agency § 228(1)(b), conduct falls within the scope of employment when it "occurs substantially within the authorized time and space limits." This formulation does not naturally encompass the working circumstances of many managerial and professional employees and others whose work is not so readily cabined by temporal or spatial limitations. Many employees in contemporary workforces interact on an employer's behalf with third parties although the employee is neither situated on the employer's premises nor continuously or exclusively engaged in performing assigned work.[166]

2. Case Law

Early cases were quite strict in defining the scope of an agent's employment, sharply limiting the circumstances under which a plaintiff could recover. Consider, for example, Judge Benjamin Cardozo's opinion in *Fiocco v. Carver*,[167] which remains the classic statement of the "frolic and detour" rule. Defendants sent a

---

[165] RESTATEMENT (THIRD) § 7.07 cmt. b.

[166] *Id.*

[167] 137 N.E. 309 (N.Y. 1922).

truckload of merchandise from Manhattan to Staten Island. On the return trip, the truck's driver literally detoured to visit his mother. En route from his mother's house to the garage, the driver encountered a street carnival. Some of the young merrymakers asked the driver for a ride, to which request he acceded. After driving the boys around the neighborhood for a while, the driver stopped at a pool hall to visit a friend. While the truck was stopped, one of the boys climbed onto it. When the driver started the truck up again, the boy fell off and was injured. Cardozo held that the driver had departed from his service to the master and had not returned from this frolic and detour before the injury occurred:

> We are not dealing with a case where, in the course of a continuing relation, business and private ends have been coincidently served. We are dealing with a departure so manifest as to constitute an abandonment of duty, exempting the master from liability till duty is resumed. . . . Whether we have regard to circumstances of space or of time or of causal or logical relation, the homeward trip was bound up with the effects of the excursion, the parts interpenetrated and commingled beyond hope of separation. Division more substantial must be shown before a relation, once ignored and abandoned, will be renewed and re-established.

Similarly, in *Brill v. Davajon*,[168] plaintiff David Brill was driving his automobile east on Foster Avenue in Chicago. It was a cold night, the street was icy, and Brill was proceeding slowly. As he approached the intersection of Foster and Ashland Avenue, Brill noticed a taxicab trying to push another car. The cab was driven by Frank McFarland, an employee of Checker Taxi Company. The stalled car belonged to one Joel Davajon. Somehow Brill's and Davajon's cars collided. The testimony at trial disagreed sharply as to whether McFarland or Brill was at fault in the resulting accident. What was not in dispute was that the accident occurred while McFarland was using his cab to push Davajon's car, a task for which Davajon had offered to pay him the whopping sum of $1. Checker admitted that McFarland was its servant, but defended on scope of the employment grounds. First, it argued, McFarland's use of the cab as a makeshift tow truck was not incidental to his employment as a cab driver. Second, McFarland had violated company regulations by using the cab for this purpose. Finally, McFarland had been motivated by his selfish desire for the $1 gratuity rather than by any desire to serve Checker. The court agreed on all counts, holding that McFarland was acting outside the scope of his employment.

---

[168] 201 N.E.2d 253 (Ill. App. 1964).

Rigorous application of the scope of the employment doctrine, such as in *Fiocco* or *Brill*, however, has fallen by the wayside. A series of doctrinal developments in fact have substantially eroded the doctrine. The process began with a willingness of courts to find that the servant was acting on behalf of the master on the most tenuous of facts.

Many courts, for example, have held that a brief departure from the master's business is not enough to establish a frolic and detour that would remove the conduct from the scope of the employment. In *Clover v. Snowbird Ski Resort*,[169] for example, Chris Zulliger collided with plaintiff while making a blind jump during a ski run on one of the defendant ski resort's intermediate slopes. Zulliger was employed by the resort as a chef at one of its restaurants and as a supervisor of other restaurants. He was expected to ski between restaurant locations and, like many other employees, had a season ski pass. After visiting the Mid-Gad Restaurant on the mountain, while on the employer's business, he took about four runs and then headed for the bottom of the mountain to resume his work as chef at the resort's Plaza Restaurant. It was on this last run that the accident took place. The Supreme Court concluded that summary judgment should not have been granted in favor of the ski resort and remanded for trial. According to the court, the only doubt about scope of employment arose because Zulliger did not return to the Plaza immediately after monitoring the Mid-Gad. It concluded that a jury could reasonably find that "Zulliger had resumed his employment and that [his] deviation was not substantial enough to constitute a total abandonment of his employment." In other words, a brief departure from business for personal pleasure is not enough to put the employee outside the scope of the employment.

We see a similar erosion of the scope of the employment doctrine in cases involving intentional torts. It had long been the rule that intentional torts were not motivated by a desire to serve the master. In the famous drunken boatswain case, *Nelson v. American-West African Line*,[170] however, Judge Learned Hand rejected that rule. In that case, a drunken ship's boatswain had rousted the plaintiff seaman out of his bunk with the words "Get up, you big son of a bitch, and turn to," which fighting words were accompanied by a clout across the face with a wooden bench. A fight ensued, in which the boatswain wreaked further injuries on the plaintiff. Judge Learned Hand held that even though the boatswain "had made himself incompetent to further the ship's business . . .

---

[169] 808 P.2d 1037 (Utah 1991).
[170] 86 F.2d 730 (2d Cir. 1936).

the owner had selected him to command, whatever his defects and his addictions. If he really meant to rouse the plaintiff and send him upon duty, if he really meant to act as boatswain and for the ship, however imbecile his conduct it was his master's." From the fact that the boatswain ordered the plaintiff to "turn to," Judge Hand inferred that the boatswain intended to act "for the ship." Hence, the boatswain had the requisite purpose to serve his master, and his acts were within the scope of his employment, even though (a) he was drunk and (b) his conduct involved intentional torts.

Courts also began finding the requisite purpose where the employee's intentional tort was a "response to the plaintiff's conduct which was presently interfering with the employee's ability to perform his duties successfully. This interference may be in the form of an affirmative attempt to prevent an employee from carrying out his assignments."[171] In *Manning v. Grimsley*,[172] as described at the beginning of this section, the Baltimore Orioles argued that pitcher Russ Grimsley's tortious response to the heckling did not fall within this rule. The heckling may have annoyed Grimsley, but it did not prevent him from warming up. The court disagreed, concluding that the jury reasonably could find that the heckling had the effect of rattling Grimsley so that he could not pitch effectively. You will not doubt agree that this seems quite a stretch. If you retaliated against hecklers, would it be because they were keeping you from working or because you were angry?

The erosion of the scope of the employment doctrine in relation to intentional torts eventually culminated in cases like *Lyon v. Carey*,[173] which the court acknowledged was "perhaps at the outer bounds" of vicarious liability. Lyon was waiting in her sister's apartment for a delivery of furniture from George's Radio and Television. Pep Line Trucking and George's Radio and Television had an independent contractor relationship under which Pep Line's employees delivered furniture for George's. Michael Carey, an employee of Pep Line came to the apartment to deliver a mattress and box springs for George's. Carey obtained entry to the apartment by showing Lyon a receipt with George's name on it. A dispute thereupon arose. Lyon wanted him to take the mattress and springs upstairs so that she could inspect them before giving him the check. Carey didn't want to bring in the furniture without getting paid and, in any event, wanted cash not a check. At this point what had been a fairly ordinary commercial disagreement took a tragic turn. Carey assaulted Lyon, raping, beating and stabbing her. The court

---

[171] Miller v. Federated Department Stores, Inc., 304 N.E.2d 573, 580 (Mass. 1973).

[172] 643 F.2d 20 (1st Cir. 1981).

[173] 533 F.2d 649 (D.C. Cir. 1976).

held that plaintiff had made out a case for the jury that Pep Line was liable for her injuries, setting out the following standards: If the assault was motivated by purely personal reasons, there could be no agency-based liability. If there was any purpose to serve the master, liability can arise. Here a purpose to serve the master could be found from the fact that the dispute arose out of the very transaction that had brought Carey to the apartment and out of the employer's instruction to get cash before delivery. Consequently, it is within the scope of the employment if the deliveryman, serving the master, is brought into situations where friction is likely to arise and violence to result. It does not matter that the particular nature of the violence was not foreseen.

A later opinion from the same court elaborated on the standard applicable to intentional torts, as follows:

> To qualify as conduct of the kind he was employed to perform, the electrician's actions must have either been "of the same general nature as that authorized" or "incidental to the conduct authorized." Restatement (Second) § 229. . . .

According to the D.C. Court of Appeals, conduct is "incidental" to an employee's legitimate duties if it is "foreseeable." "Foreseeable" in this context does not carry the same meaning as it does in negligence cases; rather, it requires the court to determine whether it is fair to charge employers with responsibility for the intentional torts of their employees. To be foreseeable, the torts must be "a direct outgrowth of the employee's instructions or job assignment." It is not enough that an employee's job provides an "opportunity" to commit an intentional tort. The D.C. Court of Appeals does not distinguish between intentional torts that involve physical contact and those that do not.[174]

Perhaps no court has gone further in eviscerating the scope of the employment doctrine than did the Second Circuit (per Judge Friendly) in *Ira S. Bushey & Sons, Inc. v. U.S.*[175] The Coast Guard ship Tamaroa was being overhauled in a Brooklyn drydock. per the Coast Guard's contract with the drydock's owner, the ship's crew continued to live aboard and therefore were allowed to come and go freely. Late one night Seaman Lane, a member of the crew, returned to the ship in an intoxicated state. As Judge Friendly explained: "For reasons not apparent to us or very likely to Lane, he took it into his head, while progressing along the gangway wall, to turn each of three large wheels some twenty times; unhappily . . . these wheels controlled the water intake valves." The drydock began

---

[174] Haddon v. United States, 68 F.3d 1420, 1424 (D.C. Cir. 1995) (citations omitted).

[175] 398 F.2d 167 (2d Cir. 1968).

to fill with water. The Tamaroa floated free of its supporting blocks and then toppled over against the drydock. Bushey, the corporate owner of the drydock, sued the U.S. government for the resulting damage to its drydock. The trial court ruled that Bushey was entitled to damages in an amount to be determined. The United States appealed, claiming that Lane's act was outside the scope of his employment.

Obviously, no purpose to serve the master could be found in Lane's conduct—no matter how hard you look. The trial court nevertheless found for plaintiff Bushey. Under the trial court's approach, plaintiffs no longer would be required to show that the agent was motivated by a purpose to serve the master. Instead, it would suffice to show that the conduct arose out of and in the course of the employment. The trial court's analysis amounted to virtually a rule of strict liability for the torts of an employee as long as any connection in time and space could be made between the conduct and the employment.

The trial court's holding was grounded in economic theory. The court argued that imposing liability on the principal would cause the principal to internalize the negative externalities of its agents conduct. On appeal, however, Judge Friendly rejected this analysis. From a deterrence perspective, as he correctly pointed out, forcing the principal to internalize the costs of particular misconduct by an agent only makes sense if the principal can take steps to prevent future instances of such misconduct. If the principal cannot do so, imposing liability effectively makes the principal an insurer of its agents. On the facts of *Bushey,* it is far from clear how imposing liability on the government would induce principals to take cost-effective precautions: "It could well be that application of the traditional rule might induce drydock owners, prodded by their insurance companies, to install locks on their valves to avoid similar incidents in the future, while placing the burden on ship owners is much less likely to lead to accident prevention."

Despite his rejection of the trial court's economic analysis, Judge Friendly nevertheless thought the government should be held liable. Instead of economic efficiency, he relied on rather vague fairness concerns; namely, the "deeply rooted sentiment that a business enterprise cannot justly disclaim responsibility for accidents which may fairly be said to be characteristic of its activities."[176] To implement that sentiment, he adopted a

---

[176] Query how the negligence of a drunken seaman "may fairly be said to be characteristic of [the Coast Guard's] activities." Indeed, most instances of employee negligence are hardly "characteristic" of the employer's activity in any meaningful sense of the word. *See* Gary T. Schwartz, *The Hidden and Fundamental Issue of Vicarious Liability,* 69 S. CAL. L. REV. 1739, 1749–50 (1996).

foreseeability standard: (1) If some harm is foreseeable, the principal is liable, regardless of the fact that the particular type of harm was unforeseeable. Why was it foreseeable on these facts that some harm would result? Because the government insisted that the seamen be able to stay on board the boat and be able to go to and fro. (2) Conduct by the servant which does not create risks different from those attendant on the activities of the community in general will not give rise to liability. (3) The conduct must relate to the employment. The notion here seems to be that the existence of the employment relationship causes the employee to encounter unusual circumstances which he or she otherwise would not.

Consider the application of Judge Friendly's standard to following hypothetical: Mary owns a gas station. She hires Sam to work as a pump attendant. Assume Sam is a servant. Sam smokes cigars. One day Sam is smoking while he fills a patron's gas tank. An explosion results, injuring the patron. Is the conduct within the scope of the employment? Older cases said smoking was merely a personal convenience and hence outside the scope of the employment. Some modern courts say smoking is necessary to the servant's comfort while on the job and therefore foreseeable harms are within the scope of the employment.[177] Surely this harm is at least as foreseeable as that involved in *Bushey.*

Now suppose Shirley works as a cashier in the gas station. After years of inhaling Sam's smoke, she comes down with lung cancer. If she sues Mary, is Sam's conduct within the scope of the employment? Arguably it is foreseeable, as we are routinely told that passive inhalation of smoke may cause cancer. On the other hand, Judge Friendly did say that conduct by the servant which does not create risks different from those attendant on the activities of the community in general will not give rise to liability. But then again, the harm did occur within the physical boundaries of the enterprise, which does tend to distinguish it from the examples he cites. It would be foolhardy to pretend to know how this last case would come out. One can say this much, however: Judge Friendly

---

[177] *See, e.g.,* Iandiorio v. Kriss & Senko Enterprises, Inc., 517 A.2d 530 (Pa. 1986), in which the dissent cited RESTATEMENT (SECOND) § 229 for the proposition that "personal acts of employees may be within the scope of employment when they are part of the work, but not when they are for 'personal convenience of the employees and are merely permitted by the master in order to make the employment more desirable. . . .' Smoking is an activity which is in no way related to the work of remodeling a service station, and is permitted solely for the personal convenience of the employees to make their work more desirable. The conclusion is inescapable, therefore, that smoking is not within the scope of employment applying Section 229 and that the employer, therefore, is not vicariously liable for the injuries. . . ." *Id.* at 536 (emphasis removed). In contrast, the majority held that an employer could be held liable it "not only knew that its employees smoked at work, but, in fact, dictated where employees should take breaks and smoke." *Id.* at 534.

was absolutely right when he said "the rule we lay down lacks sharp contours."

In any event, *Lyon* and *Haddon* illustrate that not all courts have retreated as completely from the purpose test as Judge Friendly did in *Bushey*. Instead, most courts do what the D.C. courts did in *Lyon* and *Haddon*—i.e., retain the language of the purpose test but frequently finding that such a purpose exists even in attenuated fact patterns.

What should the rule be? Judge Friendly's economic analysis made more sense that his sentiments about justice. The analysis ought to be grounded in the economics of deterrence. When a principal hires an agent to carry out a particular task, there may well be negative externalities from that activity. If the principal is the cheapest cost avoider, it makes sense to impose liability on the principal, as we have seen at several points in our treatment of agency law.[178] In many cases, of course, the principal will have the requisite comparative advantage. The principal can take care in selecting agents, in the tasks it assigns to them, in the equipment and working conditions it provides, and so on. In other cases, of which *Bushey* itself would seem to be a prime example, however, it seems likely that the injured third party is in a better position to take appropriate precautions.

D. Liability for Agent's Fraud

The cause of action for fraud evolved out of both contract and tort precedents (some refer to fraud as a "con-tort") and still has elements of both. This evolutionary process has important implications for agency law.

In some jurisdictions, the courts analyze the principal's liability for an agent's frauds under tort liability rules.[179] They thus focus on whether the fraudulent conduct fell within the scope of the employment, applying tests quite similar to those discussed in the preceding section. Many of these cases emphasize motive issues. A fraud for the benefit of the employee is never within the scope, while a fraud that benefits the employer as well is within the scope.[180]

---

[178] As Ribstein and Lipshaw caution, however, "even if the firm can reduce the risk of harm by controlling the employee, perhaps it should not be liable if the employment did not increase the likelihood of the harm occurring." RIBSTEIN & LIPSHAW at 55. This is so, they argue, because the question of "whether liability is socially justified depends on whether the costs of reducing socially beneficial activities outweighs the benefit of reducing accident costs." *Id.* In other words, the cost-benefit analysis must include not only the direct costs of precautions by employers but also the possibility that the employer will cut back production.

[179] *See, e.g.,* Entente Mineral Co. v. Parker, 956 F.2d 524 (5th Cir. 1992).

[180] *See, e.g.,* Adler v. Helman, 564 N.Y.S.2d 828 (App. Div. 1991).

Other jurisdictions, however, treat a principal's liability under the rules governing contract liability. Accordingly, in these jurisdictions, the issue normally is whether the agent had apparent authority.[181] Note carefully the following point: it is not necessary in these cases to show that the principal authorized the fraud itself (although of course that would help). Rather, the issue typically is whether the agent had apparent authority to engage in the transaction which led to the fraud.

Although the latter approach (apparent authority) is supported by "the great weight of authority,"[182] the former approach (scope of employment) is preferable from an efficiency perspective. The cheaper cost avoider perspective argues that the principal should only be held liable if it is the party who is in the best position to take cost-effective precautions. In fraud cases, however, such precautions often will be unavailable. As the late U.S. Supreme Court Justice Lewis Powell once observed, "no set of rules and regulations, and no procedures however elaborate, can protect adequately against fraud and disloyalty.... [An agent] bent on fraud could forge evidence or otherwise circumvent most safeguards. In practice, a rule of apparent authority can be a rule of strict liability...."[183]

Instead of rehashing the tort and contract liability theories, however, perhaps a practice pointer would be more helpful. In analyzing a fraud case under agency law principles, you can often predict the outcome of the case by looking at how much of a nexus is there between the agency relationship and the fraud. Thus, to predict whether the court will find apparent authority on the part of the agent or find that the conduct fell within the scope of the agent's duties you should ask yourselves several questions:

First, did the principal put the agent in a position which had the effect of facilitating the agent's fraud. Could the agent have perpetrated the fraud without making use of the facilities provided by the principal? If the existence of the agency relationship assisted the agent in carrying out the fraud, then it becomes more likely that the principal will be held liable.

Second, to what extent did the principal monitor the agent's behavior? If adequate monitoring by the principal would have detected the misconduct and the principal fails to adequately monitor the agent, it becomes more likely that the principal will be held liable.

---

[181] *See, e.g.,* Grease Monkey Int'l, Inc. v. Montoya, 904 P.2d 468 (Colo. 1995).

[182] HYNES & LOEWENSTEIN at 317.

[183] American Soc. of Mechanical Engineers, Inc. v. Hydrolevel Corp., 456 U.S. 556, 591 n.17 (1982) (Powell, J., dissenting).

Third, to what extent did the principal benefit (even unknowingly) from the fraud? If the organization benefited in any significant way from the fraudulent conduct, it becomes more likely that the principal will be held liable.

These questions aren't part of the black letter law, but over time they have proven to be a powerful predictor of outcomes. Thus, if there is a strong nexus between the organization and the fraud, you can say with some confidence that a court will hold the principal liable.

E. Statutory Claims

What liability should an employer have for an employee's violation of statute? This has become an especially important issue in the civil rights conduct, where employers are sought to be held liable for racial discrimination or sexual harassment committed by their employers. Although such cases arise under federal law, in the absence of clear statutory direction to the contrary courts frequently look to state agency law to inform the decision as to whether the employer is vicariously liable.[184]

In *Arguello v. Conoco, Inc.,*[185] for example, a group of Hispanic and African–American consumers filed suit under the federal civil rights laws alleging racial discrimination by an employee of a gas station owned by Conoco. Defendant Conoco argued that the racist employee was animated by personal prejudice and therefore was acting outside the scope of her employment.

Recall that the D.C. Circuit held in *Haddon* that: "To be foreseeable, the torts must be 'a direct outgrowth of the employee's instructions or job assignment.' It is not enough that an employee's job provides an 'opportunity' to commit an intentional tort."[186] Query whether the use of racial epithets by Conoco's employee meets that standard.

On the other hand, recall that *Lyon* suggested that a purpose to serve the master can be found from the fact that the dispute arose out of the very transaction that had brought the parties together.[187] Consequently, it is within the scope of the employment if the servant, serving the master, is brought into situations where friction is likely to arise and misconduct to result. It therefore

---

[184] *See, e.g.,* Faragher v. City of Boca Raton, 424 U.S. 775, 803 n.3 (1998) ("our obligation ... is to adapt agency concepts to the practical objectives of Title VII").

[185] 207 F.3d 803 (5th Cir. 2000).

[186] Haddon v. United States, 68 F.3d 1420, 1424 (D.C. Cir. 1995) (citations omitted).

[187] Lyon v. Carey, 533 F.2d 649 (D.C. Cir. 1976).

doesn't matter that the particular nature of the misconduct was not foreseen.

The *Arguello* court rejected "the presumption that because [Conoco employee] Smith behaved in an unacceptable manner that she was obviously outside the scope of her employment." Instead, as suggested by the analogy to *Lyon*, the court emphasized that "although Conoco could not have expected Smith to shout racial epithets at Arguello and Govea, Smith's actions took place while she was performing her normal duties as a clerk." Smith's misconduct occurred during a sales transaction of the sort Smith was employed to conduct. Setting aside the racial epithets used, moreover, Smith's other conduct in the transaction was consistent with that in which she was authorized to engage (such as using the cash register and intercom). The appeals court therefore reversed the trial court's grant of summary judgment to Conoco and remanded for trial.[188]

F.   Liability for Torts of Independent Contractors

As we saw above, agency law generally limits vicarious liability to the acts of servants. At common law, at least, a principal was not liable for tortious conduct by independent contractors. Over time, however, that rule underwent gradual erosion. Today there are a number of well-established exceptions to the independent contractor rule.

1.   The Principal Retains Control

A principal who retains control over the aspect of the activity in which the tort occurs is liable for tortious acts of an independent contractor. If the employer controls or has the right to control the physical performance of the task, of course, the employee is a servant not an independent contractor. This exception thus implies is that one could be an independent contractor for some purposes and a servant for others.

2.   The Principal Hires an Incompetent Independent Contractor

The principal can be held liable if it employed an incompetent independent contractor. The key issue here is the extent of the inquiry, if any, the principal must make into the independent contractor's competence. In *Hixon v. Sherwin-Williams Co.*,[189] the principal hired a flooring contractor to install linoleum tile. Because the job site had a cement sub-floor, it was necessary to install a

---

[188] *See also* Mains v. II Morrow, Inc., 877 P.2d 88 (Or. App. 1994) (reversing and remanding for trial as to whether sexual harassment was within the scope of a supervisor's employment).

[189] 671 F.2d 1005 (7th Cir. 1982).

layer of plywood before laying the linoleum. The contractor, who had never laid a plywood floor on cement, used a flammable glue to attach the plywood. A fire broke out and severely damaged the home. Judge Richard Posner observed that a principal may be held liable if it was negligent in "failing to select a competent contractor." In *Hixon*, the contractor had a good reputation, which was known to the principal. Although the principal was unaware of the contractor's lack of experience with plywood flooring, the principal "had no duty to quiz him concerning the details of his experience."[190] Hence, it seems, the principal has little obligation to conduct due diligence when hiring a contractor.

There is considerable dispute as to whether hiring a financially irresponsible independent contractor—e.g., one without adequate insurance—is tantamount to hiring an incompetent one. In *Becker v. Interstate Properties*,[191] the Third Circuit held a real estate developer (the principal) could be held liable for hiring a contractor who lacked adequate assets and/or insurance to satisfy the plaintiff's tort claims. The *Becker* court invoked the cheaper cost avoider concept to justify its holding, but on closer examination it becomes clear that *Becker* really was about compensating tort victims by allowing them the deepest pocket:

> The choice of the party to bear the loss falls between the developer and the victim. Where, as here, the developer is a substantial entrepreneur and a member of an industry that carries large liability insurance policies as a matter of course, there is little question but that he is in the better position to bear the loss of such an accident. Moreover, the developer can spread the increased costs of insurance or liability to ultimate users of the project. It is only in rare circumstances that a victim will have a similar option.

Becker was a diversity case applying New Jersey law. Dicta in an older New Jersey supreme court opinion, *Majestic Realty Assoc., Inc. v. Toti Contracting Co.*,[192] supported extending the incompetent contractor exception to the case of a financially incompetent contractor. Post-*Becker*, however, two intermediate New Jersey appellate courts rejected the *Majestic Realty* dicta and declined to so extend the incompetent contractor exception.[193] Acknowledging

---

[190] *Accord* Richmond v. White Mount Recreational Ass'n, 674 A.2d 143 (N.H. 1996) ("there is no duty to take any great pains to ascertain whether [the contractor's] reputation is good or not"); *see generally* RESTATEMENT (SECOND) § 213 (the principal is liable "if he is negligent or reckless ... in the employment of improper persons or instrumentalities in work involving risk of harm to others").

[191] 569 F.2d 1203 (3d Cir. 1977).

[192] 153 A.2d 321 (N.J. 1959).

[193] *See* Cassano v. Aschoff, 543 A.2d 973 (N.J. Super. 1988); Miltz v. Borroughs-Shelving, Div. of Lear Siegler, Inc., 497 A.2d 516 (N.J. Super. 1985).

those holdings, the Third Circuit disavowed *Becker* in *Robinson v. Jiffy Executive Limousine Co.*[194] Beyond simply following New Jersey precedents, moreover, the Third Circuit went on to expressly reject *Becker*'s policy analysis. The court explained that "any person or entity which contracted for transportation service . . . would be obliged [by *Becker*] to make a diligent and continuing inquiry into the financial qualifications of the contractor before calling upon him to perform the transportation service, in order to guard against potential imputed negligence liability. Such a duty would not only be unprecedented, but would indeed impose prohibitive obligations on employers of independent contractors beyond what we are prepared to predict the New Jersey Supreme Court will adopt."

Perhaps both Third Circuit opinions erred in seeking a hard-and-fast rule. Perhaps a case-by-case analysis might be superior. In some cases, after all, the principal could at low cost ensure that the contractor carries adequate insurance and has a good credit rating. Indeed, given the ready availability of credit data, it is probably easier for a principal to investigate the financial health of a contractor than its competence. On the other hand, a hard-and-fast rule does have the advantage of certainty.

3. *Inherently Dangerous Activities*

The principal can be held liable where the contractor's performance involves an inherently dangerous activity. In the *Majestic* case discussed in the preceding section, the Parking Authority of the City of Paterson hired Toti Contracting to demolish a building adjacent to one owned by Majestic Realty.[195] A wrecking ball operated by a Toti employee knocked a section of wall onto the Majestic building's roof, causing extensive damage. Humorously, the Toti employee explained: "I goofed." Majestic sued the Authority. The trial court held that Toti was an independent contractor and, accordingly, that the Authority could not be held liable. The New Jersey supreme court reversed, on grounds that demolition was "inherently dangerous." Conduct will be deemed inherently dangerous, the court explained, where it involves "an activity which can be carried on safely only by the exercise of special skill and care, and which involves grave risk of danger to persons or property if negligently done."

Majestic distinguished inherently dangerous activities from ultra-hazardous ones. (The latter was defined as an activity that "(a) necessarily involves a serious risk of harm to the person, land or chattels of others which cannot be eliminated by the exercise of

---

[194] 4 F.3d 237 (3d Cir. 1993).

[195] Majestic Realty Assoc., Inc. v. Toti Contracting Co., 153 A.2d 321 (N.J. 1959).

the utmost care, and (b) is not a matter of common usage.") Under *Majestic*, the principal is liable with respect to both types of activities. The difference is that the principal is vicariously liable with respect to liable ultra-hazardous activities without regard to the negligence of the contractor. As the *Majestic* court put it, "liability is absolute where the work is ultra-hazardous." As to inherently dangerous activities, however, *Majestic* imposes vicarious liability only where the contractor was negligent.

Judge Posner advanced an economic justification for the ultra-hazardous exception—which he called the "abnormally dangerous" activity exception—in *Anderson v. Marathon Petroleum Co.*[196] In general, Posner argued, a principal does not directly supervise the independent contractor's work. Accordingly, the principal typically has little ability to prevent negligence on the part of the independent contractor (or the latter's employees). Where an activity is abnormally dangerous, however, it is by definition one that "might very well result in injury even if conducted with all due skill and caution." With respect to such activities, Posner argued:

> [I]t is important not only that the people engaged in it use the highest practicable degree of skill and caution, but also—since even if they do so, accidents may well result—that the people who have authorized the activity consider the possibility of preventing some accidents by curtailing the activity or even eliminating it altogether. . . . The fact that a very high degree of care is cost-justified implies that the principal should be induced to wrack his brain, as well as the independent contractor his own brain, for ways of minimizing the danger posed by the activity. And the fact that the only feasible method of accident prevention may be to reduce the amount of the activity or substitute another activity argues for placing liability on the principal, who makes the decision whether to undertake the activity in the first place.

Note that this analysis seemingly would not justify an exception to the no liability rule where the conduct is merely inherently dangerous. Because inherently dangerous activities by definition can be conducted safely with special care and precautions, there seems less justification for requiring the principal to "wrack his brain" for precautions.[197]

---

[196] 801 F.2d 936 (7th Cir. 1986).

[197] In *Anderson*, Posner also drew a distinction between tort suits brought against the principal by employees of the independent contractor and suits brought by injured third parties. As to the former, the "abnormally dangerous" exception does not apply. The common law rules are trumped by the "bedrock principle" that worker's compensation statutes are the exclusive means of redress for injured workers with respect to job-related injuries. That principle protects not only the

4. Nondelegable Duties

Where the principal owes a nondelegable duty to some third party, the principal may not legal responsibility for the performance of that duty by assigning the task to an independent contractor. Hence, if the principal does delegate the task to such a contractor, the principal is liable for any harm caused by the contractor's negligence. The chief difficulty here is determining whether the duty owed to the third party by the principal, if any, was nondelegable. Professor Hynes notes that nondelegable duties tend to arise on one of three situations: (1) Where the defendant has some special status, such as a common carrier. (2) A contractual relationship, such as landlord and tenant, exists between the principal and the third party. (3) The principal has invited the third party onto his premises.[198] To this list we might add a fourth category of cases in which a statute imposes duties on the principal.

In *Reith v. General Telephone Co. of Illinois,*[199] the defendant principal was a telephone company. Pursuant to state statute, a utility was obliged to obtain written permission from local and state officials before digging ditches to install cables. in litigation arising out of an accident in which a pedestrian fell into a ditch dug by a contractor hired by the phone company, the court held that the company "had an affirmative, non-delegable duty to take precautions against the possible and probable injuries around an excavation site constructed through its franchise or permission obtained from the state and local authority." The court's rationale for this rule was neither detailed nor especially persuasive. In the court's view, the required official permission gave the phone company a license to dig a ditch. In turn, a license is not assignable absent express authorization therein. In addition, the court implied a condition of the purported license consisting of a duty to ensure that the work was conducted safely. If all this seems formalistic and hyper-technical, that is because it is formalistic and hyper-technical.

Another example may serve to adequately illustrate the general lack of coherence associated with the nondelegable duty doctrine. In *Kleeman v. Rheingold,*[200] the plaintiff hired the defendant attorney to bring a medical malpractice suit against her doctor. Just two days before the statute of limitations was about to expire, the defendant hired a process server—Fisher's Service

immediate employer—i.e., the independent contractor—but also the principals who contract with them.

[198] HYNES at 185.
[199] 317 N.E.2d 369 (Ill. App. 1974).
[200] 598 N.Y.S.2d 149 (1993).

Bureau—to serve the doctor. Fisher's agent served the papers on the doctor's secretary rather than the doctor himself. In the medical malpractice case, the trial court held that the service of process was defective, as the doctor had to be personally served. Because the statute of limitations had run by that time, the medical malpractice case was dismissed. The litigious plaintiff thereupon sued her lawyer and his law firm for legal malpractice. They defended by arguing that they were not liable for the negligence of their independent contractor (i.e., Fisher's and its agent).

The majority held that lawyers have a nondelegable duty to see that process is validly served. Accordingly, lawyers may not avoid responsibility for the process server's negligence by hiring an independent contractor. The court cited several aspects of the legal ethics in support of its position, such as the rule that that lawyers are not allowed to limit their malpractice liability exposure by contract or otherwise. Second, both the code of legal ethics and general public perception expect lawyers to control and supervise the entire litigation process. In turn, timely service of process is an "integral part" of the lawyer's task.

A concurring judge argued that the majority's rule requires attorneys to "inquire beyond any facially sufficient affidavit of service of process to verify personally the facts that underlie it." In effect, the concurrence argued, the majority's holding created a strong incentive for lawyers to personally assume the role of process servers—or at least to exercise direct supervision and control over their process servers—instead of relying on outside specialists. As such, the majority gave a competitive advantage to large firms, which typically have in-house process servers, over small firms and solo practitioners.[201] In addition, the concurrence pointed out that the majority opinion had ramifications extending beyond process serving to such issues as selection of expert witnesses and the like. Instead of relying on the nondelegable doctrine, the concurrence would have remanded for trial on the narrower question of whether the lawyer had negligently hired an incompetent process server.

To its credit, the *Kleeman* court forthrightly acknowledged that the nondelegable duty doctrine lacks certainty and predictability:

> There are no clearly defined criteria for identifying duties that are nondelegable. Indeed, whether a particular duty is properly

---

[201] The concurrence is correct so far as it went, but could also have noted that even if a lawyer hired its process servers directly, the lawyer still would not want to accept a server's assurance that service was performed correctly. To be sure, the lawyer could ask an in-house server exactly how he served it. But the lawyer could ask that of an independent process server, as well. While an independent process server could lie about what it did, moreover, so could an in-house server.

categorized as "nondelegable" necessarily entails a sui generis inquiry, since the conclusion ultimately rests on policy considerations.

No court has yet devised a clear and concise statement of when a duty will be deemed nondelegable. Instead, at best, one gets murky and verbose platitudes. If this exception is not to swallow the rule, accordingly, courts should be loath to expand it.

IV. Attribution of Agent's Knowledge and Notice to Principal

Facts known to the agent or of which the agent is given notice are often attributable to the principal. In other words, agency law commonly treats the principal as having knowledge or notice of facts—as the case may be—that are actually known only to the agent or of which only the agent has notice. This concept is of particular importance where the principal is a legal person, such as a corporation, rather than a natural person. After all, how could a corporation know something unless the people who work for it know that information? On the other hand, however, should a corporation be deemed to know something when it is actually known only to a very junior and unimportant employee? In other words, when should an agent's knowledge be imputed to the principal?

Restatement (Third) § 4.01(3) provides that an agent has notice of a fact if the agent "knows the fact, has reason to know the fact, has received an effective notification of the fact, or should know the fact to fulfill a duty owed to another person." The term "notification" is defined in § 5.01(1) as "a manifestation that is made in the form required by agreement among parties or by applicable law, or in a reasonable manner in the absence of an agreement or an applicable law, with the intention of affecting the legal rights and duties of the notifier in relation to rights and duties of persons to whom the notification is given." Knowledge is not a defined term in either the Restatement (Second) or the Restatement (Third), but the drafters of the former indicated in commentary that knowledge means subjective "awareness of a fact or condition."[202]

In general, a principal is charged with notice of facts that the agent knows or has reason to know. In other words, facts an agent knows or has reason to know are imputed to the principal.[203]

---

[202] RESTATEMENT (SECOND) § 9 cmt. c.

[203] RESTATEMENT (THIRD) § 5.03. In the context of a corporate principal, "[t]he knowledge possessed by a corporation about a particular thing is the sum total of all the knowledge which its officers and agents, who are authorized and charged with the doing of the particular thing, acquire while acting under and within the scope of their authority." Upjohn Co. v. New Hampshire Ins. Co., 476 N.W.2d 392 (Mich. 1991). Put another way, "the corporation is considered to have acquired the collective

The theory, known as the "imputed knowledge rule," upon which imputation of knowledge from an agent to its principal rests is that, when the agent acts within the scope of the agency relationship, there is identity of interests between principal and agent. The presumption upon which imputation rests is that the agent will perform his duty and communicate to his principal the facts that the agent acquires while acting within the scope of the agency relationship.[204]

If the agent is acting adversely to the principal or has a duty to someone else not to disclose the facts to the principal, however, the agent's knowledge will not be imputed to the principal.[205] Section 5.04 carves out an exception to this rule, providing that where the agent acts adversely to the principal, the agent's knowledge nevertheless will be imputed to the principal "(a) when necessary to protect the rights of a third party who dealt with the principal in good faith; or (b) when the principal has ratified or knowingly retained a benefit from the agent's action." In turn, this exception is subject to the proviso that the agent's knowledge will not be imputed if the third party knows or has reason to know that the agent is acting adversely to the principal. The drafters offer these illustrations of those rules in action:

> 2. P retains A to negotiate terms for the purchase of Blackacre for P, promising to pay A a percentage commission of the purchase price if A can persuade Blackacre's owner, T, to agree to sell and if A finds no defects in T's title to Blackacre. In investigating T's title, A discovers that L has an unrecorded equitable interest in Blackacre. A does not reveal L's interest to P, fearing that P will not otherwise agree to buy Blackacre and thus that A would not receive a commission. P agrees to buy Blackacre from T. Although A acted adversely to P, notice of the fact of L's interest in Blackacre is imputed to P. T acted

---

knowledge of its employees." U.S. v. TIME-DC, Inc., 381 F. Supp. 730, 738 (W.D. Va., 1974).

[204] In re Waswick, 212 B.R. 350, 352 n.3 (Bkrtcy. D. N.D. 1997). Conversely, however, a principal's knowledge is not imputed to the agent. *See, e.g.,* S.O.G.–San Ore–Gardner v. Missouri Pacific R.R. Co., 658 F.2d 562, 567 (8th Cir.1981) (stating that it is "well settled" that a principal's "undisclosed knowledge is not imputed" to an agent); Hunt Trust Estate v. Kiker, 269 N.W.2d 377, 382 (N.D. 1978) (holding that a principal's knowledge is not imputed to the agent).

[205] RESTATEMENT (THIRD) § 5.03. *See, e.g.,* American Standard Credit, Inc. v. National Cement Co., 643 F.2d 248 (5th Cir. 1981) (stating that "a well established rule of imputed knowledge holds that 'where an officer is dealing with the corporation in his own behalf, or is, for any other reason, interested in a transaction adversely to the corporation, knowledge possessed by him in the transaction is not imputable to the corporation' "); In re National Century Financial Enterprises, Inc., 783 F.Supp.2d 1003, 1016 (S.D. Ohio 2011) ("Courts [applying the imputed knowledge rule] have typically found that an agent who uses his office to loot corporate assets has acted adversely to his principal.").

in good faith, and imputation is necessary to protect T's rights. T may not enforce the contract against P if T knew or had reason to know of A's failure to disclose the existence of L's interest to P.

> 3. Same facts as Illustration 2, except that A does not reveal L's interest in Blackacre because T bribes A not to do so. Notice of the fact of L's interest in Blackacre is not imputed to P. In accepting the bribe from T, A acted for A's own or T's own purposes. T did not act in good faith.

Section 5.02 of the Restatement (Third) states that when someone gives a notification to an agent the notice will be effective as to the principal "if the agent has actual or apparent authority to receive the notification, unless the person who gives the notification knows or has reason to know that the agent is acting adversely to the principal . . . ." In other words, notice to an agent authorized to receive such notices puts the principal on notice, whether the agent relays the information to the principal or not. The drafters offer this illustration of that rule:

> P, who owns a garden center, employs A to manage it. P enters into a contract with T providing that T shall supply the garden center's requirements for mulch for five years. The contract provides that either party may cancel by giving the other 60 days' written notice and further provides that any notice to P shall be given to A. T mails a written notice canceling the contract to A. A opens and reads T's notification but does not tell P. T's notification is effective against P.

V. Duties of Agents to Principals and Vice-Versa

Recall that the Restatement defines agency as "the *fiduciary* relation which results from the manifestation of consent by one person to another that the other shall act on his behalf and subject to his control, and consent by the other so to act."[206] As fiduciaries, all agents owe to their principals a duty of loyalty. In short, the agent may not put his own interests or the interests of some third party ahead of the interests of the principal.[207] Consequently, unless the principal validly consents, the agent may not derive any benefits—such as secret profits—from the agency relationship other than those promised by the principal:

> The fundamental duties of an agent include the duty of utmost loyalty and fidelity to the interests of his principal and the

---

[206] RESTATEMENT (SECOND) § 1(1) (emphasis supplied).

[207] RESTATEMENT (SECOND) § 387 ("Unless otherwise agreed, an agent is subject to a duty to his principal to act solely for the benefit of the principal in all matters connected with his agency.").

duty not to put himself in a position where his own interests may conflict with the interests of his principal. This duty includes not only the duty to act solely for the benefit of the principal on matters within the scope of his agency but also the duty not to take advantage of his position as agent. The law presumes that the principal expects, and is entitled to expect, that the agent will use the skill and experience for which he was retained to further the interests of his principal. If the agent instead promotes his own interest at the expense of the principal's, he violates the agency relationship and is subject to liability for any loss occasioned to the principal by reason of the agent's breach.[208]

So strong is this duty of loyalty that aspects of it continue to bind the agent even after the agency relationship has terminated.

In addition to the fundamental duty of loyalty, an agent also "must act in good faith, confine his acts within the scope of his actual authority, obey his principal's instructions, and use due care and reasonable diligence in the transaction of the business entrusted to him."[209] We discuss these duties at the end of this section.

A. Duties During Agency

During the course of an agency relationship there are several fairly common situations in which the duty of loyalty is implicated. The first is where the agent receives a payment from a third party in connection with some transaction between the principal and the third party.[210] The second entails competition between principal and agent, including where the agent acts as, or on behalf of, an adverse party. Finally, the third entails abuse by the agent of his position to earn side profits not authorized by the principal. Because the agency relationship is consensual, the duty of loyalty in its various forms can be trumped by agreement. If the principal consents in advance following full disclosure, there generally is no problem.

1. *Secret Profits*

The comments to Restatement (Second) § 388 provide that: "an agent who, without the knowledge of the principal, receives something in connection with, or because of, a transaction conducted for the principal, has a duty to pay this to the principal even though otherwise he has acted with perfect fairness to the

---

[208] Gussin v. Shockey, 725 F. Supp. 271, 274–75 (D. Md. 1989).

[209] Echevarias v. Lopez, 572 A.2d 671, 675 (N.J. App. Div. 1990).

[210] RESTATEMENT (SECOND) § 388.

principal. . . ."[211] The improper secret profit can come in the form of a kickback demanded by the agent; e.g., the agent may refuse to direct the principal's business to the third party unless the third party makes a side payment to the agent. Alternatively, the secret profit could come in the form of a bribe paid by the third party to assure that the business will come the third party's way. Finally, it might simply be a gratuity, a tip, paid by a happy third party who wants to reward the agent for his or her hard work. Regardless of the precise nature of the side payment it still constitutes a breach of the duty of loyalty.[212]

In *Gussin v. Shockey*,[213] for example, the plaintiffs went into the thoroughbred horse breeding business. They hired defendant Shockey, an experienced breeder and dealer, to assist and advise them. Shockey acted for the plaintiffs as a go-between and negotiator in a series of horse transactions in which he took kickbacks. In one, for example, he told the plaintiffs the horse's price was $650,000. In fact, however, the seller had agreed to take only $525,000, with the remaining $125,000 going to Shockey as a "commission." The court held that Shockey was obliged to make full disclosure of all material facts to the plaintiffs and obtain their consent before taking the challenged commissions. Because Shockey had not done so, he was liable.

2.   *Acting For or as an Adverse Party; Competition*

An agent also may not make a secret profit from the agency relationship by competing with the principal. There are several ways in which such competition could occur, all potentially violations of the duty of loyalty. First, the agent might act as an adverse party in a transaction involving the principal. "Unless otherwise agreed, an agent is subject to a duty not to deal with his principal as an adverse party in a transaction connected with the agency without the principal's knowledge."[214] Thus, if a principal hires an agent to sell her house the agent must not sell the house to himself without first disclosing his intention to the principal and obtaining her consent.

Second, the agent might act on behalf of an adverse party. Absent agreement to the contrary, an agent may not act for an adverse party in connection with a transaction involving the principal. In the real estate context, for example, unless both buyer

---

[211] RESTATEMENT (SECOND) § 388 cmt. a.

[212] RESTATEMENT (SECOND) § 388.

[213] 725 F. Supp. 271 (D.Md. 1989).

[214] RESTATEMENT (SECOND) § 389.

and seller agree, a real estate agent may not act as "dual agent" representing both sides:[215]

> An agent cannot accept another agency that creates tension with an earlier agency unless he first informs the principal and receives the principal's consent. If an agent "acts for more than one principal in a transaction," he must "disclose to each principal . . . all other facts that the agent knows, has reason to know, or should know would reasonably affect the principal's judgment unless the principal has manifested that such facts are already known by the principal or that the principal does not wish to know them." This requirement ensures that the principal will have "a focused opportunity to assess risks" once the agent identifies potentially problematic circumstances.[216]

The Restatement (Third) provides a general rule covering such situations, which provides that:

> An agent who acts for more than one principal in a transaction between or among them has a duty (a) to deal in good faith with each principal, (b) to disclose to each principal (i) the fact that the agent acts for the other principal or principals, and (ii) all other facts that the agent knows, has reason to know, or should know would reasonably affect the principal's judgment unless the principal has manifested that such facts are already known by the principal or that the principal does not wish to know them, and (c) otherwise to deal fairly with each principal.[217]

Third, the agent might compete with the principal. This violates the duty of loyalty even when the agent acts on his own time or uses his own supplies. Suppose that you are a sixth year associate at a big law firm, one year away from making partner. You're working 70 hours a week and are making lots of money for the firm. In salary and overhead, the firm is paying $175,000 a year for your services. Your billings total $700,000 a year. So the firm is making a profit of $525,000 a year off of you. You decide to cut back to about 55 hours a week. This reduces your annual billings by about 20 percent, to say about $560,000. So the firm is now making only about $385,000 off of you. During the 15 hours a week you've now freed up, you start your own law office. You don't tell the firm and you don't give the firm a share of the profits from your sideline. Have you violated your fiduciary duty? In short, yes. "Unless

---

[215] *See generally* J. Clark Pendergrass, *The Real Estate Consumer's Agency and Disclosure Act: The Case Against Dual Agency*, 48 ALA. L. REV. 277 (1996).

[216] Estate of Eller v. Bartron, 31 A.3d 895, 898–99 (Del. 2011).

[217] RESTATEMENT (THIRD) § 8.06(2).

otherwise agreed, an agent is subject to a duty not to compete with the principal concerning the subject matter of his agency."[218]

3. Abuse of Position

An agent has "not only the duty to act solely for the benefit of the principal on matters within the scope of his agency but also the duty not to take advantage of his position. . . ."[219] Usually this duty comes into play where the agent usurps a business opportunity that should have gone to the principal. Occasionally, however, one encounters situations in which the agent uses his position to make a personal profit from transactions and/or persons wholly unrelated to the principal.

The English King's Bench decision in *Reading v. Regem* is a well-known example of the latter sort of abuse of position case.[220] A British soldier stationed in Egypt during World War II fell into bad company—to wit, a smuggler who prevailed upon the sergeant to abuse his position with the military. While in uniform, the sergeant escorted the smuggler's trucks through the streets of Cairo. By virtue of the sergeant's presence, the trucks were allowed to pass civilian police checkpoints without being inspected. For these services, the smuggler paid the sergeant some £20,000. The army's Special Investigation Branch found him out and seized his bank account and cash found in his apartment. Cheekily, the sergeant sued to recover the money.

The court rejected the sergeant's claim, holding that an agent is required to pay over to the principal—here, His Majesty's Government—any secret profits made as a result of his misuse of the agency position. The sergeant "[took] advantage of his service and violate[d] his duty of honesty and good faith to make a profit for himself." Where "the wearing of the King's uniform and his position as a soldier is the sole cause of his getting the money and he gets it dishonestly, that is an advantage which he is not allowed to keep."

Although it is hard to see how His Majesty's Government was injured in this case, as is often true in such cases, the law nevertheless holds that taking secret profits constitutes a breach of duty. Put another way, part of the agent's duty of loyalty includes a responsibility not to use the agency position—let alone the principal's property or facilities—for the agent's own benefit without the principal's consent.

What is more noteworthy about *Reading* is the tenuous connection between the secret profits and the business of the

---

[218] RESTATEMENT (SECOND) § 393.

[219] Gussin v. Shockey, 725 F. Supp. 271, 274–75 (D.Md. 1989).

[220] [1948] 2 KB 268.

principal. The general statement of the duty of loyalty in Restatement (Second) § 387 speaks of "matters connected with" the agency relationship. Likewise, the general liability provision in § 388 only requires disgorgement of secret profits made "in connection with transactions conducted by [the agent] on behalf of the principal. . . ." In what way, other than the weak link provided by his use of his uniform, was the sergeant's misconduct connected with his agency relationship? The Restatement's drafters seemingly contemplated that use of a uniform is a sufficient connection standing alone. Restatement (Section) § 404 states in pertinent part:

> An agent who, in violation of duty to his principal, uses for his own purposes or those of a third person assets of the principal's business is subject to liability to the principal for the value of the use. If the use predominates in producing a profit he is subject to liability, at the principal's election, for such profit. . . .

But is the uniform an asset of the principal? The comments to § 404 offer an illustration that appears to be based on *Reading* and to confirm its result:

> A soldier uses his official uniform and position to smuggle forbidden goods into a friendly country and thereby makes large profits. The country by which he is employed is entitled to the profits.[221]

4.   *Usurpation of Opportunities*

Cases like *Reading* are relatively rare. The more usual abuse of position case is one in which the agent uses information learned during the course of the agency relationship for personal profit.[222] Perhaps most commonly, this problem arises when the agent usurps a business opportunity that properly belongs to the principal. Consider, for example, the dispute between General Automotive and its key employee John Singer.[223] General Automotive was a small machine shop. Singer was an experienced machinist and manufacturer's representative. General Automotive

---

[221] RESTATEMENT (SECOND) § 404 illus. 3.

[222] *See* RESTATEMENT (SECOND) § 395 ("Unless otherwise agreed, an agent is subject to a duty to the principal not to use or to communicate information confidentially given him by the principal or acquired by him during the course of or on account of his agency or in violation of his duties as agent, in competition with or to the injury of the principal, on his own account or on behalf of another, although such information does not relate to the transaction in which he is then employed, unless the information is a matter of general knowledge."). In the corporate context, of course, the use of confidential information by an agent or other fiduciary can present the special set of problems known as insider trading. *See generally* STEPHEN M. BAINBRIDGE, SECURITIES LAW—INSIDER TRADING (1999).

[223] 120 N.W.2d 659 (Wis. 1963).

hired Singer as its general manager. His compensation was set by contract as a salary plus 3 percent of gross sales. His contract called for him to devote his "entire time, skill, labor and attention" to the job, and to work 5 ½ days per week. A customer, Husco, sent some business to General Automotive that Singer determined General Automotive could not handle. Singer sent the work out to other shops, charging a finder's fee. When General Automotive discovered this and comparable transactions, it sued. In his defense, Singer argued that he was running a separate brokering business with respect to orders that General Automotive could not handle.

Although the contract's "entire time . . ." clause seemed to bar Singer from conducting a sideline business of any sort, the court relied on fiduciary obligation rather than breach of contract. The court held that Singer had a duty to "exercise good faith by disclosing to Automotive all the facts regarding this matter." Since he failed to disclose the transactions, Singer was liable. Presumably, of course, disclosure alone would not have sufficed. Instead, Singer needed General Automotive's informed consent.[224]

5.   *Principal's Remedies*

When an agent breaches the duty of loyalty, the principal is entitled to a constructive trust on the agent's ill-gotten gains. As Restatement (Second) § 388 puts it: "Unless otherwise agreed, an agent who makes a profit in connection with transactions conducted by him on behalf of the principal is under a duty to give such profits to the principal." In addition, where the agent has acted adversely to the principal's interest, the principal need not compensate the agent.[225]

Imposition of disgorgement in the absence of loss to the principal is a prophylactic rule designed to constrain the conflict of interest inherent in secret profit transactions. The case-by-case inquiry necessary if proof of loss is an element of the principal's case might require litigation of various issues not readily susceptible of proof and, moreover, runs counter to the general thrust of property rights analysis. (Note that the nature of the remedy effectively gives the principal a property right in the secret profits.) In general, creation of a property right with respect to a particular asset is not dependent upon there being a measurable

---

[224] *See* RESTATEMENT (SECOND) § 387 (agent must act solely for principal's benefit absent agreement to the contrary).

[225] *See, e.g.*, Gelfand v. Horizon Corp., 675 F.2d 1108, 1111 (10th Cir. 1982); Gussin v. Shockey, 725 F. Supp. 271, 278 (D.Md. 1989); Canon v. Chapman, 161 F. Supp. 104, 111 (D.Okl. 1958); Craig v. Parsons, 161 P. 1117, 1119 (N.M. 1916). Courts are divided as to whether the principal is entitled to recover compensation already paid to the agent during the period of disloyalty. HYNES & LOEWENSTEIN at 115 (citing cases).

loss of value resulting from the asset's use by someone else. Indeed, creation of a property right is appropriate even if any loss in value is entirely subjective because subjective valuations are difficult to measure for purposes of awarding damages. As with other property rights, the law therefore should simply assume (although the assumption will sometimes be wrong) that protection of the principal's interest maximizes social welfare.

Another justification for the harsh disgorgement remedy rests on the economics of deterrence.[226] In order to deter people from engaging in this type of misconduct, the expected sanction must exceed the expected benefit. The expected sanction is a multiple of the probability of conviction times the nominal sanction. In these cases, the probability of conviction is low. It is relatively rare that a plaintiff is able to detect violations of the duty of loyalty. Moreover, violations can be hard to prove. The high level of damages offered by the disgorgement remedy significantly increases the nominal sanction, thereby offsetting the low probability of conviction and creating a reasonably high expected sanction. It also has the effect of compensating successful plaintiffs for the large amount of resources that must be invested in prosecuting one of these cases.

6.   *Consent by the Principal*

The Restatement (Second) had no broad provision dealing with the effect of a principal's consent to conduct by an agent that would otherwise violate the duty of loyalty, although many sections dealing with that duty stated or implied that such consent would preclude liability. The Restatement (Third), in contrast, contains a broad provision under which a principal may give such consent:

> Conduct by an agent that would otherwise constitute a breach of [the duty of loyalty] does not constitute a breach of duty if the principal consents to the conduct, provided that (a) in obtaining the principal's consent, the agent (i) acts in good faith, (ii) discloses all material facts that the agent knows, has reason to know, or should know would reasonably affect the principal's judgment unless the principal has manifested that such facts are already known by the principal or that the principal does not wish to know them, and (iii) otherwise deals fairly with the principal; and (b) the principal's consent concerns either a specific act or transaction, or acts or transactions of a specified type that could reasonably be expected to occur in the ordinary course of the agency relationship.[227]

---

[226] *See generally* Gary S. Becker, *Crime and Punishment: An Economic Approach*, 76 J. POL. ECON. 169 (1968).

[227] RESTATEMENT (THIRD) § 8.06(1).

Note that this provision contemplates either that the principal can consent on a case-by-case basis as conflicts arise or may give a blanket consent at the outset of the relationship dealing with future conflicts of the types specified by the parties in their agreement.

7.   Summation

The bottom line thus can be stated fairly simply: Unless the principal and the agent have expressly agreed otherwise, the only compensation the agent may receive by virtue of the agency relationship is the compensation the principal agreed to pay or, in the absence of an agreed amount, a reasonable payment for the value of the agent's services. Any other benefits received by the agent, which reasonably can be said to arise out of the agency relationship or by virtue of the agency relationship, from whatever source derived, must be paid over to the principal.

B.   Duties After Termination of Agency

As a consensual relationship, an agency relationship terminates whenever either side withdraws its consent that the agent should act on behalf of the principal and subject to the principal's consent. Termination of the relationship ends the agent's actual authority to conduct business on the principal's behalf, although apparent authority can persist as to third parties unaware that the relationship has ended. For present purposes, however, the key point is that certain fiduciary obligations persist post-termination.

In particular, a former agent remains subject to the obligation not to make use of confidential information learned during the course of the agency relationship.[228] Operationalizing this obligation has gotten quite complicated, however. To a considerable extent the relatively straightforward agency law limits on grabbing and leaving have been supplanted by the far more complex law of trade secrets—a subject well beyond the scope of this text.

As a matter of agency law, an agent is free to compete with the principal after termination of their relationship.[229] Indeed, the agent may make preparations for competition even while the agency relationship is still in force.[230]

---

[228] RESTATEMENT (SECOND) § 396(b) (the former agent "has a duty to the principal not to use or to disclose to third persons, on his own account or on account of others, in competition with the principal or to his injury, trade secrets, written lists of names, or other similar confidential matters given to him only for the principal's use or acquired by the agent in violation of duty. The agent is entitled to use general information concerning the method of business of the principal and the names of the customers retained in his memory, if not acquired in violation of his duty as agent. . . .").

[229] RESTATEMENT (SECOND) § 396(a).

[230] RESTATEMENT (SECOND) § 393 cmt. e.

Once one gets down to brass tacks, however, the rules begin to lose coherence—and even common sense. Suppose you are a senior associate at a large law firm and are considering leaving to start your own firm. You are not permitted to solicit clients of your present firm while still employed at that firm.[231] Could you, however, talk to some fellow associates about leaving with you? What about your secretary or law clerk? The Restatement (Second) is simultaneously opaque and equivocal:

> The limits of proper conduct with reference to securing the services of fellow employees are not well marked. An employee is subject to liability if, before or after leaving the employment, he causes fellow employees to break their contracts with the employer. On the other hand, it is normally permissible for employees of a firm, or for some of its partners, to agree among themselves while still employed, that they will engage in competition with the firm at the end of the period specified in their employment contracts. However, a court may find that it is a breach of duty for a number of the key officers or employees to agree to leave their employment simultaneously and without giving the employer an opportunity to hire and train replacements.[232]

Hardly the sort of analysis that lends itself to providing advice to a client hoping for some degree of certainty. In fairness to the Restatement's drafters, however, context doubtless is quite important. As a result, these issues tend to be decided on a case-by-case basis.[233]

As a practical matter, of course, job mobility in the legal profession and other service industries depends mainly on your ability to bring a portfolio of clients with you to the new firm. As we have seen, the Restatement takes the position that one cannot solicit clients before leaving the former firm. But what about after you leave?

According to Restatement (Second) § 396(b) a former agent may not use a customer list—"written lists of names"—even after the agency relationship terminates. Section 396(b) goes on to state,

---

[231] RESTATEMENT (SECOND) § 393 cmt. e (agent is not "entitled to solicit customers for [a] rival business before the end of his employment").

[232] Restatement (Second) § 393 cmt. e.

[233] In Bancroft-Whitney Co. v. Glen, 411 P.2d 921 (Cal. 1966), for example, liability was imposed on the president of a division of a publishing company who grabbed and left with a bunch of subordinates in large measure because the president, who had a duty to defend the company from raids on its employees, used confidential firm salary information to lure away the employees and lied to superiors by denying rumors of an impending raid. If the president had refrained from using proprietary firm information and/or told the truth when asked by his superiors, liability likely would not have been imposed.

however, that the "agent is entitled to use . . . the names of the customers retained in his memory, if not acquired in violation of his duty as agent. . . ." If that is not confusing enough, it is this issue of customer lists that has gotten most thoroughly bollixed up with trade secret law.[234] On top of which is the further complicating factor that many employment contracts in service industries include covenants not to compete, whose enforceability is the subject of yet another body of law that lacks coherence.[235]

Under these conditions, an example may do more harm than good, but perhaps we can risk a few words on a decision that appears in several leading casebooks. In *Town & Country House & Home Service, Inc. v. Newbery*,[236] the plaintiff corporation operated a maid service in suburban New York. The wife of the company's president had put together a list of customers by telephoning people in several neighborhoods. The defendants were former Town & Country employees who quit, then called their old customers, and built their business from that base. The court held that the defendants breached their fiduciary duty by calling clients of their employer, even though they waited until after they had resigned. In addition, the court held that the list was a trade secret.

The decisive factor seems to have been the court's opinion that:

> The customers of plaintiff were not and could not be obtained merely by looking up their names in the telephone or city directory or by going to any advertised locations. . . . In most instances housewives do their own house cleaning. The only appeal which plaintiff could have was to those whose cleaning had been done by servants regularly or occasionally employed, except in the still rarer instances where the housewife was on the verge of abandoning doing her own work by hiring some outside agency.

It had taken years of hard work to build up a clientele of such customers. The defendants were not entitled to free ride on that work.

---

[234] *See* GREGORY & HURST at 314–16; HYNES & LOEWENSTEIN at 118–125; *see generally* Henry J. Silberberg & Eric G. Lardiere, *Eroding Protection of Customer Lists and Customer Information Under the Uniform Trade Secrets Act*, 42 BUS. LAW. 487 (1987).

[235] *See* HYNES & LOEWENSTEIN at 125–131; *see generally* Robert W. Hillman, *Law Firms and Their Partners: The Law and Ethics of Grabbing and Leaving*, 67 TEX. L. REV. 1 (1988); Stuart L. Pachman, *Accountants and Restrictive Covenants: The Client Commodity*, 13 SETON HALL L. REV. 312 (1983).

[236] 147 N.E.2d 724 (N.Y. 1958). If the court's opinion strikes you as paternalistic and politically incorrect by today's standards, that's because it is paternalistic and politically incorrect. But it was decided in the Ozzie & Harriet era, after all.

Is the *Town & Country* rule fair to the customers? A rule that prohibited a client from following its lawyer to a new firm would seem unfair to the client. Arguably, people would like to keep the same person cleaning their house as well. As we have seen, however, Town & Country spent lots of time and money building the customer list. Presumably some barrier to competition is necessary to encourage firms like Town & Country to make that effort. On yet another hand, however, as a capitalist society we encourage people to better themselves by finding new jobs. Giving customer lists strong protection might discourage job mobility. Because these policy goals usually are in direct conflict in any given fact pattern, one often sees courts trying to strike a middle ground, which has led to ever-growing confusion.

C. Other Duties

In addition to the core duty of loyalty, the Restatement identifies a slew of additional fiduciary obligations the agent owes the principal. Some of these supplement the duty of loyalty by helping the principal to better monitor the agent's conduct. Under Restatement (Second) § 381, for example, the agent is obliged to alert the principal to information the agent is on notice that "the principal would desire to have." Under Restatement (Second) § 382, to take another important example, the agent is obliged to keep an account of all "money or other things which he has received or paid out on behalf of the principal" and to render such accounts to the principal.

Other duties respond to the risks of vicarious liability associated with a principal's reliance on an agent. An agent is obliged, for example, "not to conduct himself with such impropriety that he brings disrepute upon the principal."[237] Likewise, the agent is obliged to obey "all reasonable directions" by the principal.[238]

In an attempt to minimize the risk that a principal will be bound by unauthorized acts of the agent, Restatement § 383 forbids the agent from acting "except in accordance with the principal's manifestation of consent." If the agent lacked actual authority to make a contract deemed binding on the principal, as where the agent had apparent or inherent authority, the principal can recover from the agent any loss suffered thereby.[239]

The key non-loyalty fiduciary obligation, however, is the duty of care. A compensated agent must "act with standard care and with the skill which is standard in the locality for the kind of work

---

[237] RESTATEMENT (SECOND) § 380.

[238] RESTATEMENT (SECOND) § 385(1).

[239] RESTATEMENT (SECOND) § 401.

which he is employed to perform and, in addition, to exercise any special skill that he has."[240] In many agency relationships, of course, this standard is supplemented and/or displaced by more specific legal regimes; medical and legal malpractice being good examples.[241]

D. Duties of Principal to Agent

Although most litigation involves duties owed by the agent to the principal, agency law does recognize a number of duties running in the other direction. As a practical matter, of course, the most significant duty owed by principals to their agents is the duty of compensation. The principal owes a duty to the agent to reasonably compensate the agent for her services, unless the agent has agreed to act gratuitously. Absent evidence that the relationship was gratuitous, moreover, it will be inferred that the principal agreed to compensate the agent.[242] In the normal business agency relationship, of course, the employment agreement will provide for set payments to the agent. But if the agreement does not so provide, a court can force the principal to pay the agent the reasonable value of the services rendered.[243] Although the agent is thus entitled to compensation from the principal, we have seen in preceding sections that the duty of loyalty forbids the agent from receiving any other compensation in connection with the agency relationship unless the principal knowingly agrees to the contrary.

Restatement (Third) § 8.14 provides that the principal has a duty to indemnify the agent "in accordance with the terms of any agreement between them" and, "unless otherwise agreed":

---

[240] RESTATEMENT (SECOND) § 379(1). A gratuitous agent is only obliged to exercise "the care and skill which is required of persons not agents performing similar gratuitous undertakings for others." RESTATEMENT (SECOND) § 379(2).

[241] An interesting duty of care issue is presented when the principal is a corporation. As employees of the corporation, corporate managers are its agents. As such, they owe a duty of care to the corporation. *See, e.g.,* MODEL BUS. CORP. ACT ANN. § 8.42(a)(2) (2003) (requiring that officers exercise the "care that a person in a like position would reasonably exercise under similar circumstances"). Unfortunately, it is not well-settled whether officers get the benefit of the business judgment rule. *Compare* Galef v. Alexander, 615 F.2d 51, 57 n.13 (2d Cir. 1980) (holding that the business judgment rule "generally applies to decisions of executive officers as well as those of directors"); FDIC v. Stahl, 854 F. Supp. 1565, 1570 n.8 (S.D.Fla. 1994) (holding that the rule "applies equally to both officers and directors") with Platt v. Richardson, 1989 WL 159584 at *2 (M.D.Pa. 1989) (holding that the rule "applies only to directors of a corporation and not to officers."). At least one court claims that the former view is the majority position, rejecting an argument that "the business judgment rule applies only to the conduct of corporate directors and not to the conduct of corporate officers" on grounds that it was "clearly contrary to the substantial body of corporate case law which has developed on this issue." Selcke v. Bove, 629 N.E.2d 747, 750 (Ill. App. 1994).

[242] RESTATEMENT (SECOND) § 441.

[243] RESTATEMENT (SECOND) § 443 (agent is entitled to be paid "the fair value of his services).

(a) when the agent makes a payment (i) within the scope of the agent's actual authority, or (ii) that is beneficial to the principal, unless the agent acts officiously in making the payment; or

(b) when the agent suffers a loss that fairly should be borne by the principal in light of their relationship.

Note that the indemnification rights of corporate agents typically are defined by the state's business corporation statute rather than the common law of agency, although courts sometimes look to the common law for guidance in interpreting the statutes.

Restatement (Third) § 8.15 creates a broad duty requiring the principal to deal fairly and in good faith" with the agent. The duty includes an obligation to inform the agent about risks—both fiscal and financial—potentially posed by the work to be done by the agent. In *Taylor v. Cordis Corp.*,[244] for example, a medical device salesman sought a judicial declaration that his employment contract was void on grounds that his employer had failed to disclose to him information relating to problems that the employer had discovered in its pacemakers. The salesman argued that he repeatedly suffered considerable embarrassment when obliged to disclose product recalls to doctors, which ultimately damaged his business reputation. The court agreed with the salesman "that a principal has a duty to deal fairly and in good faith with an agent, which includes and obligation "to provide the agent with any information which might subject the agent to physical or pecuniary loss in dealing with the product."[245] The principal's duty of good faith duty further requires that the principal refrain from conduct that would "harm the agent's business reputation or reasonable self-respect."[246] The court rejected plaintiff's claim, however, on grounds that the employer did not have a duty to inform the salesman of "product problems" or "consumer complaints."[247] "The duty to inform its sales agents of product problems attached only when the company, in the exercise of reasonable diligence, knew that specific product defects posed a threat of harm to consumers and a concomitant threat to the professional reputation of the sales agent."[248]

---

[244] 634 F. Supp. 1242 (S.D. Miss. 1986).

[245] *Id.* at 1246.

[246] *Id.* (citing the comments to RESTATEMENT § 437).

[247] *Id.* at 1247.

[248] *Id.*

Chapter 3

PARTNERSHIPS

A partnership is an association of two or more persons as co-owners of a business for profit. The partnership thus is distinguished from the sole proprietorship in that at least two people must have ownership rights in the enterprise. As we shall see, a great many consequences flow from that distinction.

The partnership is a very old form of business organization. Roman law, for example, had a well-developed system of partnership law. Modern partnership law, however, is most directly traced to the Law Merchant—the international law governing medieval traveling merchants and their fairs—which was gradually incorporated into English and then American common law. Indeed, the "black letter law" of partnerships as late as the mid-1800's still closely resembled the rules of the Law Merchant.

Unlike agency law, which was a creation of (and remains a matter of) the common law, modern partnership law is a mixture of statutory and common law rules. In 1914, the National Conference of Commissioners on Uniform State Laws promulgated the Uniform Partnership Act as a model statute for state legislatures to adopt.[1] The UPA (1914) eventually was adopted by almost every state, with a high degree of uniformity. In 1994, the Commissioners promulgated a revised uniform partnership statute. Substantially revised versions followed in 1996 and 1997.

The revised Uniform Partnership Acts updated and expanded the 1914 statute in many respects.[2] As of late 2013, 37 states had adopted one of the various versions of the revised act. Because multiple versions were promulgated within a short period of time, and because some of the revised act's provisions proved controversial, there is less uniformity than existed under the 1914 statute. Some states had moved early, adopting one of the preliminary drafts. Although NCCUSL intended the final 1997 version to supersede the earlier drafts, some of the states that had adopted one of the earlier drafts chose not to adopt the 1997 version. In addition, unlike the 1914 Act, which most states adopted verbatim, many states modified some provisions of whichever

---

[1] The National Conference of Commissioners on Uniform State Laws consists of practicing lawyers, judges, and law professors who are appointed by the 50 state governments to draft proposals for uniform and model statutes and to work toward their enactment in the state legislatures.

[2] The UPA (1997) is also sometimes referred to as the Revised Uniform Partnership Act or RUPA.

version of the revised act they had adopted. States nevertheless are gradually coalescing around the final Revised Act, which is now more commonly known as the UPA (1997), so it will be our focus herein.

Thus far we have been referring to the most basic form of partnership, which is sometimes called the general partnership to distinguish it from other forms.[3] In addition, the law has long recognized the so-called limited partnership. Unlike a general partnership, in which all partners are fully liable for partnership debts and obligations, a limited partnership provides limited liability for some of its members. In recent years, the law has also developed two additional partnership forms: the limited liability partnership and the limited liability limited partnership. We take these forms up at the end of this Chapter.

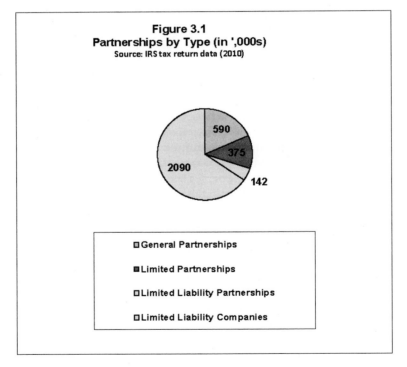

Figure 3.1
Partnerships by Type (in ',000s)
Source: IRS tax return data (2010)

- General Partnerships
- Limited Partnerships
- Limited Liability Partnerships
- Limited Liability Companies

I. Partnership Defined

The general partnership, like the sole proprietorship, but unlike almost every other form of business organization, requires no formalities for its creation. No document need be filed with any

---

[3] In this text, the terms "partnership" and "general partnership" are used interchangeably.

government official nor is the approval of any governmental body required to form a partnership.[4] All that is required is that two or more persons agree to carry as co-owners a business for profit. In this sense, the general partnership is a default form of business organization. If the parties fail to more formally define and establish their firm, their relationship defaults to partnership status.

Suppose two lawyers, Alice and Bob, share office space. Sometime later the question arises whether Alice and Bob are partners or solo practitioners who happen to be co-tenants of the office. How do we decide?

A. General Principles

UPA (1997) § 101(6) defines a partnership as "an association of two or more persons to carry on as co-owners a business for profit."[5] The key concepts here are co-ownership and business. Section 101(1) broadly defines "business" to include "every trade, occupation, and profession." In most cases, this definition is sufficiently sweeping to encompass just about any for profit venture. The requirement that the parties "carry on" such a business, however, occasionally creates issues. To "carry on" a "trade, occupation or profession" implies something more than a single, isolated transaction. There must be some on-going business relationship. Indeed, it is this factor that distinguishes the partnership from the otherwise similar joint venture, which is discussed below.[6]

The co-ownership requirement also can pose problems. Suppose Alice and Bob purchased their office suite rather than leasing it. Co-ownership of property does not itself establish a partnership. But now suppose the office suite they purchased has three offices. Alice and Bob rent out the third office to lawyer Zelda, sharing the rent proceeds equally. Does that make them partners? Ownership of property by joint or common tenancy does not by itself establish a partnership, even if the co-owners share any profits from use of the property.[7] Rather, the alleged partners must be co-

---

[4] As with a sole proprietorship, however, a partnership may be required to register under a Fictitious Business Name statute in order to conduct business under a name other than those of the partners. In addition, if the partnership is formed to engage in some regulated business, a state or local license to conduct such business may be required. Finally, and most significantly, the partnership must file tax returns.

[5] The UPA (1914) provisions are essentially identical in effect.

[6] *See, e.g.,* Scandinavian Airlines System Denmark-Norway-Sweden v. McDonald's Corp., 947 F. Supp. 1257, 1259 (N.D.Ill. 1996) ("A joint venture is an association of two or more persons to carry on a single enterprise for profit.").

[7] UPA (1914) § 7(2); UPA (1997) § 202(c)(1).

owners of a trade, occupation, or profession for profit.[8] Here one could argue that the lawyers really aren't in the business of real estate management. Instead, they just happen to jointly own an asset that they are leasing to some third party. In any event, even if the two lawyers might be partners in a real estate venture, they do not become partners of a law firm simply by virtue of jointly owning the office suite. Instead, it must be shown that they agreed, either explicitly or implicitly—either in writing or orally—to associate together to act as co-owners of a business.

Because an agreement is required, which contemplates some sort of meeting of the minds, it is sometimes said that the parties must have intended to become partners. This is error, however. It is perfectly possible to create a partnership without realizing you're doing so. The relevant question is whether the parties intended to act as co-owners of a business for profit. If so, the law will treat them as partners, whether or not they knew that they were creating a particular type of business entity known as a partnership and carrying with it specific legal consequences.[9] Consequently, courts will look behind the parties stated intentions to determine whether or not their actions in fact created a partnership.[10]

Does it matter how the parties described their relationship? Suppose that the lawyers filed separate tax returns, each claiming solo practitioner status. Could you still find a partnership? Yes. How the parties described the business is a relevant but not determinative factor.[11]

Suppose that Alice's practice was booming and she asked Bill to help out on some of the excess cases. Does that establish a law firm partnership between them? No, because sharing workloads on an occasional would not itself establish that they were co-owners of

---

[8] *See* Dalton v. Austin, 432 A.2d 774, 777 (Me. 1981) (stating that "the right to participate in control of the business is the essence of co-ownership").

[9] *See, e.g.,* Truck Ins. Exchange v. Industrial Indemnity Co., 688 P.2d 1243, 1245 (Mont. 1984) ("If the intended action of the parties creates a partnership in fact, what the parties call their arrangement or intend their arrangement to be is irrelevant."). Accordingly, it is not necessary that the parties have intended to become partners, "it is only necessary that [they] intended [their] actions and that [their] actions created a partnership in fact." MacArthur Co. v. Stein, 934 P.2d 214, 218 (Mont. 1997). The requisite intent may be inferred "from all the facts, circumstances, actions, and conduct of the parties." *Id.* at 217. *See also* Arnold v. Erkmann, 934 S.W.2d 621, 630 (Mo.Ct. App. 1996) ("The primary criterion is the parties' intention to enter a relationship which in law constitutes a partnership; intent to form a partnership is not necessary.")

[10] Where there is clear evidence of the parties' subjective intent, courts are more likely to defer to that apparent intent when the litigation involves a dispute between the purported partners than when the rights of a third party are involved. RIBSTEIN & LIPSHAW at 83.

[11] Arnold v. Erkmann, 934 S.W.2d 621, 630 (Mo.Ct. App. 1996).

a business for profit.[12] This would be true even if they shared gross receipts from excess cases.[13]

Suppose, however, that Alice and Bob agreed to pool their gross receipts from both law practice and office rentals in a single account, pay all expenses out of the joint account, and then split the profits. Is that a partnership? In the absence of evidence to the contrary, yes. Division of profits is prima facie evidence that a partnership exists.[14] But what if Alice had originally paid the entire purchase cost of the office suite and argues that the sharing of profits was Bob's way of repaying her for his half of the purchase price? If true, sharing of profits as payments on a loan will rebut the presumption that a partnership exists. The same would be true if the profit sharing really was a form of rent payment.

B. Proving Partnership

If the question of whether a partnership exists arises in a litigation setting, the party claiming that a partnership exists has the burden of proof.[15] Normally, the burden of proving a partnership exists is a preponderance of the evidence. "However, where the evidence contains writings of the parties that distinctly indicate a relationship other than a partnership, the assertion that a partnership exists must be based on very clear and convincing evidence."[16]

The existence of a partnership is a mixed question of law and fact:

> "The question of whether a partnership exists between particular persons is a mixed question of law and fact. This means that what constitutes a partnership under established facts is a question of law for the court, but the existence of the facts necessary to bring the relation within the tests of partnership, or the determination whether a partnership exists under the evidence and the inferences reasonably drawn from the evidence, is a question of fact for the jury." In other words, "where the facts are . . . susceptible of only one reasonable inference, the question of whether a partnership exists between particular persons is one of law for the court."[17]

---

[12] They might be joint venturers with respect to any given case in which they collaborated, however.

[13] UPA (1914) § 7(3); UPA(1997) § 202(c)(2).

[14] UPA (1914) § 7(4); UPA(1997) § 202(c)(3).

[15] *See, e.g.,* Miller v. Salabes, 169 A.2d 671, 672 (Md. 1961); Blaustein v. Lazar Borck & Mensch, 555 N.Y.S.2d 776, 777 (N.Y. App.Div. 1990).

[16] Seidmon v. Harris, 526 N.E.2d 543, 546 (Ill. App. 1988).

[17] Lenoble v. Best Temps, Inc., 352 F.Supp.2d 237, 250 (D. Conn. 2005) (citations and footnote omitted). *See also* Robinson v. Parker, 11 App. D.C. 132 (D.C.

C.   Some Examples

As should be obvious by now, there is no bright-line test defining a partnership. Instead, analysis proceeds on a case-by-case basis in a highly fact-dependent way.[18] As such, a few examples from leading cases may be more helpful than abstract discussion. In this section, we consider two of the most common situations in which the existence of a partnership comes into dispute: employment and lending. In the first category, the question is whether the parties' relationship is one of partners or employer-employee. In the second, the question is whether the parties' relationship is one of partners or debtor-creditor. As we shall see, both can involve fine distinctions: and even a bit of luck.

1.   Partner or Employee?

Carl Zajac and George Harris operated an automobile salvage business that purchased wrecked automobiles from insurance companies and then either rebuilt them or cannibalized them for parts. Harris used his own money to buy some of the cars used by the firm, which Zajac knew, although Zajac had never expressly approved of Harris doing so. Zajac paid Harris one half of the profits derived from the firm's sales, including sales of cars financed solely by Zajac. They eventually had a falling out and Harris sued. Harris claimed that they had formed a partnership and, accordingly, that Harris was entitled to a half interest in the alleged partnership's assets and profits. Zajac contended that Harris was a mere employee, working on commission. The court held that sharing of profits constituted prima facie evidence that a partnership existed.[19] Zajac attempted to rebut the resulting presumption of partnership status by showing that he controlled the business' books and records, no partnership income tax return was ever filed, Harris was treated as an employee in that federal withholding and Social Security taxes were paid upon his share of the profits, and workmen's compensation insurance was carried for

---

App. 1897) ("Whether or not the necessary elements exist to constitute a partnership is a question of fact for the jury, and as to whether such facts when proved to exist are sufficient to create a copartnership, is a question of law for the court.").

[18] *See, e.g.,* Southex Exhibitions, Inc. v. Rhode Island Builders Ass'n., Inc., 279 F.3d 94, 100 (1st Cir. 2002) (" 'Partnership' is a notoriously imprecise term, whose definition is especially elusive in practice. . . . Since a partnership can be created absent any written formalities whatsoever, its existence *vel non* normally must be assessed under a 'totality-of-the-circumstances' test."); *see also* Ingram v. Deere, 288 S.W.3d 886, 899–903 (Tex. 2009) (holding that "whether a partnership exists must be determined by the totality of the circumstances"); Madden Invest. Co. v. Stephenson's Apparel, 832 N.E.2d 780, 782 (Ohio App. 2005) ("The existence of a partnership may be express, as by an agreement, or implied from the conduct of the persons concerned. An implied partnership must be found to exist from the totality of the attendant facts and circumstances.").

[19] Zajac v. Harris, 410 S.W.2d 593 (Ark. 1967).

Harris's protection. The court rejected Zajac's argument on two grounds, however.

First, because Harris was illiterate, Harris likely did not appreciate the significance of those practices. This aspect of the court's argument is not very persuasive. It is not enough for Harris to believe that he was a partner in the business. Zajac must have agreed to associate with Harris as co-owners of a business for profit. Zajac's evidence tended to show that he treated Harris as an employee. Under UPA (1914) § 7(4)(b), the then-applicable statute, no inference of partnership status is to be drawn from the fact that the parties shared profits if the division of profits constituted wages to an employee.

Second, the court relied on testimony by Zajac that Harris was entitled to receive half of the profits derived from business conducted by Zajac alone. Yet, this evidence did not preclude a finding that Harris was an employee. Many employee profit-sharing plans entitle employees to share in profits of the firm as a whole not just in those profits attributable the employee's own labor. On the other hand, employees generally do not contribute capital to the firm. Harris' right to share in the profits of the business as a whole must be coupled with the fact that he used his own funds in the business.[20] Taken together, these factors lend some credence to the court's holding.

As illustrated by *Fenwick v. Unemployment Compensation Commission*,[21] however, a partnership will not always be found where two parties share profits from a business. In 1936, one John Fenwick opened a beauty shop in Newark, N.J. Arline Chesire joined the business a year later as a receptionist. One year after that, Chesire demanded a raise from her weekly wage of $15. Fenwick countered with an offer to make her a partner with the right to 20% of the profits, or so Fenwick later claimed.

New Jersey provided unemployment compensation to out-of-work individuals that was funded by a tax on employers. Businesses with fewer than 8 employees were exempt from paying the tax. Partners in the business did not count as employees. If Cheshire were counted as an employee, the beauty shop would have 8 employees and would have to pay the tax; if Cheshire were treated as a partner, the business would be exempt. The state

---

[20] *Cf.* MacArthur Co. v. Stein, 934 P.2d 214, 218 (Mont. 1997) ("each of the purported partners must contribute something that promotes the enterprise"). Note that a contribution of labor would suffice, however. *See* Dalton v. Austin, 432 A.2d 774, 777 (Me. 1981) ("Evidence relevant to the existence of a partnership includes evidence of a voluntary contract between two persons to place their money, effects, labor, and skill, or some or all of them, in lawful commerce or business with the understanding that a community of profits will be shared.").

[21] 44 A.2d 172 (N.J. 1945).

Unemployment Compensation Commission sued Fenwick to collect the tax. Fenwick defended by claiming Cheshire was a partner. The court decided Cheshire was Fenwick's employee.

Unlike Zajac and Harris, Fenwick and Cheshire had a written partnership agreement. In addition, Fenwick and Cheshire held themselves out to as partners at least insofar as tax issues were concerned. They filed a partnership income tax return and Fenwick's personal income tax returns indicated that his income came from the partnership. In addition, their filings with the Commission itself claimed that Cheshire and Fenwick were partners. Finally, and perhaps most importantly, the agreement provided for an 80–20 split of profits, which by statute should have created a prima facie case that a partnership existed.

Despite these indicia of partnership, however, the court treated Cheshire as an employee. Under UPA (1914) § 7(4)(b), evidence that the parties' sharing of profits was in fact payment of wages to an employee rebuts the presumption that a partnership exists. Here the court determined that Chesire's share of the profits were in fact wages. In the court's view, Cheshire lacked any of the indicia of being a partner. Cheshire made no capital contribution. The agreement provided that Cheshire was not responsible for any losses by the firm. The agreement gave Cheshire no right to assets of the business upon dissolution. Finally, and most significantly, the agreement expressly provided for "the control and management of the business" to be vested solely "in Fenwick."

No one of these factors, standing alone, should suffice to rebut the presumption of partnership created by sharing profits. Nothing in the UPA requires a capital contribution from every partner; or, indeed, from any partner. So-called service partnerships, in which one or more partners contributes solely services, in fact are very common. Although the default UPA rule is that partners share losses equally, the statute also provides that that rule can be changed as the partners see fit by contrary agreement.[22] The same is true with respect to control rights. Although the UPA default rule is that each partner is entitled to participate in firm management on a one partner-one vote basis, that rule is also subject to modification by contrary agreement.[23]

In many respects, the relationship at issue in *Fenwick* thus had considerably more indicia of partnership than did that in *Zajac*. Why then the seemingly counter-intuitive result? One need not be a

---

[22] UPA (1914) § 18(a); UPA (197) § 401(b). *See* In re Senior Living Properties, L.L.C., 309 B.R. 223, 257 (Bkrtcy.N.D.Tex. 2004) ("a partnership may exist without the sharing of losses").

[23] UPA (1914) § 18(e); UPA (197) § 401(f).

cynic to think that context mattered. *Zajac* was a dispute between
the partners *inter se*, in which it appeared that Zajac was taking
advantage of the illiterate Harris. In contrast, although the
Fenwick court went out of its way to note that the Commission was
not alleging tax fraud, there can be little doubt that the court saw
the Fenwick-Cheshire relationship as a sham intended as a tax
dodge. One need not think the government always wins tax cases to
believe that court is more likely to find a partnership in cases
involving internal disputes than those that impact the rights of
third parties.

From a planning perspective, the key issue thus is what
Fenwick could have done in structuring his relationship with
Cheshire to buttress his claim. Perhaps nothing, given the court's
apparent conclusion that the deal was just a tax gimmick. A good
lawyer, however, could have camouflaged the relationship a bit
better and thus made it harder for the court to find against
Fenwick. After all, much transactional lawyering consists of
building a paper record so that a dubious position later can be
defended with a straight face.

The money quote in *Fenwick* reads: "The next [consideration] is
community of power in administration, and the reservation in the
agreement of the exclusive control of the management of the
business in Fenwick excludes this element so far as Mrs. Chesire is
concerned." The court went on to explain that someone would be
treated as an employee rather than a partner when "such a person
had no control over the operation of the firm, and could not direct
its investments, nor prevent the contracting of debts; in other
words, had none of the prerogatives of a principal in the
management and control of the business."

Assume that Fenwick desired sole control and that Cheshire
was willing to go along. The transactional planning problem thus
becomes one of giving Cheshire the appearance of control rights,
without the reality thereof. Instead of the language vesting control
in Fenwick, the agreement might say something like: "The partners
shall confer on all business decisions and, in the event of
disagreement, shall vote." Elsewhere in the agreement it could be
provided that each partner shall have that number of votes equal to
her or his percentage share of the partnership's profits. This gives
Fenwick 80 votes and Cheshire only 20, so Fenwick would retain *de
facto* control. These provisions make Chesire's vote meaningless,
but are consistent with the common practice of altering the basic
UPA rule on voting by making votes proportional to interests in the
partnership. Query whether a court would be impressed, however,
on the facts of *Fenwick*. At the end of the day, after all, a tax dodge
is still a tax dodge.

An example of particular interest to readers of this text is the question of whether so-called income or non-equity partners of a law firm are partners or employees. In *Davis v. Loftus*,[24] for example, Terry Davis filed a legal malpractice complaint against the partners in the law firm of Gottlieb & Schwartz. One of the partners named in the complaint as a defendant, Anthony Frink, filed a motion to dismiss the claims against him on grounds that he was not a partner in Gottlieb & Schwartz for purposes and thus not subject to vicarious liability for torts committed by the firm. Frink relied on Gottlieb & Schwartz' partnership agreement, which listed him—and several others—as so-called "Income Partners." According to the agreement, income partners did not share in either partnership profits or losses. Instead, the agreement provided for the firm to pay each income partner "a fixed level of compensation determined on an annual basis by the Executive Committee," plus a bonus. Each income partner made a "capital contribution" of $10,000 to the firm, which they got back—"without any adjustment for the growth or profits of the firm from the time of the capital contribution" if they left the firm. Income partners had no voting rights and were not eligible to serve on the executive committee.

The court agreed that Frink and the other income partners were not liable. They are not true partners, because a true partner shares in the profits and control of the firm and the so-called income partners shared in neither.[25]

On the other hand, attorney Douglas Richmond argues that:

> It is difficult for law firms to convincingly argue that non-equity partners are not partners for agency law or vicarious-liability purposes given the fashion in which they hold them out to the world as partners. It is similarly disingenuous for non-equity partners to hold themselves out as partners when it is beneficial to do so but then deny or disclaim partner status when it has negative ramifications. To deny partnership in either instance is to arguably engage in multiple ethical violations.

---

[24] 778 N.E.2d 1144 (Ill. App. 2002).

[25] Note that if Frink were the lawyer who committed the malpractice, then his status as "income partner" would again be irrelevant. Lawyers are liable for their own malpractice, partner or no.

Note also that if the firm holds an "income partner" out to the public as a partner, the income partner may be liable for the debts of the partnership under apparent partner principles. The question turns on § 308 of the UPA (1997), which provides in pertinent part that "[i]f a person . . . consents to being represented by another as a partner, . . . the purported partner is liable to a person to whom the representation is made, if that person, relying on the representation, enters into a transaction with the actual or purported partnership." See the discussion of partnership by estoppel in Chapter 3.I.D.

For example, for a firm's equity partners to claim that a non-equity partner who has been held out as a partner is not one is to potentially acknowledge deceit, dishonesty, and misrepresentation in those activities, and thus to admit violations of [Model Rules of Professional Conduct, Rule] 8.4(c). Such a claim might also be alleged to violate Model Rule 7.1, which prohibits lawyers from making false or misleading communications about their services; Model Rule 7.5(a), which forbids lawyers from using a professional designation that violates Rule 7.1; and Model Rule 7.5(d), which provides that lawyers may state or imply that they practice in a partnership only when that is the fact. . . . On the law firm side, all equity partners will end up being liable under Model Rule 5.1(a) for allowing those violations to occur. From the individual lawyer's perspective, the fact that the firm allowed or encouraged her to hold herself out as a partner is no defense to alleged violations of Rules 7.1, 7.5, and 8.4(c), because lawyers are bound by ethics rules even when they are acting at the direction of another person.[26]

2.   *Partner or Lender?*

Shortly after the First World War, the brokerage firm of Knauth, Nachod & Kuhne ("KNK") got into financial difficulty as a result of unwise speculative investments. One of the firm's partners, a John Hall, had three wealth friends—Peyton, Perkins, and Freeman ("PPF")—upon whom he prevailed to loan KNK $2.5 million worth of marketable securities. KNK then used those securities as collateral for a bank loan. Unfortunately, the loan failed to turn around KNK's finances and the firm eventually folded. KNK's creditors then sued PPF, claiming that PPF had entered into a partnership with KNK and, accordingly, were liable for KNK's debts. Fortunately for PPF, the New York Court of Appeals (per famed Judge William Andrews) disagreed.[27]

If PPF had lost the case, and were deemed to be partners in KNK, two very bad things would have happened. First, recall that KNK owes them $2.5 million. As partners, their claims come last.[28] In bankruptcy, all other creditors get paid before the partners get a dime. Thus, they stand to lose their whole $2.5 million investment. But it gets worse. As we'll see below, partners are personally liable for all firm debts.[29] Thus, PPF stood to lose not only the $2.5 million

---

[26] Douglas R. Richmond, *The Partnership Paradigm and Law Firm Non-Equity Partners*, 58 U. KAN. L. REV. 507, 530–31 (2010).

[27] Martin v. Peyton, 158 N.E. 77 (N.Y. 1927).

[28] UPA (1914) § 40(b); UPA (1997) § 807(a).

[29] UPA (1914) § 15; UPA (1997) § 306.

they put into the firm, but also as much of their personal fortunes as needed to pay off KNK's creditors.

The agreement between KNK and PPF provided for PPF to continue collecting the dividends on their securities, entitled them to 40% of KNK's profits, with a minimum payment of $100,000 and a maximum of $500,000, and have them an option to buy up to a 50% equity interest in KNK. PPF had inspection rights and the right to veto speculative transactions. The agreement also provided that Hall was to provide the "directing management" of KNK. Finally, PPF all the other KNK partners submitted signed resignations to be accepted by Hall at his discretion. Despite these precautions, KNK continued its unwise speculations and eventually failed.

Although sharing of profits is *prima facie* evidence a partnership exists, UPA (1914) § 7(4)(a) rebuts the presumption of partnership if sharing of profits is done in payment of principal or interest on a debt. As the court analyzed the agreements, it deemed the various rights and protections demanded by PPF to be consistent with the role of lender. Hence, the presumption did not control.

The court's conclusion seems correct. PPF needed to protect its loan due to the risky nature of KNK's business. What better way to protect themselves than to insist that their friend Hall be in charge? Indeed, such a provision is quite similar to common terms of bank loans that prohibit changes in a corporation's board of directors or CEO without the bank's permission.

Yet, it is also clear that PPF had a very close call. Judge Andrews observed: "a point may come where stipulations immaterial separately cover so wide a field that we should hold a partnership exists. As in other branches of the law, a question of degree is often the determining factor. Here that point has not been reached."[30] From a transactional planning perspective, how could

---

[30] *Martin*, 158 N.E. at 80. Judge Andrews' point of demarcation was reached in *In re Senior Living Properties, L.L.C.*, 309 B.R. 223 (Bkrtcy.N.D.Tex. 2004), where defendant Zurich was deemed to be a partner of the business in question rather than a mere creditor for the following reasons:

Zurich contracted to share in the profits of SLP's business, which is the essential term for a partnership under Illinois law. Zurich contracted to obtain a residual interest of seventy to ninety percent of the fair market value of SLP as a going concern; that is, Zurich contracted for a distribution of equity. Zurich acted as an owner in contracting for the payment of all operating expenses, debt service and capital improvement expenditures before distribution of profits. Zurich contracted to cover debt service if SLP's revenue would not pay operating expenses and the mortgage. Zurich contracted to assure that creditors were paid before excess cash was distributed to equity level interests. Zurich had ultimate control of the hiring and termination of the management of the nursing homes. Zurich took control of the cash management system of SLP and could dictate the priority of payments of expenses and debt obligations, with a level of control over SLP's operations extending to dictating deviations from the contractual provisions of the waterfall.

PPF have modified the agreement to provide themselves with additional cover without sacrificing important protections?

It was unwise of PPF to demand a right to be consulted on business decisions and to take the resignations of all the partners. Both tend to give PPF a degree of control consistent with a finding of partnership. Instead, the agreement should have provided that KNK would not engage in any "speculative or injurious" investments, without giving PPF a veto power over such investments. Alternatively, PPF could have avoided any reference to control and simply demanded that a minimum equity cushion be maintained. If so, they would have also wanted a provision rendering failure to maintain that cushion an act of default, so the loan would become due and payable.

As in the preceding section, it may prove instructive to compare the outcome of *Martin v. Peyton* with a case whose facts seem quite similar but in which the opposite result was reached. In the 1950s, frozen concentrated orange juice manufacturer Minute Maid Corporation entered into a long-term contract to sell its products to United Foods, Inc. If United Foods carried a sufficiently large inventory of Minute Maid products, it would receive substantial volume allowances. Unfortunately for it, United Foods lacked the financial resources to carry the necessary level of inventory. A second firm, United States Cold Storage Corporation, was willing to lend United Foods the necessary funds. Unbeknownst to Minute Maid, United Foods and Cold Storage agreed that Cold Storage would advance the necessary funds to United Foods for inventory purchases. The inventory would be stored in a Cold Storage warehouse, for which Cold Storage would receive its normal rental fees. The volume-based allowances received from Minute Maid would be deposited into a special account carrying 6% interest, with the interest being paid to Cold Storage. United Foods and Cold Storage subsequently would split the allowances 50–50. When United Foods got into financial difficulty and was unable to pay some $143,000 it owed Minute Maid, Minute Maid sued Cold Storage, claiming that the latter had entered into a partnership agreement with United Foods and was

---

Zurich had the authority to extend the mortgage maturity date and to control the disposition of SLP's capital assets, both to protect its interest in equity. Zurich controlled the prepayment of the mortgage, not as a surety, but to protect its interest in equity. Zurich hired professional persons for SLP. Zurich exercised a degree of control as an equity holder in negotiating credit for SLP without SLP involvement in the negotiations. Zurich controlled the distribution of profits and controlled the salary of the members of SLP. Zurich negotiated indemnification of managers and members working at SLP. Zurich shared in the risk of loss. The parties actually implemented the SLP transaction, with SLP engaged in the nursing home business. *Id.* at 266.

therefore liable for the purported partnership's debts. The court agreed.[31]

Cold Storage argued that its relationship with United Foods was that of a debtor and creditor. The court agreed with that characterization, but held that where a debtor and creditor create a separate business enterprise over which they each exercise control, a partnership exists. Here, "the arrangement whereby Cold Storage furnished the financing and warehouse facilities to make possible United's use of its relationship as a direct buyer of Minute Maid products in such quantities and under such terms as would turn a profit for both of them" was a separate business enterprise entered into by the parties over which they each "had joint control." A strong dissent argued that the profit-sharing relationship was merely a way for United Foods to pay interest on its debts to Cold Storage and thus was not evidence of a partnership.[32]

Query what the *Minute Maid* majority would have made of the arrangement in *Martin v. Peyton?* Was the relationship between KNK and PPF any less a separate business enterprise than that of United Foods and Cold Storage? Indeed, on paper, PPF arguably had more control rights than did Cold Storage.

A couple of factors, however, distinguish the two cases sufficiently to make sense of the disparate outcomes. First, PPF's direct control consisted only of its right to veto speculative investments. In practice, moreover, PPF had no way of controlling what was going on at KNK, except through their friend Hall, who let them down. Hence, in *Martin,* you have a limited share in profit and a passive indirect form of control. In contrast, Cold Storage was actively involved in decision making. Indeed, the *Minute Maid* court quoted a United Foods employee, who testified that "the [Cold Storage] could have stepped in and written me [United] off pretty damned fast."

The significance of such control rights is confirmed by the outcome in *Lupien v. Malsbenden*, which also appears in a number of the leading casebooks.[33] Frederick Malsbenden and Stephen Cragin created a loan arrangement where Malsbenden received a portion of the sales from Cragin's business, York Motor Mart, as repayment of monies advanced by Malsbenden used by York Motor Mart to purchase car kits, parts and equipment and to pay wages. Plaintiff Robert Lupien contracted with Cragin for a kit car from

---

[31] Minute Maid Corp. v. United Foods, Inc., 291 F.2d 577 (5th Cir. 1961).

[32] One objection raised by the dissent was a Texas statute that forbade corporations from entering into partnerships. At one time, it was a "hotly-disputed question" whether corporations were permitted to be partners. DEMOTT at 503. Today, all corporation statutes give corporations the power to join partnerships. *Id.*

[33] 477 A.2d 746 (Me. 1984).

York Motor Mart. When Cragin disappeared and the kit car was never provided, Lupien sued Malsbenden based on a partnership liability theory. The court upheld Malsbenden's liability for breach of contract as Cragin's partner. Pointing out that a partnership agreement may be expressed or implied, the court noted that two or more persons could form a partnership even if one was never intended. Thus, when two or more persons agree to share profits from a business created by their combined skill, labor or money, they create a partnership, even if they label the endeavor otherwise. Although Malsbenden likened his involvement with York Motor Mart to that of a "banker," the court concluded that, based on his financial interest and involvement in the day-to-day business operations, he was in fact a partner. First, Malsbenden's financial contributions were not structured as a loan of fixed sums but more as day-to-day purchases when needed. The "loan" carried no interest. Also, repayment was not in the form of fixed payments at designated times but was contingent upon the sales of York Motor Mart. Second, Malsbenden participated in the day-to-day operations of the business. He often opened the business in the mornings, ordered parts, and paid salaries. Plaintiff often dealt directly with Malsbenden rather than Cragin when he visited the business. Further, Malsbenden continued doing business at York Motor Mart after Cragin disappeared. Thus, their arrangement amounted to a "pooling of Malsbenden's capital and Cragin's automotive skills, with joint control over the business and intent to share the fruits of the enterprise."

A second factor distinguishing *Martin* and *Minute Maid* is the equities of the situation. Cold Storage and United Foods kept their relationship secret from Minute Maid so as to take advantage of the volume allowances. In addition, with Cold Storage's apparent cooperation, United Foods undertook a scheme whereby it took possession of Minute Maid products from storage warehouses but delayed informing Minute Maid. On balance, the court may have felt that their collaborative deception of Minute Maid justified treating them as partners so that Cold Storage could be held liable.

Even if these factors justify the disparate outcomes, however, it should be clear that PPF had a very close call. Once again, the take-home lesson is that good transactional planning is essential. If one wishes to avoid the legal consequences of partnership, a good paper record is essential.

3. Partner or Family Member?

Some courts have suggested that purported partnerships between family members should be viewed with a "raised eyebrow."[34] As a result, acts and circumstances between spouses may not have the same significance . . . as the same acts and circumstances between strangers might have."[35] In *Schlichenmayer v. Luithle*,[36] for example, a husband and wife jointly purchased a cattle farm. Proceeds from the farm operations were used for family expenses and to pay the mortgage on the land. The wife did not participate on a daily basis in the purchase or sale of the cattle, although she did occasionally assist in the operation by milking cows and taking on other chores. The court found that this evidence presented "no credible evidence to support a claim of partnership."

In recent years, courts have also been reluctant to find a partnership where the parties were in an unmarried domestic relationship. In *Ontiveros v. Silva*,[37] for example, one member of an unmarried couple tried to end run the fact that New Mexico does not recognize common law marriages, and thus there was no family law basis for a division of property, by claiming that the parties had created a partnership. The court rejected that argument, because there was no evidence that the parties intended "to combine their money, property, or time, and to share profits and losses."

D. Partnership by Estoppel

So far we've focused on true partnerships: on in which there is an agreement, express or implied, between the parties. UPA (1914) § 16, however, contemplates that non-partners sometimes can be treated as though they were partners:

> When a person, by words spoken or written or by conduct, represents himself, or consents to another representing him to any one, as a partner in an existing partnership or with one or more persons not actual partners, he is liable to any such person to whom such representation has been made, who has, on the faith of such representation, given credit to the actual or apparent partnership, and if he has made such representation or consented to its being made in a public manner he is liable to such person, whether the representation has or has not been made or communicated to such person so giving credit by or with the knowledge of the apparent partner making the representation or consenting to its being made.

This basis of liability is known as partnership by estoppel, which like agency by estoppel only creates rights in third parties. It is not

---

[34] Schneider v. Kelm, 137 F.Supp. 871, 874 (D. Minn. 1956).

[35] Sunkyong International v. Anderson Land & Livestock Co., 828 F.2d 1245, 1249 (8th Cir.1987).

[36] 221 N.W.2d 77 (N.D.1974).

[37] 2011 WL 704497 (N.M. App. 2011).

a theory one alleged partner can use as against the other member of the alleged partnership.

Interestingly, by the plain text of § 16, statutory partnership by estoppel relates only to the creation of liability to third persons who, in reliance upon representations as to the existence of a partnership, have "given credit" to the purported partnership. What about tort victims? UPA (1997) § 308(b) raises similar questions by limiting the purported partner's liability to "persons who enter into transactions in reliance upon the representation."

Suppose lawyers Anne and Bob share an office. A client of Anne's settles a case and is due to receive a substantial payment. The settlement check is delivered to Anne, who forges the client's endorsement on the check, and absconds with the proceeds. The client then sues Bob, seeking to hold him liable for Anne's breach of trust. Because Anne and Bob were not partners, but merely office-mates, the client relies on partnership by estoppel. Although § 16 seemingly does not apply to such situations, a number of courts have held that someone in the client's position nevertheless may invoke partnership by estoppel to hold Bob liable.[38]

In order to establish a partnership by estoppel, four elements must be proven: (1) Plaintiff must establish a representation, either express or implied, that one person is the partner of another—i.e., that there was a holding out of a partnership.[39] (2) The making of the representation by the person sought to be charged as a partner or with his consent. (3) A reasonable reliance in good faith by the third party upon the representation. (4) A change of position, with consequent injury, by the third person in reliance on the representation.[40] Some courts omit the fourth factor or collapse it into the third.[41] In any case, failure to establish any of these requirements precludes recovery on an estoppel theory.[42]

---

[38] *Compare* Frye v. Anderson, 80 N.W.2d 583 (Minn. 1957) (partnership by estoppel available in tort cases) *with* Pruitt v. Fetty, 134 S.E.2d 713 (W.Va. 1964) (not available).

[39] Where an individual holds himself out as being a member of an existing partnership, only those partners who know about and consented to the holding out will be held liable.

[40] Brown v. Gerstein, 460 N.E.2d 1043, 1052 (Mass. App. 1984). *See also* Gosselin v. Webb, 242 F.3d 412, 415 (1st Cir. 2001) ("To prevail under [the partnership by estoppel] doctrine, a plaintiff must prove four elements: '(1) that the would-be partner has held himself out as a partner; (2) that such holding out was done by the defendant directly or with his consent; (3) that the plaintiff had knowledge of such holding out; and (4) that the plaintiff relied on the ostensible partnership to his prejudice.')".

[41] *See, e.g.,* Howick v. Lakewood Village Ltd. Partnership, 2009 WL 1110829 at *6 (Ohio App. 2009) (holding that "partnership by estoppel has three prongs: a misrepresentation prong (prong one); a reliance prong (prong two); and a credit prong (prong three)").

[42] Brown v. Gerstein, 460 N.E.2d 1043, 1052 (Mass. App. 1984).

Two points should be noted about the application of this standard to the hypothetical. First, Bob must have made the representation or, at least, knowingly consented to Anne's making such a representation. Evidence that Bob held himself out or consent to Anne holding him out "may consist of 'words spoken or written or . . . conduct.' "[43] Anne cannot hijack Bob into her business unilaterally. Second, it must be established that the client, to whom the holding out was made, reasonably relied upon the representation that a partnership existed to her legal detriment. The alleged partners must have created an expectation in the client's mind that they stood behind each other, and that they would make good any malfeasance that one might commit.

Both UPA (1914) § 16 and UPA (1997) § 308 draw a distinction between private and public holdings out. If Bob held himself out as Anne's partner only to this particular client, other creditors of Anne cannot pursue him on a partnership by estoppel theory. Suppose, however, that Anne and Bob decided to save money not only by sharing office space but also by printing up common stationery, the letterhead of which states: "The Law Offices of Anne & Bob."[44] If Bob consented to being held out as a partner in this public manner, then Bob is liable to any third party who extends credit to Anne's business in reliance on that holding out.[45]

E. The Joint Venture

A joint venture is commonly described as an association or cooperative agreement between two or more persons or companies to carry out a single specific undertaking for profit.[46]

A joint venture is " 'an association of two or more persons to carry out a single business enterprise for profit, for which purpose they combine their property, money, effects, skill and knowledge.' " A party seeking to establish the existence of a

---

[43] Gosselin v. Webb, 242 F.3d 412, 415 (1st Cir. 2001).

[44] *See, e.g.,* Glazer v. Brookhouse, 471 F.Supp.2d 945, 949 (E.D.Wis. 2007) ("Brookhouse's name is listed on the letterhead. Based on that letterhead, Glazer could reasonably believe that the firm was a partnership."); Andrews v. Elwell, 367 F.Supp.2d 35 (D.Mass. 2005) (holding that "listing the names of attorneys together [on letterhead] constitutes 'holding out' those attorneys as partners"). On the other hand, although having one's name appear on the letterhead constitutes the requisite holding out, the mere fact that one's name appears on the letterhead—standing alone—does not prove that one has consented to being held out as a partner or that the third party reasonably relied on such holding out. *See, e.g.,* Standard Oil Co. v. Henderson, 265 Mass. 322, 326 (1928) (holding that "the use of a person's name in a business, even with that person's knowledge, is too slender a thread to warrant a favorable finding on the consent element").

[45] *See* National Premium Budget Plan Corp. v. National Fire Ins. Co., 234 A.2d 683, 729–32 (1967), aff'd, 106 N.J.Super. 238, 254 A.2d 819 (1969); Reisen Lumber and Millwork Co. v. Simonelli, 98 N.J.Super. 335, 237 A.2d 303, 306–08 (1967); Pruitt v. Fetty, 148 W.Va. 275, 134 S.E.2d 713 (W.Va.Sup.Ct.1964); but see Gilbert v. Howard, 64 N.M. 200, 326 P.2d 1085, 1087 (1958).

[46] 46 Am. Jur. 2d *Joint Ventures* § 1 (2002).

joint venture under New York law must demonstrate the following elements: (1) the existence of a specific agreement between two or more persons to carry on an enterprise for profit; (2) evidence in the agreement of the parties' intent to be joint venturers; (3) a contribution of property, financing, skill, knowledge, or effort by each party to the joint venture; (4) some degree of joint control over the venture by each party; and (5) the existence of a provision for the sharing of both profits and losses. The existence of a joint venture is generally a question of fact. The party asserting the existence of the joint venture bears the burden of proof to establish these elements. Failure to establish any element of the joint venture will be fatal to the party asserting the existence of the joint venture.[47]

As suggested by the opening sentence of the preceding quotation, the distinction between a joint venture and a partnership is based on the idea that joint ventures involve a single transaction of limited duration, while partnerships are ongoing business enterprises. Thus, a joint venture is distinguishable from a partnership by the narrowness of its purpose and scope.[48]

Courts generally apply the law of partnerships to joint ventures; indeed, many courts have often ignored any differences between joint ventures and partnerships.[49] These courts comment that "a joint venture is a form of partnership"[50] or that "it is sometimes difficult, and often unnecessary, to distinguish in particular cases between joint adventures and partnerships."[51] Other courts have recognized the differences between joint ventures and partnerships but view them as insubstantial in determining which law to apply, noting that "a joint adventure is not identical with a partnership but is so similar in its nature and in the

[47] In re Cohen, 422 B.R. 350, 377 (E.D.N.Y. 2010).

[48] *See* Hagerman v. Schulte, 181 N.E. 677, 681 (Ill. 1932) (referring to joint venture as a "limited partnership—not limited in the statutory sense as to the liabilities of the partners but as to its scope and duration").

[49] The rights and duties of partners in a partnership generally have been applied to members of a joint venture. Early on, Judge Cardozo noted that joint adventurers "like copartners, owe to one another, while the enterprise continues, the duty of the finest loyalty," the standard for which he went on to note was "the punctilio of an honor the most sensitive." Meinhard v. Salmon, 164 N.E. 545, 546 (N.Y. 1928). Other courts have followed in finding that a fiduciary relationship exists between joint adventurers and imposing upon adventurers the duties of loyalty, good faith, fairness, and honesty in dealings with each other. Greenup v. Hewett, 235 S.W.2d 1000, 1002 (Ky. Ct. App. 1951). Additionally, the act of one adventurer has been held to bind the entire joint venture. Singer Housing Co. v. Seven Lakes Venture, 466 F. Supp. 369, 376 (D. Colo. 1979). Furthermore, once the venture is bound, joint adventurers have been held to be jointly and severally liable for the obligations of the venture. In re Chandler Airpark Joint Venture, 163 B.R. 566, 570 (Bankr. D. Ariz. 1992).

[50] Paragom Building Corp. v. Banker Trust Co., 567 P.2d 1216, 1217 (Ariz. Ct. App. 1977).

[51] Greenup v. Hewett, 235 S.W.2d 1000, 1002 (Ky. Ct. App. 1951).

contractual relations created thereby that the rights as between adventurers are governed practically by the same rules that govern partnerships."[52]

While it is generally agreed that partnership law should govern joint ventures, a narrower question has been answered by a number of courts: which partnership law? Some cases have been concerned with whether common law partnership rules or partnership rules under the Uniform Partnership Act should govern. The Connecticut Supreme Court has ruled that common law partnership principles should govern the joint venture.[53] Similarly, Massachusetts courts have ruled, at least in situations where a joint venture includes corporate members, that application of UPA rules is not mandatory and should be treated as relevant to joint ventures with corporate members "only by way of analogy and only when the use of the analogy in particular circumstances will achieve a just result."[54]

F.   An Aggregate or Entity?

A question that long bedeviled partnership law was that of whether the partnership is an aggregate or its members or a separate entity. Although the tone of the debate often was reminiscent of Scholastic arguments over how many angels could dance on the head of a pin, it had non-trivial implications. For example, if the partnership is an entity it can sue and be sued in its own name. If it is an aggregation of individuals, however, then each and every partner must be joined to any suit involving the partnership. Procedural complications relating to diversity jurisdiction in federal courts, joinder of parties, personal jurisdiction, and venue all resulted. Numerous non-litigation examples also could be cited, such as the names in which partnership property must be registered on a deed or certificate of title.

The UPA (1914) did not come down squarely on one side or the other of this debate; rather, it treats the partnership as an entity for some purposes and as an aggregate for others. UPA (1997)

---

[52] Simpson v. Richmond Worsted Spinning Co., 145 A. 250, 254 (Me. 1929); *see also* Hagerman v. Schulte, 181 N.E. 677, 681 (Ill. 1932) ("a joint adventure is not identical with a partnership ... [but] the relationship between the parties is so similar that their rights and liabilities are usually tested by the rules which govern partnerships."); Bank of California v. Connolly, 36 Cal. App.3d 350, 364 (1973) ("incidents of both relationships are the same in all essential respects").

[53] Travis v. St. John, 404 A.2d 885, 888 (Conn. 1978).

[54] Eastern Electrical Co. v. Taylor Woodrow Biltman Constr. Corp., 414 N.E.2d 1023, 1027 (Mass. Ct. App. 1981) (emphasis in original); *see also* Infusaid Corp. v. Intermedics Infusaid, Inc., 739 F.2d 661, 663 (1st Cir. 1984) (holding UPA applicable to joint venture between corporations since "just result" would be achieved and intent of the parties was that UPA partnership law would apply).

§ 201(a), in contrast, purports to answer the question definitively: "A partnership is an entity distinct from its partners." In fact, however, even the 1997 statute effectively treats the partnership as though it were an aggregate for some purposes. For example, the 1997 still treats partners as being personally liable for partnership obligations and does not provide for automatic continuation of the business when a partner dies or retires.

II. Management Rights of Partners

All partners have an equal right to participate in the firm's management on a one-partner/one-vote basis.[55] Most partnership decisions are to be made by majority vote.[56] Admission of new partners, acts outside the ordinary scope of partnership business, and amendments to the partnership agreement, however, require unanimous consent.[57]

Each of the foregoing principles, of course, are default rules. Partners are free to vary all of them by agreement to the contrary.[58] They are thus free to set up any decisionmaking structure they prefer. In the small firm setting, the one-partner, one-vote rule often makes perfect sense; but even in that setting, unequal bargaining positions may lead to unequal voting rights. Suppose that Alice was a 50 year old lawyer, with lots of money and clients. Bob and Charles are young associates at Alice's law firm. The three of them decide to split off and form their own law firm. Alice says that because she is contributing most of the capital and most of the clients, she ought to be able to out-vote the other two lawyers. So she proposes that there be a total of 100 votes, divided up so as to Alice 55 votes, to Bob's 25 and Charles's 20. Alice also proposes that they use majority rule on all questions, including those where the UPA requires unanimous consent. If Bob and Charles agree, these changes are all valid and, in the event of subsequent dispute, will be enforced by courts.

In the large firm setting, of course, the one-partner/one-vote democratic style of firm government is especially unmanageable. Take, for example, the case of a large national law firm with many offices in different parts of the country and several hundred partners. It would be unworkable for such a firm to try to make every decision, or even every important decision, by majority rule. Even worse, unanimity would be almost impossible to achieve; indeed, it would create holdout incentives for the partners. Because partnership law permits the parties great flexibility, however, we

---

[55] UPA (1914) § 18(e); UPA (1997) § 401(f).

[56] UPA (1914) § 18(h); UPA (1997) § 401(j).

[57] UPA (1997) § 401(i)–(j).

[58] UPA (1997) § 103(a).

see a wide variety of decisionmaking structures in this setting, ranging from partnerships essentially run by one person to partnerships that delegate substantial amounts of authority to one or more committees that make decisions by consensus among the committee members to partnerships (even rather large ones) that retain the traditional one-partner/one-vote democratic model. Again, courts will defer to the parties' choice of governance arrangements.[59]

A. Every Partner an Agent: Management Rights and Liabilities

Each partner is an agent of the partnership for carrying on its business. A partner, of course, may have actual authority to conduct business on behalf of the partnership. Since each partner is an agent of the partnership, with an equal right to conduct partnership business, actual authority to bind the partnership is inherent in the position. There are, however, some extraordinary acts as to which a partner has no authority without the consent of his fellow partners. As to such acts, actual authority may be created by the partnership agreement (e.g., the agreement states Anne shall have authority to assign the partnership's real property, Anne therefore has actual authority to do so) or a vote by the partners (if a majority of the partners vote to give Bill authority to assign the partnership's real property, Bill has actual authority to do so).[60]

In the absence of actual authority to bind the partnership, such as where the partnership agreement forbids the partner from making a contract of the type in question, a partner may still have apparent authority to do so.[61] In most partnership cases, the agency law requirement of a holding out by the principal is satisfied by the mere fact that one is a partner. Just as hiring an agent to a position customarily carrying certain powers constitutes the requisite holding out, so does appointment of someone to partnership status. Where a partner enters into an unusual transaction having little direct relation to the partnership business, however, some courts require evidence that the firm held the partner out as having authority to conduct such transactions.[62]

---

[59] *See, e.g.,* Day v. Sidley & Austin, 394 F. Supp. 986 (D. D.C. 1975), *aff'd,* 548 F.2d 1018 (D.C. Cir. 1976) (upholding partnership agreement that delegated "complete authority" to an executive committee).

[60] UPA (1914) § 9; UPA (1997) § 301.

[61] Note that while each partner is an agent of the partnership, he is not necessarily the agent of the other partners as individuals. A partner thus has power to bind the partnership as a firm, but no automatic power to bind the other partners in their individual capacities. FDIC v. Kagan, 871 F. Supp. 1522, 1525 (D. Mass. 1995).

[62] *See, e.g.,* McGarity v. Craighill, Rendelman, Ingle, & Blythe, P.A., 349 S.E.2d 112 (N.C. 1987) (lawyer solicited funds from client to invest in securities; court

Unlike most rules of partnership law, which the partners may modify by agreement amongst themselves, the rules governing a partner's authority are mandatory. This is done to protect the reasonable expectations of third parties and to lower transaction costs. If the partners could adopt any arrangements relating to authority to act on behalf of the firm that suited them, it would be very difficult for outsiders to discover what idiosyncratic internal rules had been adopted. Accordingly, without standard, mandatory rules regarding authority to act for the partnership, transactions between the firm and third parties would involve very high transaction costs.

1.　Apparent　Authority:　What　is　the　Business　of　the Partnership?

UPA (1997) § 301(1) states:

> Each partner is an agent of the partnership for the purpose of its business. An act of a partner, including the execution of an instrument in the partnership name, for apparently carrying on in the ordinary course the partnership business or business of the kind carried on by the partnership binds the partnership, unless the partner had no authority to act for the partnership in the particular matter and the person with whom the partner was dealing knew or had received a notification that the partner lacked authority.

UPA (1914) § 9(1) is substantially similar, except that it omits the phrase "apparently carrying on in the ordinary course . . . business of the kind carried on by the partnership." On its face, this omission from the 1914 statute seems to substantially limit a partner's apparent authority. Suppose two partners—Adam and Zelda—have long operated a grocery store. Most grocery stores in their locality sell alcoholic beverages, but their store has never done so. Zelda enters into a long-term contract with a beer distributor to begin selling beer at the store. When Adam learns of the contract, he objects. Is the contract binding?

By the plain text of the 1914 statute, the answer should be no. The 1914 statute provides apparent authority only where the partner was "apparently carrying on in the usual way the business of the partnership of which he is a member."[63] Hence, one could argue, only evidence of past practice of that particular partnership is relevant; evidence of community practice would be irrelevant. This interpretation of the statute is inconsistent with both agency

---

required client to prove that law firm had held the lawyer out as being authorized to do so).

[63] UPA (1914) § 9(1).

law, where custom in the community or industry is relevant to the scope of apparent authority, and good sense. The whole point of apparent authority, after all, is to eliminate the need for third parties to inquire into the peculiarities of the agent or partnership with whom they do business. The drafters of the 1997 statute thus properly clarified the issue by adding the phrase "business of the kind," which clearly makes evidence of customary practice in the community or industry relevant.[64]

Even with that clarification, however, it still can be difficult in many cases to tell whether a particular transaction was one "apparently carrying on in the ordinary course the partnership business." In the leading case of *Cook v. Brundidge, Fountain, Elliott and Churchill*, for example, Warren Lyon was a partner in the Texas law firm of Brundidge, Fountain, Elliott & Churchill. He represented one Betty Cook in a divorce proceeding and also prepared her will. During a conference concerning the divorce, Cook asked Lyon whether he knew of someone with whom she could discuss investing an anticipated inheritance in real estate. Lyon informed Cook that he was a silent partner in a real estate firm and suggested several investments. Cook chose to invest in a fast-food franchise Lyon was setting up. The franchise went belly up and Cook sued both Lyon and the law firm.[65]

The issue thus presented was whether attorney Lyon had been acting in the ordinary course of the law firm's business such that the firm was bound by and could be held liable for his actions. The trial court granted summary judgment to the law firm on this issue, but the Texas appellate court reversed and remanded for trial.

A strong dissent emphasized that Lyon specifically told Cook that he was a silent partner in a different firm in a different field. Cook should have realized he was talking about a different business than the business of the law firm. The dissent also made a great deal out of the fact that the law firm did not know of or benefit from

---

[64] There is little case law on point under UPA (1914) § 9(1), but some courts interpreted the statute sensibly rather than strictly. In Burns v. Gonzalez, 439 S.W.2d 128 (Tex. Civ. App. 1969), for example, the court explained: "As we interpret Sec. 9(1), the act of a partner binds the firm, absent an express limitation of authority known to the party dealing with such partner, if such act is for the purpose of 'apparently carrying on' the business of the partnership in the way in which other firms engaged in the same business in the locality usually transact business, or in the way in which the particular partnership usually transacts its business." *Id.* at 131. The principle is a long-standing one in Texas, dating to well before the promulgation of the 1914 UPA. *See, e.g.,* Randall v. Meredith, 13 S.W. 576, 581 (Tex. 1890) ("Between the partners themselves, and between the firm and persons dealing with it through a partner, there is no doubt that the usages of firms engaged in the same character of business in the same country, as well as the general usage of the firm in the conduct of its business, may be looked to ascertain the implied powers possessed by a partner.").

[65] Cook v. Brundidge, Fountain, Elliott and Churchill, 533 S.W.2d 751 (Tex. 1976).

the transaction. While those facts arguably go more to the issue of whether there was actual authority, they do tend to indicate that this was not the type of activity the firm ordinarily engaged in.

On the other hand, the majority could point to a number of factors tending to show that what Lyon did was within the ordinary scope of the business. First, many lawyers, particularly those in general practice dealing with individuals rather than big businesses, act as trustees and financial advisors. Accordingly, it may well be reasonable for a client to believe that such an attorney is acting within the scope of ordinary legal business when offering investment advice. As the Oregon supreme court explained in a similar case involving investment advice provided by a partner in an accounting firm:

> If a third person reasonably believes that the services he has requested of a member of an accounting partnership [are] undertaken as a part of the partnership business, the partnership should be bound for a breach of trust incident to that employment even though those engaged in the practice of accountancy would regard as unusual the performance of such service by an accounting firm. The reasonableness of a third person's belief that a partner is acting within the scope of the partnership should not be tested by the profession's own description of the function of its members. Those who seek accounting services may not understand the refinements made by accountants in defining the services they offer to the public.[66]

Second, the check by which Cook made her investment was made payable to Lyon as her attorney and mailed to Lyon at the law firm. Third, the investment advice arose out of a transaction in which Lyon was acting as attorney for Cook.

Cases in other jurisdictions are sharply divided on whether soliciting investment funds from clients is within the ordinary course of law practice.[67] The outcome in any given case, of course, will be highly fact-dependent. In general, however, the *Cook* majority has the better argument. As between Cook and the law firm, the latter—more precisely, the firm's other partners—is in the best position to monitor Lyon's conduct of business. The firm could prevent these losses by requiring its members to abstain from conducting outside business with firm clients or, at least, to abstain from doing so on firm time and on the firm's premises. Indeed,

---

[66] Croisant v. Watrud, 432 P.2d 799 803 (Ore. 1967).

[67] *Compare* Zimmerman v. Hoag & Allen, P.A., 209 S.E.2d 795 (N.C. 1974) (within scope) *with* Sheinkopf v. Stone, 927 F.2d 1259 (1st Cir. 1991) (not within scope); Heath v. Craighill, Rendelman, Ingle & Blythe, P.A., 388 S.E.2d 178 (N.C. App. 1990) (same); Rouse v. Pollard, 21 A.2d 801 (N.J. 1941) (same).

many law firms have just this type of prohibition. By imposing liability, the court arguably put the loss on the party who could have most cheaply prevented it in the first instance and thereby created the proper incentives.

2. Apparent Authority: Must the Third Party Inquire?

Under pre-UPA(1997) law, there was some precedent for the proposition that a third party dealing with the partnership may have a duty to inquire into the scope of a partner's authority.

3. Extraordinary Acts

UPA (1914) § 9(3) lists five specific actions that a partner has no authority to take absent express authorization by his fellow partners:

> Unless authorized by the other partners or unless they have abandoned the business, one or more but less than all the partners have no authority to: (a) Assign the partnership property in trust for creditors or on the assignee's promise to pay the debts of the partnership, (b) Dispose of the good-will of the business, (c) Do any other act which would make it impossible to carry on the ordinary business of a partnership, (d) Confess a judgment, (e) Submit a partnership claim or liability to arbitration or reference.

Note that all of these actions lie outside of the ordinary scope of day-to-day business; most of them go to the very existence of the partnership; at the very least, all of them are actions that can be expected to have a considerable impact on the partnership's success and viability.

The 1997 UPA contains no comparable provision. The comments to § 301, however, state that most of the acts proscribed by § 9(3) "probably remain outside the apparent authority of a partner" under the 1997 statute as well.[68] The outer limits of a partner's apparent authority are thus left to the courts, who will presumably be influenced both by case law developed under the 1914 statute and the large body of relevant agency cases.[69]

4. The Effect of Restrictions on Authority

Under both the 1914 and 1997 statutes, a person with knowledge of a restriction on a partner's actual authority may not rely on apparent authority to validate a disputed contract with the firm.[70] In addition, the 1997 statute expressly denies apparent

---

[68] UPA (1997) § 301 cmt. 4.

[69] For discussion of the relevant agency law cases, see Chapter 2.II.G *supra*.

[70] UPA (1914) § 9(4); UPA (1997) § 301(1).

authority-based recovery to third persons on notice of such a restriction.[71]

A key distinction between the 1914 and 1997 statutes arises from their differing definitions of "knowledge." UPA (1914) § 3(1) defines "knowledge" of a fact as not only actual knowledge thereof, but also knowledge of such other facts as in the circumstances shows bad faith. In contrast, the 1997 limits knowledge to cases of actual knowledge. To be sure, the 1997 statute does not bind the partnership where the third party had received notice of the restriction. UPA (1997) § 102(b), however, draws a difference between being on notice and having received notice. For the latter condition to be satisfied, the recipient must have actually received a notice. The fact that the third party was on notice—i.e., had reason to know—of the restriction thus does not preclude the contract from binding the partnership so long as the third person had not actually received a notice of the restriction. The comments to § 301 note this change but offer no justification for it. It is hard to see why the drafters wished to encourage willful blindness by a third party who has reason to know of a restriction on a partner's authority. Surely a third party who is on notice of such a restriction is the cheaper cost avoider.

B. Deadlock

In partnerships with an even number of members, especially those with just two members, deadlock is a potentially serious problem. The leading opinions on deadlock are *National Biscuit Company v. Stroud* and *Summers v. Dooley*.[72] In the former case, Stroud and Freeman formed a partnership to operate a grocery store. In late 1955, Stroud informed National Biscuit that he would not be personally liable for any more bread National Biscuit sold to the store. During February 1956, however, Freeman ordered more bread for the store and National Biscuit delivered it. On February 25, 1956, Stroud and Freeman dissolved their partnership, with all assets going to Stroud. National Biscuit, not having been paid for the bread ordered by Freeman, sued Stroud for to recover the whopping sum of $171.04. Why they bothered, let alone appealing to the state supreme court, is one of life's little mysteries. Surely even in 1959, when the supreme court opinion came down, the two sides' legal bills exceeded $171.

---

[71] Section 303 of the 1997 statute also introduced a novel mechanism for restricting partners' apparent authority to conduct real property transactions. If the partnership files a written statement of authority with the appropriate officials—usually the Secretary of State and the local Recorder of Deeds—partners not identified in the statement as having the power to conduct real property transactions lack both actual and apparent authority to do so.

[72] Summers v. Dooley, 481 P.2d 318 (Idaho 1971); National Biscuit Co. v. Stroud, 106 S.E.2d 692 (N.C. 1959).

If the partnership is liable on the contract, Stroud is personally liable for that debt. The question therefore is whether Freeman had authority to order the bread. Recall that under UPA (1914) §§ 9(1) and 9(4) a partner cannot have apparent authority where the third party with whom the partner dealt knew that the partner has no actual authority to make the contract. In the *National Biscuit* case, why didn't Stroud's letter give plaintiff knowledge that Freeman had no authority to buy bread?

The answer, of course, is that Freeman had actual authority. Up until February 23, 1956, the grocery store was still a going concern. As a partner, Freeman had an equal right to conduct the business of the firm. As a partner, Freeman therefore had actual authority to bind the partnership. Stroud could not unilaterally restrict that authority. Partnership decisions are governed by a majority vote of the partners. In a two-person partnership, a 1-1 vote yields no majority. Because there was no majority vote of the partners to terminate Freeman's authority to buy bread, Stroud's unilateral act was unavailing: "The partnership being a going concern, activities within the scope of the business should not be limited, save by the expressed will of the majority deciding a disputed question; half of the members are not a majority." The partnership therefore was bound by Freeman's orders.

In *Summers v. Dooley*, the contending parties had equal stakes in a trash-collection partnership. A dispute arose as to whether the firm should hire a third worker, with Summers favoring doing so and Dooley opposed. Despite Dooley's opposition, Summers went ahead and hired the third worker. Initially Summers paid the new worker out of his own pocket, but later tried to bill the partnership for the cost.

The court held that Summers was not entitled to recover the third worker's wages. Partnership matters are decided by majority vote and Summers doesn't control a majority: "business differences must be decided by a majority of the partners provided no other agreement between the partners speaks to the issues. . . . [Dooley] did not sit idly by and acquiesce in the actions of his partner."

How do you reconcile *Summers* and *National Biscuit*? The cases are distinguishable in the first instance by the nature of the claim at issue. In *National Biscuit*, suit was brought by a third party seeking to hold the partnership liable for the acts of one of the partners. In *Summers*, suit was brought by one partner against the other for contribution towards an alleged partnership expense.

In *National Biscuit*, Freeman could bind the partnership to third parties because ordering bread was an act in the "usual way of business" for his firm—see UPA (1914) § 9(1). As a partner,

Freeman is a general managerial agent of the business, with actual authority to conduct the affairs of the partnership in the "usual way of business." The partnership could have restricted that authority, but not without a majority vote and Stroud did not control a majority.

Why does that principle not apply in *Summers*? Arguably, Summers never purported to hire the man on behalf of the firm, so the authority principles of UPA (1914) § 9(1) never kicked in. Yet even if those principles applied, they would only have governed the partnership's liability to the third party (here, the employee).[73] They would not have governed the allocation of expenses among partners. For the latter question, we must look to UPA (1914) §§ 18(b) and 18(h). Although § 18(b) allows partners to obtain reimbursements for "ordinary" partnership expenses, § 18(h) requires a majority vote in the case of disagreement among partners. The burden is on the party wishing to change the status quo. If Summers wants to be reimbursed for an act changing the status quo, he needs a majority vote, even if the act would have bound the partnership to a third party under the apparent authority principles of § 9(1).

Evidence that the proposed change would benefit the partnership as a whole is not enough to change the legal result.[74] Even evidence that the dissenting partner benefits personally from resisting the proposed change is not enough. Instead, "absent an enforceable agreement covering such circumstances of disagreement, when both partners in a two-partner partnership disagree on an advantageous prospective business transaction, it is dissolution, not an action for breach of fiduciary duty, that is the appropriate avenue of relief."[75]

In sum, the best way of looking at this problem is to see it as a conflict between two basic principles of partnership law—i.e., the rule that all partners are agents of the partnership with power to bind the partnership and the rule that all partners have equal rights to participate in the management of the partnership. As

---

[73] Suppose the partnership had sufficient cash to pay the employee. Summers hires the employee, purporting to do so on behalf of the firm. Summers then pays the employee out of firm funds. This reduces the profits, cutting into Dooley's partnership draw. Dooley objects. Who wins that case? It depends on whether Summers had authority to hire someone. If so, Summers had an equal right to conduct the business of the firm. Dooley could not unilaterally restrict that authority. One partner cannot unilaterally cut off another partner's apparent authority. Only the partnership acting collectively can do so (and even then it may not be effective as against third parties who lack knowledge of the restriction).

[74] Sanchez v. Saylor, 13 P.3d 960, 977 (N.M. 2000); Covalt v. High, 675 P.2d 999, 1002 (N.M. App. 1983).

[75] Sanchez v. Saylor, 13 P.3d 960, 977 (N.M. 2000). *See also* Mack v. Mack, 613 N.W.2d 64, 68 (S.D. 2000).

between the partners and some third party, the former principle controls (*National Biscuit*). As between the partners, the latter controls (*Summers*).[76]

From a planning perspective, a lawyer advising a two person partnership must anticipate and deal with the deadlock question. Unfortunately, it can sometimes prove intractable. Would any prospective partner agree to putting up half the capital but not getting half the voice in the business? Matters do not improve if one of the partners obtained a majority voting interest in exchange for a majority capital investment, because then the minority partner (who presumably is still putting up substantial capital) would always be outvoted. Another possibility is to name a third party as a tie breaker. But who? Still another possible rule would require unanimous partner consent to doing business with any supplier, with appropriate notification of creditors. But this does not eliminate the possibility of apparent authority vis-à-vis creditors without notice of the restriction. For better or worse, two-person partnerships will always be fragile beasts.

III. Partnership Property and Accounts

A. Capital Contributions and Accounts

Neither the UPA (1914) nor (1997) requires any initial capital contribution from the partners. Some or all partners may contribute only services. As we shall see in the section on dissolution, these so-called "service partnerships" can present special difficulties when the partnership is dissolved.

If capital contributions were made, the UPA (1914) treated them differently than profits in several respects. Most importantly, in the event of dissolution, partners were entitled to be repaid their capital contributions before any remaining sums were distributed as profits.[77] The UPA (1997) largely ignores the distinction between capital contributions and profits. Section § 401(a) provides that:

> Each partner is deemed to have an account that is: (1) credited with an amount equal to the money plus the value of any other property, net of the amount of any liabilities, the partner contributes to the partnership and the partner's share of the partnership profits; and (2) charged with an amount equal to the money plus the value of any other property, net of the

---

[76] *See* Covalt v. High, 675 P.2d 999, 1002 (N.M. App. 1983) ("as between the partners themselves ... an act involving the partnership business may not be compelled by the co-partner. If the parties are evenly divided as to a business decision affecting the partnership ... the power to exercise discretion on behalf of the partners is suspended so long as the division continues. The rule is different, however, as to transactions between partners and third parties.").

[77] UPA (1914) § 40.

amount of any liabilities, distributed by the partnership to the partner and the partner's share of the partnership losses.

Both capital contributions and profits thus go into a single pot, from which losses and distributions are deducted from time to time, and from which any remainder is distributed upon dissolution.

B. Profits and Losses

Absent contrary agreement, and a limited exception for the winding up period during dissolution, a partner is not entitled to compensation for services rendered to the partnership.[78] Instead, under UPA (1997) § 401(b), a "partner is entitled to an equal share of the partnership profits and is chargeable with a share of the partnership losses in proportion to the partner's share of the profits."

Note that the statute is silent on the question of when profits are distributed. The well-drafted partnership agreement will contain provisions governing the partners' draw. In the absence of a formal agreement, draws are normally paid by consensus on an ad hoc basis. UPA (1914) § 18(a) is essentially identical in all material respects.

Why is equal sharing the default rule? Other options suggest themselves, after all. Division of profits in accordance with capital contribution—the corporate law rule—is but one plausible alternative.[79] Also, why the curious rule that losses follow profits?

Two principles immediately suggest themselves as being highly relevant to the problem at hand. First, outcomes of indeterminate games tend to cluster around prominent solutions: Sally is going out to buy a used car. The first car she looks at has a sticker price of $10,650. She bargains with Bill, the dealer. What will be the final sales price of the car? Probably $10,000—it is a prominent solution to an otherwise indeterminate outcome. Round numbers stick out like sore thumbs and thus results of indeterminate games tend to cluster around them.[80] More generally, prominent solutions reduce transaction costs by avoiding the need for extensive information gathering, exacting calculations of costs and benefits, and lengthy bargaining.

Second, equal division—share and share alike; 50/50—is a social norm of considerable power. In ORDER WITHOUT LAW, which

---

[78] UPA (1914) § 18(f); UPA (1997) § 401(h).

[79] As the commentary to the UPA (1997) explains, that option was considered and expressly rejected: "Thus, under the default rules, partners share profits per capita and not in proportion to capital contributions as do corporate shareholders or partners in limited partnerships." UPA (1997) § 401 cmt. 3.

[80] J. KEITH MURNIGHAN, BARGAINING GAMES: A NEW APPROACH TO STRATEGIC THINKING IN NEGOTIATIONS 41–46 (1992).

studied social norms governing cattle ranching in Shasta County California, Robert Ellickson reported that: "When the base ranches of two full-time cattleman adjoin, a well-engrained norm requires that they divide evenly the costs of building and maintaining their common share of fence."[81] Behavioral economist Richard Thaler likewise reports that the results of ultimatum game experiments cluster around 50–50 divisions of the pot.[82]

Equal division thus is both a prominent solution and also one that enjoys the benefit of strong social support. Hence, it would be surprising if the default rule for partnerships was anything other than equal shares.[83]

The perhaps somewhat curious phrasing of the profit and loss provision is intended to ensure that losses follow profits. If partners Alan and Barbara agree to split profits 60–40, but say nothing about division of losses, losses also would be split 60–40. This rule admits of easy justification. Probably nobody goes into a business expecting it to fail, just as nobody goes into a marriage expecting it to fail. The failure rates for both are quite depressing, of course, but it would be natural for parties to tend to assume that theirs will succeed. Partners who bargain over division of profits thus may well ignore the equally important but far less pleasant task of bargaining over division of losses.[84] Accordingly, if the parties agree to a division of profits that departs from the equal shares default

---

[81] ROBERT C. ELLICKSON, ORDER WITHOUT LAW 72 (1991). Ellickson reports that a different norm governs relationships between full-time ranchers and owners of small ranchettes. In that situation, an all-or-nothing norm prevailed under which the full-time rancher paid the whole cost of maintaining a shared fence. Id. at 72–73. Because general partners have equal rights to participate in the management of the business, their relations are more closely akin to the case of adjoining ranchers.

[82] *See* RICHARD H. THALER, THE WINNER'S CURSE: PARADOXES AND ANOMALIES OF ECONOMIC LIFE 21–35 (1992) (summarizing results of numerous studies). In an ultimatum game, two players bargain over division of a sum of money. In a typical example, one player is given $10 and instructed to propose a division of that sum to the second player. If the latter accepts the offer, the sum is divided amongst the two players as per the accepted offer. If the offer is rejected, however, neither player receives anything. Rational choice theory posits that the offeror should offer only a nominal sum to the second player, because that maximizes her wealth, while the recipient should accept any non-zero offer, because that any non-zero amount makes him better off. Experimental results consistently depart from the predictions of rational choice theory. Recipients reject offers perceived as unfair, while offerors tend to make offers that cluster around a 50–50 split. Id.

[83] It is equally unsurprising that corporations use a different allocation of profits and losses. Social norms of fairness are most important among players who are part of a close-knit group in which they repeatedly interact. Partnership law is designed for small businesses in which the owners closely cooperate. By contrast, corporate law is designed for large enterprises with diffuse and fluid ownership. The corporate rule that allocates profits and losses in accord with capital contribution is efficient in that setting because it facilitates the development of orderly and liquid secondary trading markets.

[84] As the commentary to the UPA (1997) explains: "If partners agree to share profits other than equally, losses will be shared similarly to profits, absent an agreement to do otherwise. That rule, carried over from the UPA, is predicated on the assumption that partners would likely agree to share losses on the same basis as profits, but may fail to say so." UPA (1997) § 401 cmt. 3.

rule, we may safely assume that that division reflects the parties' view of their relative economic position within the firm. If the agreement is silent as to division of losses, providing for division of losses on the basis of the way in which they divided profits thus is likely to do rough justice.

C. Partnership Property

Lawyer Alice wants to sell her share in a law firm partnership to Xavier. To what extent can Alice's membership in the partnership be transferred?

If Alice enters into an agreement by which she purports to sell her membership in the firm to Xavier, does Xavier thereby become a member of the firm? Hardly. Unless the partnership agreement otherwise specifies, no one can become a member of the firm without the unanimous consent of all other partners.[85]

If Alice enters into an agreement by which she purports to sell her share of the partnership's assets to Xavier, does Xavier take title to those assets? No. A partner's ownership interest in partnership property is a special form of property known as the tenancy in partnership.[86] "A tenancy in partnership is *sui generis*" with "severely limited" rights and incidents.[87] Although Alice has an equal right with her copartners to possess and use partnership property for partnership purposes, she has no right to possess or use such property for non-partnership purposes.[88] Nor can she unilaterally sell or assign such property.

1. Assignment of Partnership Interest

By the nature of tenancy in partnership, a partner's rights to partnership property are not assignable except in connection with an assignment of the rights of all the partners (e.g., a sale of the partnership as a whole).[89] Does lawyer Alice have any right she can assign to Xavier? Yes, but not much of one. Alice can assign Xavier her "interest" in the firm. The partner's interest in the firm is the partner's share of firm profits. The partner's interest is her personal property.[90] Hence, while Alice cannot unilaterally transfer or assign her share of the partnership's assets, she can assign to Xavier her right to receive the stream of income generated through the use of partnership assets.

---

[85] UPA (1914) § 18(g); UPA (1997) § 401(i).

[86] UPA (1914) § 25(1).

[87] NCNB Nat. Bank of North Carolina v. O'Neill, 401 S.E.2d 858, 860 (N.C. App. 1991).

[88] UPA (1914) § 25(2)(a); UPA (1997) § 501.

[89] UPA (1914) § 25(2)(b); UPA (1997) § 502.

[90] UPA (1914) §§ 26–27; UPA (1997) § 503.

The rights Xavier receives, however, are severely limited. When a partnership interest is assigned, the assignee gets none of the general rights of a partner—the assignee can not interfere in firm management, can not demand any information about the firm and may not inspect the firm's records.[91] All the assignee gets is the right to be paid the profits to which the assigning partner would otherwise be entitled.

2. Creditor Access to Firm and Personal Assets

From time to time partnerships, like any business, run into financial difficulties. The issue in such situations is how the firm's remaining assets and the individual assets of the partners will be divided amongst the firm's creditors and the partner's personal creditors. These issues are somewhat easier to handle if we identify which the basic fact patterns with which one is most likely to be faced.

Pattern 1: A creditor of the firm seeks to attach personal assets of a partner. Very often when a partnership goes belly-up, one or more of the partners will be left with substantial personal assets. Because each partner is personally liable for all firm debts and obligations, creditors of the partnership may recoup their losses by seizing some or all of those partners' personal assets.[92] Because this potential liability is unlimited, moreover, each partner could be forced to pay his or her share of the obligation to the full extent of his or her personal assets.

Although UPA (1914) § 15 did not expressly require that creditors exhaust partnership assets before seeking to collect against the personal property of individual partners, the common law in most jurisdictions required a creditor to exhaust its remedies against the partnership before going after the individual partners.[93]

---

[91] UPA (1914) § 27; UPA (1997) § 503(a).

[92] UPA (1914) § 15; UPA (1997) § 306(a).

[93] *See, e.g.*, Matter of Fowler, 407 F. Supp. 799 (W.D.Okla. 1975) ("In the ordinary course of events a partner's individual liability on a partnership debt accrues only after partnership assets are depleted."); In re Heafitz, 85 B.R. 274, 278 (Bankr.S.D.N.Y. 1988) ("In New York, an individual partner is liable for a partnership obligation only if the partnership property is insufficient to pay the firm debt and it appears that there can be no effective remedy without resort to individual property."); Horn's Crane Service v. Prior, 152 N.W.2d 421, 423 (Neb. 1967) ("In an action seeking a personal judgment against the individual members of a partnership or a joint adventure the petition does not state a cause of action if it fails to state that there is no partnership property or that it is insufficient to satisfy the debts of the partnership or joint adventure."); *see generally* McCune & McCune v. Mountain Bell Tel., 758 P.2d 914, 917 (Utah 1988) (citing numerous authorities). *But see* Catalina Mortg. Co., Inc. v. Monier, 800 P.2d 574, 578 (Ariz. 1990) (holding that where "a general partner is jointly and severally liable," rather than merely jointly, a "partner may be sued severally and his assets reached even though the partnership or other partners are not sued and their assets not applied to the debt"); Head v. Henry Tyler Const. Corp., 539 So.2d 196, 197–98 (Ala.1988). According to RIBSTEIN & LIPSHAW at 160, most courts require exhaustion only where liability is joint rather than joint and several.

UPA (1997) § 307(d) codifies that rule, while providing that a creditor may proceed directly against the estate of an individual partner if (1) the partnership is in bankruptcy, (2) the partner agreed to be held liable without exhaustion of partnership assets, (3) the creditor obtains a court order, typically on grounds that collecting against the partnership would be too burdensome or otherwise inequitable, or (4) the partner has liability directly without regard to his status as a partner, as might be the case where the partner committed a tort against the plaintiff-creditor who then sues both the partner and the firm.

Pattern 2: A personal creditor of an individual partner seeks to attach firm assets. As we saw above, a partner's ownership interest in partnership property is that of a tenant in partnership. As such, the partner has no right to possess or use such property for non-partnership purposes. Accordingly, a partner's rights to partnership property are not subject to attachment or execution by personal creditors.[94] The creditor, however, may reach the partner's interest—the partner's share of firm profits—by going to court to get a "charging order."[95] The charging order functions as a lien on the partner's interest, upon which the creditor may then seek foreclosure and sale of the interest. The purchaser of the interest at the foreclosure sale becomes an assignee of the interest with the same rights as a voluntary assignee. The purchaser may thereafter petition the court to dissolve the partnership, provided that the partnership was "at will" at the time of the charging order. If the partnership had a specific term or was organized for a specific undertaking, the purchaser can only demand a dissolution at the termination of the set term or undertaking.[96] If dissolution is ordered, the creditor will receive the partner's *pro rata* share of any unpaid profits and firm assets.

Because a charging order can lead to a foreclosure sale of the partner's interest and, in turn, to a dissolution, this process has significant implications not only for the debtor partner but also for all the other partners. Under both UPA (1914) § 28(2) and UPA (1997) § 504(c), the other partners are entitled to redeem the interest being charged at any time prior to the foreclosure sale. In addition, they may purchase the interest at the foreclosure sale. Partnership funds may be used to affect the purchase provided that all partners (excepting the debtor) consent.

---

[94] UPA (1914) § 25(2)(c); UPA (1997) § 504(e).

[95] UPA (1914) § 28; UPA (1997) § 504.

[96] UPA (1914) § 32(2); UPA (1997) § 801(6). UPA (1997) § 801(6) clarifies that the court should only order dissolution if "it is equitable" to do so.

Pattern 3: Creditors of the partnership and creditors of the individual partners are going after both firm and personal assets at the same time. Suppose the firm of A&B goes belly up and, at the same time, A and B as individuals go into bankruptcy. The firm's creditors will go after A and B's personal assets, while their personal creditors will try to go after their interest in the firm.

UPA (1914) § 40 adopted the so-called "jingle rule," pursuant to which personal creditors must first satisfy their claims out of personal assets and firm creditors must satisfy their claims out of partnership assets. The "jingle rule," however, was superseded for all practical purposes by the federal bankruptcy code. Under federal law, the firm's creditors are paid out of firm assets and then have equal rights to participate with personal creditors in dividing up personal assets. The 1997 UPA eliminated the jingle rule, deferring to the federal approach.

3. Is Property Personal or Partnership?

The sharp restrictions on partner and creditor access to property of the partnership make it essential to determine whether a particular asset is property of the partnership or of an individual partner. UPA (1997) § 204 made a major contribution towards cleaning up this area of the law by laying out some basic common-sense rules.

Property belongs to the partnership if one of two conditions is met: First, any asset acquired in the name of the partnership is partnership property. This condition is satisfied either by (1) a transfer directly to the partnership in its own name or (2) by a transfer to one or more partners so long as they are acting in their capacity as partners and the name of the partnership appears on the transfer document. Second, property acquired by one or more partners is partnership property even if the partnership is not named so long as the document transferring title indicates the partner was acting in his capacity as a partner. Property purchased with partnership funds is presumed to be partnership property, moreover, even if neither of the foregoing conditions is satisfied.

IV. Partner Liabilities

In the section on partnership management, we saw that a partner can bind the partnership to a contract. Likewise, the tortious or other wrongful conduct of a partner can be binding on the partnership. The partnership is liable for a tort committed by a partner with actual authority or one "acting in the ordinary course of the business of the partnership" (i.e., with apparent authority).[97]

---

[97] UPA (1914) §§ 13 & 14(a); UPA (1997) § 305(a). Under the co-principal doctrine, UPA (1914) § 13 did not allow a partner of the firm who was the victim of a

In addition, the partnership is strictly liable for misappropriation of money or property received by the partner in the course of the partnership's business or with actual authority to do so.

Partnership law provides no limits on the liability of partners for debts or other obligations of the firm. Instead, the partner is fully personally liable for anything for which the firm is liable. The only exception is that persons admitted to an existing partnership generally are not personally liable for pre-existing obligations of the firm.[98] This rule is the single most important deterrent to doing business in the partnership form. As we shall see, new forms of limited liability entities—especially the limited liability company and the limited liability partnership—have been created to alleviate this problem.

UPA (1914) § 15 drew a hyper-technical distinction between tort and contract liability. As to the former, each partner was jointly and severally liable. As to the latter, the partners were only jointly liable. The distinction had mainly procedural implications, going to questions of joinder and the like. Technically, in cases of joint liability, all partners are necessary parties. Suit therefore should be dismissed if plaintiff failed to join all partners, regardless of the reason plaintiff had not done so. Many states modified this rule, however, typically by changes to their procedural codes, to provide either that the partnership could be sued in its own name without joinder of the individual partners and/or to impose joint and several liability for all partnership obligations. The UPA (1997) adopted both solutions to the problem, imposing joint and several liability for all obligations in § 306, and providing for the partnership to sue and be sued in its own name in § 307.

In order for a partner's tortious conduct to throw vicarious liability upon the partnership and his fellow partners, the partner must have been acting either in the ordinary course of partnership business or with authority from the partnership.[99] The analogy to the scope of the employment doctrine in agency law should be apparent.[100] As with agency law, one need not prove that the partnership is in the business of committing torts or that the partners authorized the commission of a tort. Instead, it suffices to show that the partner's overall course of conduct was of the type

---

tort by the firm or another partner to sue the partnership. The UPA (1997) abandoned that limitation as archaic. UPA (1997) § 305 cmt.

[98] UPA (1997) § 306(b).

[99] UPA (1914) § 13; UPA (1997) § 305(a).

[100] *See, e.g.*, Paneson v. Zubillaga, 753 So. 2d 127 (Fla.App.2000) (drawing on agency law cases dealing with scope of the employment to resolve dispute as to whether the misconduct of one partner was within the ordinary course of partnership business).

broadly authorized.[101] Note that, unlike agency law, partnership law does not draw the servant/independent contractor distinction. It suffices that one is a partner of the firm.

Under UPA (1914) § 13, the partnership was not liable for the tortious conduct of one of its members where the victim of the tort was one of the other partners. UPA (1997) § 305(a) eliminated this rule.

A.   The Limited Liability Partnership

As discussed in more detail in the Chapter on limited liability companies, the emergence of mass financial tort lawsuits in the 1980s exposed partnerships to liabilities of a scope never before seen. Law and accounting firms caught up in various corporate scandals, for example, not infrequently faced lawsuits seeking hundreds of millions of dollars in damages. A number of high-profile partnerships were forced into bankruptcy by such suits, with devastating effects for their members.

Matters came to a head in Texas in 1991, when litigation arising out of the collapse of the Texas savings and loan industry threatened lawyers for that industry with massive malpractice liability. The Texas legislature responded by creating the limited liability partnership (LLP).[102] A LLP is a standard general partnership in all respects, except insofar as the individual liability of the partnership's members is concerned. UPA (1997) § 306(c), for example, provides that:

> An obligation of a partnership incurred while the partnership is a limited liability partnership, whether arising in contract, tort, or otherwise, is solely the obligation of the partnership. A partner is not personally liable, directly or indirectly, by way of contribution or otherwise, for such an obligation solely by reason of being or so acting as a partner.

In order for a firm to become a LLP, it must file a "statement of qualification" with the requisite state official and appoint an in-state agent for the service of process.[103] Such a statement may be

---

[101] *See, e.g.,* Schloss v. Silverman, 192 A. 343 (Md. 1937) ("The test of the liability of the partnership and of the several members thereof for the torts of any one partner is whether the wrongful act was done within what may be reasonably found to be the scope of the business of the partnership and for its benefit, . . . and the scope of the authority of a partner is determined by the same principles as those which measure the scope of an agent's authority.").

[102] *See generally* Robert W. Hamilton, *Registered Limited Liability Partnerships: Present at the Birth (Nearly),* 66 U. Colo. L. Rev. 1065 (1995). Professor Hamilton notes that "more than 1,200 law firms, including virtually all of the state's largest firms, elected to become LLPs within one year after . . . enactment" of the Texas LLP legislation. *Id.*

[103] UPA (1997) § 1001. The LLP so formed also must file an annual report with the state containing its address and identifying its agent for service of process. UPA (1997) § 1003.

filed either on behalf of a newly formed partnership or an established general partnership that wishes to convert to LLP status. In the latter case, partners remain personally liable for pre-conversion obligations of the firm.

Not all states are so generous in the liability protection their LLP statute provides. Many provide limited liability only for torts caused by negligence or similar misconduct. Under such statutes, partners remain personally liable with respect to contractual obligations. Many statutes also deny the benefit of limited liability to any partner who is directly responsible for the tortious conduct (including torts committed by other partners or agents working under the partner's supervision). Finally, some require that the LLP carry require specified insurance and/or maintain specified minimum capital. The trend, however, seems to be towards the broad protection provided by the UPA (1997).

As discussed below in the Chapter on limited liability companies, courts are routinely extending the corporate law doctrine of piercing the corporate veil to LLCs. It seems likely the same will happen with respect to LLPs. In *In re Adelphia Communications Corp.*, for example, the court opined that "there is nothing about the nature of a limited liability partnership (where the limited partner is sometimes likened to a shareholder) that would preclude recourse to veil piercing as an equitable remedy in appropriate circumstances."[104] Presumably courts will apply veil piercing to LLPs in roughly the same manner as LLCs, which is discussed in more detail in the LLC chapter below. Because of the paucity of cases, however, many questions currently remain unanswered.

In all states, the partnership's name must include the acronym LLP or some similar term identifying the firm as having limited liability for its owners. The intent of these provisions is to put prospective customers and creditors of the firm that its partners do not face the full liability exposure traditionally associated with being a general partner.

V. The Fiduciary Obligations of Partners

Just as an agent is a fiduciary of the principal, so are partners fiduciaries of one another. Indeed, if you measure it by the volume of judicial rhetoric, a partner's fiduciary duties are among the strongest in organization law. Yet, as Justice Felix Frankfurter

---

[104] 376 B.R. 87, 108 (Bkrtcy. S.D.N.Y. 2007). *See also* Red River Wings, Inc. v. Hoot, Inc., 751 N.W.2d 206, 221 (N.D. 2008) ("Principles for piercing a corporate veil apply to limited liability partnerships."); Middlemist v. BDO Seidman, LLP, 958 P.2d 486, Colo. App. 1997) ("A party seeking to hold a partner of a limited liability partnership personally liable for alleged improper actions of the partnership must proceed as if attempting to pierce the corporate veil.").

once observed, "to say that a man is a fiduciary only begins analysis; it gives direction to further inquiry. To whom is he a fiduciary? What obligations does he owe as a fiduciary? In what respect has he failed to discharge those obligations?"[105] Over a century ago, the U.S. Supreme Court provided a laundry list of the obligations a partner owes as a fiduciary, which remains just as valid today as it was in 1893:

> [I]t being well settled that one partner cannot, directly or indirectly, use partnership assets for his own benefit; that he cannot, in conducting the business of a partnership, take any profit clandestinely for himself; that he cannot carry on the business of the partnership for his private advantage; that he cannot carry on another business in competition or rivalry with that of the firm, thereby depriving it of the benefit of his time, skill, and fidelity, without being accountable to his copartners for any profit that may accrue to him therefrom; that he cannot be permitted to secure for himself that which it is his duty to obtain, if at all, for the firm of which he is a member; nor can he avail himself of knowledge or information which may be properly regarded as the property of the partnership, in the sense that it is available or useful to the firm for any purpose within the scope of the partnership business.[106]

As this list suggests, much of partnership fiduciary duty is concerned with preventing self-dealing and other breaches of the duty of loyalty. In addition, however, partners also owe one another duties of care and disclosure.

A.　Duty of Loyalty

The duty of loyalty requires that partners act in good faith and treat each other fairly, which may not sound terribly demanding. In fact, however, partners frequently must subordinate their personal economic interests to those of the firm and their fellow partners.[107] This duty, moreover, has ramifications not only during the life of the partnership but both before it begins and after it ends.[108]

---

[105] SEC v. Chenery Corp., 318 U.S. 80, 85–86 (1943).

[106] Latta v. Kilbourn, 150 U.S. 524, 542 (1893).

[107] *See, e.g.,* Meinhard v. Salmon, 164 N.E. 545, 548 (N.Y. 1928) ("thought of self was to be renounced, however hard the abnegation").

[108] At least it did so historically. UPA (1914) § 21 states that a "partner must account to the partnership for any benefit, and hold as trustee for it any profits derived by him without the consent of the other partners from any transaction connected with the formation, conduct, or liquidation of the partnership...." In contrast, UPA (1997) § 404(b)(1) both omits the reference to formation of the partnership and purports to limit the scope of the duty of loyalty to the types of misconduct specifically enumerated in the statute. The drafters explain these omissions as being intended to avoid "inappropriately" extending the duty of loyalty "to the pre-formation period when the parties are really bargaining at arm's length."

UPA § 404(b) defines the modern scope of the partnership duty of loyalty:

> A partner's duty of loyalty to the partnership and the other partners is limited to the following: (1) to account to the partnership and hold as trustee for it any property, profit, or benefit derived by the partner in the conduct and winding up of the partnership business or derived from a use by the partner of partnership property, including the appropriation of a partnership opportunity; (2) to refrain from dealing with the partnership in the conduct or winding up of the partnership business as or on behalf of a party having an interest adverse to the partnership; and (3) to refrain from competing with the partnership in the conduct of the partnership business before the dissolution of the partnership.

Subsection (1) is a corollary of the rules governing partnership property. Recall that a partner is entitled to use partnership property only for partnership purposes, not for personal gain. In addition, this subsection provides a partnership version of the agency law prohibition of secret profits. Subsection (2) is the partnership law version of the corporate law interested director transaction doctrine.[109] Although § 404(b)(2) appears to prohibit transactions between a partner and the partnership, this section must be read in conjunction with § 103(b)(3)(ii), which provides: "all of the partners or a number or percentage specified in the partnership agreement may authorize or ratify, after full disclosure of all material facts, a specific act or transaction that otherwise would violate the duty of loyalty." As with the corporate law version of the doctrine, partnership law thus polices rather than prohibits conflict of interest transactions. Where the other partners consent, following full disclosure, there is no liability. Finally, subsection (3) prohibits competition with the partnership. Again, this apparent prohibition is subject to the ameliorating effects of § 103(b)(3)(ii), so that competition may be authorized, as is often the case in industries like real estate where partners are involved in multiple ventures simultaneously.

1.　The Classic Case: Meinhard v. Salmon

There is probably no more famous case in partnership law— maybe business organization law, for that matter—than Judge Benjamin Cardozo's opinion for the New York Court of Appeals in

---

UPA (1997) § 404 cmt. 2. "Pre-formation negotiations," however, "remain subject to the general contract obligation to deal honestly and without fraud." *Id.*

[109] For discussion of the corporate law doctrine, see STEPHEN M. BAINBRIDGE, CORPORATION LAW AND ECONOMICS 307–21 (2002).

Meinhard v. Salmon.[110] The case involves the same sort of conduct now prohibited by UPA (1997) § 404(b)(1) as "appropriation of a partnership opportunity." Meinhard and Salmon formed a joint venture to lease an office building. Shortly before expiration of the lease, Salmon began secret negotiations with the lessor, as a result of which Salmon's real estate corporation was able to lease the building and several adjoining lots. Salmon planned to eventually replace the existing building with a new and considerably more profitable facility. Meinhard did not learn of Salmon's new arrangement until after the new lease was finalized. At that time he demanded that the new lease be held in trust for the joint venture. Salmon refused and the lawsuit ensued.

If partners can withhold new information—such as the discovery of a new business opportunity—from each other, then each has an incentive to drive the other out so as to take full advantage of the information. As each incurs costs to exclude the other, or to take precautions against being excluded, the value of the firm declines. Accordingly, a legal rule vesting the firm with a property right to the information and requiring disclosure is more efficient than forcing the partners to draft disclosure agreements and monitor one another's behavior. Note that this rule does not discourage the production of new information; the partners still have incentives to produce information because they share in its value to the firm. As no one will withhold information, however, the firm's productivity is maximized.[111] As a result, we can confidently predict that the partners would agree ex ante to bar any one partner from taking an organizational opportunity for his personal gain.

While some such prohibition thus emerges from our hypothetical bargain as a majoritarian default, the form such a prohibition ought to take is less obvious. Does it matter if one partner is actively managing the business (as was Salmon) while the other is passive (as was Meinhard)? Should all outside business ventures be proscribed or only some? If the latter, how do we decide which are proscribed? Should we adopt a bright line rule or a flexible standard? What should be the remedy?

---

[110] 164 N.E. 545 (N.Y. 1928). *Meinhard* has been cited approvingly by many courts in many jurisdictions in a variety of settings. As one California appeals court decision put it: "The [Meinhard] doctrine was applied in this state to joint ventures in MacIsaac v. Pozzo, and is equally applicable in all situations in which a person manages or transacts business for another or for others to whom he stands in a fiduciary relation without being trustee of an express trust." Industrial Indem. Co. v. Golden State Co., 117 Cal. App. 2d 519, 533 (1953) (citation omitted).

[111] Michael P. Dooley, *Enforcement of Insider Trading Restrictions*, 66 VA. L. REV. 1, 64–66 (1980).

In a justly famous passage, Judge Cardozo adopted a wonderfully vague standard to govern these problems:

> Joint adventurers, like copartners, owe to one another, while the enterprise continues, the duty of the finest loyalty. Many forms of conduct permissible in a workaday world for those acting at arm's length, are forbidden to those bound by fiduciary ties. A trustee is held to something stricter than the morals of the market place. Not honesty alone, but the punctilio of an honor the most sensitive, is then the standard of behavior. As to this there has developed a tradition that is unbending and inveterate. Uncompromising rigidity has been the attitude of courts of equity when petitioned to undermine the rule of undivided loyalty by the "disintegrating erosion" of particular exceptions. Only thus has the level of conduct for fiduciaries been kept at a level higher than that trodden by the crowd. It will not consciously be lowered by any judgment of this court.

In applying this standard, Cardozo focused closely on the specific circumstances of the case. As such, he converted the vague default rule into one specifically tailored for the parties at bar. Hence, for example, Cardozo emphasized that Salmon was "in control with exclusive powers of direction. . . ." Salmon "was much more than a coadventurer. He was a managing coadventurer." Cardozo further acknowledged that:

> A different question would be here if there were lacking any nexus of relation between the business conducted by the manager and the opportunity brought to him as an incident of management. . . . For this problem, as for most, there are distinctions of degree. If Salmon had received from Gerry a proposition to lease a building at a location far removed, he might have held for himself the privilege thus acquired, or so we shall assume. Here the subject matter of the new lease was an extension and enlargement of the subject matter of the old one. A managing coadventurer appropriating the benefit of such a lease without warning to his partner might fairly expect to be reproached with conduct that was underhand, or lacking, to say the least, in reasonable candor, if the partner were to surprise him in the act of signing the new instrument. Conduct subject to that reproach does not receive from equity a healing benediction.[112]

---

[112] The case is further complicated by the fact that the business actually was joint venture rather than a general partnership. In dissent, Judge Andrews argued vigorously that joint venturers should be held to a lesser standard. In real estate joint ventures, it is now quite well-accepted for a managing partner to conduct multiple operations through many different partnerships. Indeed, Cardozo seems to

One of the difficult questions about this case is how seriously we ought to take Cardozo's high-flying language. Much of the opinion is devoted to lofty statements of a partner's duties. One in particular springs to mind: "the thought of self was to be renounced." What does that mean? Taken literally, this suggests that Salmon had a duty to let Meinhard share in the new opportunity. Indeed, this notion of renouncing self easily can be taken to rather silly extremes. Note the problem: Each of the partners must renounce thought of self. So Salmon says to Meinhard, "You first," and Meinhard replies, "No, no, after you," and so forth.[113]

Cardozo's rhetoric had two useful functions. First, the moralistic tone seems intended to invoke shame as a social sanction. Second, when the law is set out as a bright-line rule, people know exactly what they can get away with. This inevitably tempts them to go right up to the line. The strong judicial rhetoric found in these opinions serves to obscure the actual parameters of the law, depriving market actors of the guidance that a bright line rule would offer. By fudging the line, and by imposing severe consequences on those who skate across it, courts have sought to deter cheating. Having said all that, however, it remains true that Cardozo's deliberate ambiguities strongly suggest the need for *ex ante* planning and resolution through contract.

Assuming we have a partnership opportunity at hand, what should Salmon have done? Despite Cardozo's rhetorical flourishes, the emphasis seems to be on the duty to give notice. He emphasized, for example, that "only through disclosure could opportunity be equalized." On the other hand, even here he is quite vague. Cardozo is careful not to foreclose an obligation to do more than simply provide notice: "we need not say" whether liability would still ensure if Salmon had given notice and, moreover, Salmon had a duty, "if nothing more," to disclose the opportunity.

The idea that a partner could abscond with a new business opportunity simply by making disclosure seems inconsistent with notions of trust that are essential to a partnership. It would lead to lots of wasteful precautions. Requiring something more than disclosure—i.e., consent—is consistent with the closely related corporate opportunity doctrine. Under the prevailing view, mere disclosure of a corporate opportunity is not enough. Consent by the

---

recognize this by acknowledging that a different result might obtain is a distant property had been involved rather than a reversion of the lease that was the subject of the joint venture.

[113] UPA 91997) § 404(e) clearly rejects any such result, stating: "A partner does not violate a duty or obligation under this [Act] or under the partnership agreement merely because the partner's conduct furthers the partner's own interest."

board of directors is required. The comments to UPA (1997) § 404(b) indicate that that statute requires consent by the other partners to the taking of a partnership opportunity rather than mere disclosure by the taking partner.

2. Grabbing and Leaving

Grabbing and leaving is just as much a problem for partners as for agents. Suppose you make partner at a big law firm. You develop a large practice with many important clients. One day a recruiter approaches you with an offer to join a new firm with a higher profit share. Can you go? Can you take associates and staff with you? Can you encourage your clients to follow you? The issues here are much the same as those raised in the agency context.

Absent a contractual non-competition agreement, some things are clearly permissible. A partner is free to jump ship to a new firm. A partner who wants to start a new firm is free to start looking for new office space. Although perhaps less clear, most courts and commentators assume that departing partners are permitted to inform clients—at least those with whom the departing partner has an established professional relationship—about their new practice. The departing partner probably can even say something coy, like reminding the client of the freedom to retain counsel of one's own choice. Abandoning the firm on short notice, using confidential firm information to help lure away clients or associates, luring firm clients without disclosing one's intention to one's partners, misleading one's partners as to one's intentions, and so on are all impermissible.[114]

3. Expulsion and the Requirement of Good Faith and Fair Dealing

UPA (1914) provided no statutory right to expel a partner from the firm; nor did the common law.[115] Implicitly, however, UPA (1914) permitted a partnership agreement to contain provisions authorizing expulsion of a partner.[116] UPA (1997) § 601 likewise authorizes such provisions, but also introduced two statutory mechanisms for expelling a partner. First, under subsection 601(4) a partner may be expelled by unanimous vote of the other partners if any of four conditions are satisfied: (1) It has become unlawful to carry on the business of the partnership with the present partner.

---

[114] *See, e.g.,* Meehan v. Shaughnessy, 535 N.E.2d 1255 (Mass. 1989); Gibbs v. Breed, Abbott & Morgan, 710 N.Y.S.2d 578 (2000).

[115] Cadwalader, Wickersham & Taft v. Beasley, 728 So.2d 253 (Fla. App. 1998).

[116] *See* UPA (1914) § 31(1)(d) ("Dissolution is caused: (1) Without violation of the agreement between the partners. . . . By the expulsion of any partner from the business bona fide in accordance with such a power conferred by the agreement between the partners. . . .").

Suppose a lawyer is disbarred. Because someone who is not licensed to practice law may not be a member of law partnership, the other partners could use this provision to expel the errant partner. (2) The partner's interest has been assigned or has become subject to a charging order. (3) An incorporated partner may be expelled if it is dissolved or loses its right to conduct business. (4) A partner that is itself a partnership may be expelled if it is being dissolved.

Second, the other partners may sue to obtain a judicial expulsion if one of three conditions are satisfied: (1) The partner has engaged in wrongful conduct that adversely and materially affected the partnership's business. (2) The partner willfully or persistently violated the partnership agreement or the fiduciary duties of a partner. (3) The partner's conduct makes it impracticable to carry on the business with him.

Even where the other partners have the right by agreement or statute to expel a partner, however, they remain subject to the overarching duty of good faith and fair dealing. In this context, however, the good faith and fair dealing obligation is exceedingly narrow in scope. Courts have upheld as valid, for example, guillotine expulsion provisions under which a partner may be expelled without cause and without any procedural due process.[117] If the agreement contains such a provision, bad faith is found only when there is "a wrongful withholding of money or property legally due the expelled partner at the time he is expelled."[118] As a result, so long as the other partners pay the partner to be expelled any sums due, they are free to expel him without either good cause or even notice and hearing.[119]

A couple of examples, taken from opinions commonly used as principal cases in the major texts, may be helpful. In *Lawlis v. Kightlinger & Gray*,[120] plaintiff was a partner in the defendant

---

[117] *See, e.g.,* Holman v. Coie, 522 P.2d 515 (Wash. 1974); *see also* Bohatch v. Butler & Binion, 977 S.W.2d 543, 546 (Tex. 1998) (holding that "a partnership may expel a partner for purely business reasons," "to protect relationships both within the firm and with clients." and "in order to resolve a 'fundamental schism' within the firm").

[118] Lawlis v. Kightlinger & Gray, 562 N.E.2d 435, 443 (Ind. App. 1990).

[119] The principal case holding to the contrary is Winston & Strawn v. Nosal, 664 N.E.2d 239 (Ill. App. 1996), an intermediate appellate court decision in which the complaining partner was expelled after threatening to sue to enforce his rights to inspect the partnership's books and records. In the court's view, this claim raised a triable issue of fact. In Cadwalader, Wickersham & Taft v. Beasley, 728 So.2d 253 (Fla. App. 1998), the court upheld an award of punitive damages where the partners breached their duty of good faith by expelling a partner so as to increase their own share of the firm's profits. In that case, however, the partnership agreement contained no applicable provision authorizing expulsion. Hence, while *Beasley* is widely cited as an example of the duty of good faith in action, it is irrelevant to the issue at hand, which is how courts interpret expulsion provisions in partnership agreements.

[120] 562 N.E.2d 435 (Ind. App. 1990).

Indianapolis law firm. Lawlis was an alcoholic, but he hid his problem from the partnership until mid-1983. When he informed his partners, they outlined a series of steps for him to take. Lawlis signed a written agreement with the firm, in which he expressly acknowledged that there would be no second chance. As part of the deal, Lawlis agreed to accept a reduced share of partnership profits. Unfortunately, Lawlis resumed abusing alcohol. Despite the no second chance agreement, the firm did grant Lawlis one more chance. The partners again specified a set of steps for him to take. Lawlis claimed he was told that the firm would return him to full partnership if he complied with the program. This time, Lawlis apparently complied and broke his habit.

In 1986, Lawlis demanded that the partnership restore his full profit participation. Within a month of making this demand, another partner—one Wampler—told him that the firm would expel him. Two days after that, the firm reclaimed its files from Lawlis office. In February 1987, the firm expelled Lawlis by a 7–1 vote (Lawlis dissenting). Lawlis sued, claiming that the expulsion was unlawful.

Lawlis claimed that the firm had wrongfully expelled him. By the firm's partnership agreement, expulsion required a 2/3 vote of the partners, argued Lawlis, but he had been expelled by Wampler's unilateral announcement. The court rejected that argument, stating that Wampler simply announced what the other partners intended to do. The firm did not actually expel Lawlis until after the February vote, which followed the proper procedures to do so.

Second, Lawlis claimed that his partners had violated their fiduciary duties toward him, because they had expelled him to increase their own profit draw. Lawlis had no serious evidence of this, and the court rejected it more-or-less out of hand. In the court's view, the other partners' motives were irrelevant. The partnership agreement had a guillotine provision that allowed them to expel a member without cause so long as there was a 2/3 vote. The partners who vote to do so violate no fiduciary duty unless they wrongfully withhold money due an expelled partner.

How do we square the court's approval of the guillotine provision with Cardozo's famous proclamation in *Meinhard* that partners should be utterly selfless? We consider the extent to which partners can opt out of fiduciary duties by contract in more detail below. For now suffice it say that the expulsion cases validate a fairly expansive notion of private ordering, pursuant to which the partners can substantially limit—albeit not eliminate—the duties they owe one another.

The other leading precedent, *Bohatch v. Butler & Binion,*[121] provides a nice object lesson in intra-firm politics and office wars. Colette Bohatch was one of three partners in Butler & Binion's Washington office. She suspected that John McDonald, one of the other partners in that office, was padding his time sheets and over-billing their client Pennzoil. Bohatch reported her concerns to the firm's managing partner. McDonald was cleared after an investigation. Meanwhile, McDonald told Bohatch that Pennzoil was dissatisfied with her work. The firm subsequently expelled Bohatch. She sued for, *inter alia,* breach of fiduciary duty.

The majority declined to create a "whistleblower" exception to the general rule that a partnership may expel a partner for business reasons, including the preservation of good working relationships between the partners and with clients. The thrust of the opinion is that a partnership relationship is based on interpersonal trust and that expulsion of a partner who violates that trust is not a breach of fiduciary duty. A very strong dissent argued that the firm's other partners violated their fiduciary duty to Bohatch by expelling her as retaliation for making a good faith effort to alert the firm's leadership to possible over-billing of a client.

A concurring judge tried to find a middle ground. The concurrence took the majority to task for missing the main issue in the case. The bulk of the majority opinion focused on whether Bohatch had a right to remain a partner if a majority of her fellow partners wanted her out; the majority concluded she did not. In the concurring judge's view, however, that was not the real issue. If the other partners wanted her out, she was out. While the other partners thus may have the power to expel her, however, they may not have the right to do so. If they failed to act in good faith, Bohatch may have been entitled to damages for breach of fiduciary duty. The concurrence also expressed concern that the majority's blanket rule might deter some lawyers from reporting suspected misconduct. In light of these concerns, the concurrence argued that a law firm may, without incurring liability, expel a lawyer (such as Bohatch) who mistakenly reports what she believes to be unethical conduct, but a law firm that expels a lawyer who correctly reports unethical conduct will be liable.

The concurrence thus tried to split the baby by allowing a firm to fire a partner who mistakenly reports unethical conduct, while allowing imposition of liability when a partner is fired after correctly reporting unethical conduct. But this approach ultimately proves something less than Solomonic. Under the concurrence's

---

[121] 977 S.W.2d 543 (Tex. 1998).

approach, what rational lawyer would ever report suspected unethical conduct, except in the most mild, diffident, self-effacing way, and then only to a gentle and forgiving partner? Ethical violations are rarely clear-cut. A lawyer will often have good grounds for suspicion, but no proof. If she comes forward and turns out to be wrong, however, the concurrence would allow her to be fired without fear of liability.

The policy choice thus really boils down to whether there should be a public policy exception to the general rule allowing expulsion for any reason.[122] In the employment setting, a number of courts and legislatures have recognized statutory or common law "whistleblower" exceptions to the employment at will doctrine. In theory, of course, partners are not employees but rather are owners. In practice, however, partners in large law firms and other service industries increasingly resemble employees. It thus would not be surprising if the employment trend eventually found its way into partnership law. Indeed, one can plausibly argue that the case is even stronger in the partnership context than in the employment contract: "When a partner is expelled, his partners are effecting a forced sale or private taking, often for a purchase price that does not reflect the actual going-concern value of the business."[123]

On the other hand, the *Bohatch* majority correctly observed that trust is essential to the working of a partnership. In economic terms, a partnership is thought of as a production team. Members of a production team interact over an extended period of time and develop relationships with one another that are important in determining their conduct. In such settings, parties frequently rely on noncontractual social norms rather than legal sanctions, notably trust. Trust acts as a lubricant within teams to reduce friction. If I trust you to refrain from opportunistic behavior, I will not invest as many resources in *ex ante* contracting. If you prove trustworthy, I will not need to incur *ex post* enforcement costs. A whistleblower exception to the general rule that partners may be expelled without case would have deleterious implications for inter-personal trust within a partnership. Bohatch's charges disrupted the inter-personal relationships within the firm by making it harder for her fellow partners to work with her "to their mutual benefit and the benefit of their clients." A rule forbidding the firm from expelling

---

[122] Remember we are assuming that the partnership agreement permits expulsion without cause. If the agreement is silent, expulsion will only be permissible if (1) the firm is organized in a UPA (1997) state and (2) one of the conditions set forth by § 601 is satisfied.

[123] Paula J. Dalley, *The Law of Partner Expulsions: Fiduciary Duty and Good Faith*, 21 CARDOZO L. REV. 181, 205 (1999). *See also* Allan W. Vestal, *Law Partner Expulsions*, 55 WASH. & LEE L. REV. 1083 (1998) (arguing for adding a motive analysis to the duty of good faith and fair dealing).

her under those circumstances would exacerbate the problem because "threat of tort liability for expulsion would tend to force partners to remain in untenable circumstance—suspicious of and angry with each other—to their own detriment and that of their clients whose matters are neglected by lawyers distracted with intra-firm frictions."[124]

B.   Duty of Care

The UPA (1914) contains no direct reference to the duty of care. A number of judicial decisions, however, indicated that partners did own the firm and/or each other such a duty.[125] Whether a partner could be held liable to his fellow partners for simple negligence, however, was sharply debated.

In corporation law, of course, the business judgment rule provides a presumption that "in making a business decision the directors of a corporation acted on an informed basis, in good faith and in the honest belief that the action taken was in the best interests of the company [and its shareholders]."[126] The precise doctrinal implications of that presumption have been debated for decades. Yet, one thing remains quite clear: "liability is rarely imposed upon corporate directors or officers simply for bad judgment and this reluctance to impose liability for unsuccessful business decisions has been doctrinally labeled the business judgment rule."[127]

A substantial number of courts have extended the same principle to the partnership context, both in the case of general partnerships and limited partnerships.[128] In *Levine v. Levine*, for example, the court noted that although the business judgment rule is commonly applied in actions against corporate directors, "its rationale applies equally to partners acting as fiduciaries for the partnership and the other partners."[129] As a result, it is exceedingly

---

[124] Bohatch v. Butler & Binion, 977 S.W.2d 543, 546–47 (Tex. 1998). For a defense of *Bohatch* along the lines suggested in the text, see Eric Talley, *Taking the "T" out of "Team": Intra-Firm Monitoring and the Content of Fiduciary Duties*, 24 J. CORP. L. 1001, 1035–37 (1999).

[125] *See* Norwood P. Beveridge, Jr., *Duty of Care: The Partnership Cases*, 15 OKLA. CITY U. L. REV. 753 (1990) (analyzing cases).

[126] Aronson v. Lewis, 473 A.2d 805, 812 (Del. Supr. 1984); Smith v. Van Gorkom, 488 A.2d 858, 872 (Del. Supr. 1985).

[127] Joy v. North, 692 F.2d 880, 885 (2d Cir. 1982).

[128] *See, e.g.,* Bane v. Ferguson, 890 F.2d 11 (7th Cir. 1989); VHB Assocs. v. Orix Real Estate Equities, 2002 U.S. Dist. LEXIS 17569, *18 (C.D. Ca., Sept. 3, 2002) ("'the presumption of good faith embodied by the business judgment rule' protects ORIX's business decisions from second-guessing by the court"); Weinberg v. Lear Fan Corp., 627 F. Supp. 719, 723 (S.D.N.Y 1986) ("the decision of the general partners . . . would probably be considered a direct benefit to the limited partners and a decision entitled to protection under the business judgment rule.").

[129] Levine v. Levine, 590 N.Y.S.2d 439, 443 (1992).

rare for a partner to be held liable to the firm or his fellow partners for mere negligence. In *Bane v. Ferguson*, for example, retired lawyer Bane sued partners of his former law firm for mismanagement when their decision to merge with another firm terminated Bane's pension payments. Judge Posner held that the business judgment rule shielded the defendant partners from liability for mere negligence in the operation of their law firm.[130]

Just as in corporate law, moreover, the partnership variant of the business judgment rule has no application where the defendants engaged in self-dealing. The court in *Rabin v. Concord Assets Group*, for example, held that the business judgment rule was inapplicable to the defendants' real estate sale decisions due to the dual interests of the defendants as both managers of the limited partnership and beneficiaries from the sales.[131] The court noted that the burden was on the defendants to prove that the self-interested dealings were fair to the limited partners and the partnership, stating "when the rule is not applicable, as here, courts have broader authority to examine the relevant decision making."

Drafters of the UPA (1997) resolved the debate by imposing a statutory duty of care, but sharply limiting the scope of that duty:

> A partner's duty of care to the partnership and the other partners in the conduct and winding up of the partnership business is limited to refraining from engaging in grossly negligent or reckless conduct, intentional misconduct, or a knowing violation of law.[132]

The net effect is to codify what most observers believe was the predominant common law approach; namely, to require due care, while not allowing liability for mere negligence.

C. Duty of Disclosure

As we have seen, an obligation to disclose material facts is part and parcel of the duty of loyalty. Where the partner has a conflict of interest in connection with a particular transaction, for example, the partner must disclose his interest and any other material facts that might affect the value of the transaction to the firm. Is there any broader duty of disclosure?

---

[130] Bane v. Ferguson, 890 F.2d 11, 14 (7th Cir. 1989). *See also* Duffy v. Piazza Construction, Inc., 815 P.2d 267, 268–269 (Wash. Ct. App. 1991) ("In the ordinary management and operation of a general partnership or joint venture there is no liability to the other partners or joint venturers for the negligence in the management or operation of the affairs of the enterprise.").

[131] Rabin v. Concord Assets Group, Inc., 1995 U.S. Dist. LEXIS 16166 (S.D.N.Y., Nov. 2, 1995).

[132] UPA (1997) § 404(c).

In *Day v. Sidley & Austin*,[133] plaintiff was a senior partner in the defendant law firm and the managing partner of its Washington, DC, office. When Sidley & Austin merged with another DC law firm, Day was demoted (at least in his eyes) to co-chairman of the office. Day sued. Among other things, Day claimed that his fellow partners breached their fiduciary duties by not disclosing the effect the merger would have on internal firm governance. The court characterized Day's claim as concerning non-disclosures relating to the internal structure of the firm, as to which the court held that no duty to disclose exists: "No court has recognized a fiduciary duty to disclose this type of information, the concealment of which does not produce any profit for the offending partners nor any financial loss for the partnership as a whole." In other words, there is no freestanding duty of disclosure absent a conflict of interest.[134]

Day would be in a much better position today. UPA (1914) § 20 limited intra-partnership disclosure duties (other than access to the books) to situations in which a partner made demand for information of all things affecting the partnership. In contrast, UPA (1997) § 403(c)(1) imposes a duty to disclose, without demand, any information concerning the partnership's business and affairs reasonably required for the proper exercise of the partner's rights and duties. Because Day had a right to vote on the merger, the partnership and its partners had a duty to disclose any information relating to the merger.

D.   Role of Private Ordering, If Any

Whether the fiduciary obligations of partners could be modified by contract was sharply debated at common law. The issue arose out of the clash between two basic principles. On the one hand, contracts purporting to allow a fiduciary to violate his duties long were regarded as suspect. On the other hand, partnership law recognizes that a partnership is a consensual entity by permitting the parties to opt out by agreement of the rules concerning internal partnership governance.

Singer v. Singer[135] is a widely cited precedent for the proposition that partners can waive, or at least modify, fiduciary duties by contract. The partnership agreement provided:

---

[133] 394 F. Supp. 986 (D.D.C. 1975).

[134] There is some case law to the contrary. *See, e.g.,* Appletree Square I Ltd. Partnership v. Investmark, Inc., 494 N.W.2d 889, 892 (Minn.App.1993) ("The relationship of partners is fiduciary and partners are held to high standards of integrity in their dealings with each other. . . . Parties in a fiduciary relationship must disclose material facts to each other.")

[135] 634 P.2d 766 (Okla.Ct.App.1981).

8. Each partner shall be free to enter into business and other transactions for his or her own separate individual account, even though such business or other transaction may be in conflict with and/or competition with the business of this partnership. Neither the partnership nor any individual member of this partnership shall be entitled to claim or receive any part of or interest in such transactions. . . .

When a dispute later arose, the court upheld the validity of the provision:

We find paragraph 8 is designed to allow and is uniquely drafted to promote spirited, if not outright predatory competition between the partners. Its strong wording leaves no doubt in our minds that its drafters intended to effect such a result. . . .

The court noted that paragraph 8 would not have protected the defendant partners if they had "pirated an existing partnership asset or used partnership funds or encumbered [the firm] financially." Unfortunately, the court did not make clear whether its dicta on that score was grounded on the language of the contract or reflected a legal limitation on the freedom of partners to vary their duties by contract.

To the extent cases like *Singer* allow partners to waive fiduciary duties, as opposed to merely modifying such duties, there is case law to the contrary. In *Labovitz v. Dolan*,[136] for example, an Illinois appellate court squarely rejected "the proposition that there can be an a priori waiver of fiduciary duties in a partnership." In another Illinois decision, the court further explained that "partners are free to vary many aspects of their relationship inter se, but they are not free to destroy its fiduciary character."[137]

The drafters of the UPA (1997) settled on the modify but not waive formula. Section 103(a) embraces a broad notion of freedom of contract: "Except as otherwise provided in subsection (b), relations among the partners and between the partners and the partnership are governed by the partnership agreement." Turning then to subsection (b), we learn that the partnership agreement may not "unreasonably reduce the duty of care." It also may not "eliminate the duty of loyalty," although "the partnership agreement may identify specific types or categories of activities that do not violate the duty of loyalty, if not manifestly unreasonable." In addition, consistent with the principle that consent vitiates a breach of duty of loyalty, the subsection further provides that a transaction may be

---

[136] 545 N.E.2d 304 (Ill.App.1989).
[137] Saballus v. Timke, 460 N.E.2d 755, 760 (Ill.App.1983).

authorized by a vote of the partners. Unanimity is required unless the partnership agreement specifies otherwise.

The UPA (1997) raises almost as many questions as it solves. How does one "reduce" the duty of care? At what point does a reduction in the duty of care become "unreasonable"? What would render a modification of the duty of loyalty "manifestly unreasonable"? And so on. In fairness to the drafters, these provisions were intensely controversial.[138] Hence, it is not surprising that the drafters opted to leave the task of defining the outer limits of freedom of contract to the courts. Unfortunately, however, we lack good case law fleshing out these highly ambiguous terms.

Delaware has gone considerably further than did the drafters of the UPA (1997). Section 103(f) of the Delaware Revised Uniform Partnership Act provides that:

> A partnership agreement may provide for the limitation or elimination of any and all liabilities for breach of contract and breach of duties (including fiduciary duties) of a partner or other person to a partnership or to another partner or to another person that is a party to or is otherwise bound by a partnership agreement; provided, that a partnership agreement may not limit or eliminate liability for any act or omission that constitutes a bad faith violation of the implied contractual covenant of good faith and fair dealing.

Interpreting the same language as found in the Delaware LLC statute, the Chancery Court has held that drafters of an LLC agreement "must make their intent to eliminate fiduciary duties plain and unambiguous."[139]

As a planning matter, one issue thus seems beyond dispute. Partners who wish to relieve themselves of fiduciary duties should make their intent as clear as possible in a written partnership agreement. They should also seriously consider forming their partnership under Delaware law.

What should the law be in this area? It turns out that precisely the same issue arises in connection with limited liability companies. Discussion of the relevant policy considerations therefore is taken up in the next Chapter.

---

[138] See, e.g., J. Dennis Hynes, Fiduciary Duties and UPA (1997): An Inquiry Into Freedom of Contract, 58 LAW & CONTEMP. PROBS. 29 (1995); Larry Ribstein, Fiduciary Duty Contracts in Unincorporated Firms, 54 WASH. & LEE L. REV. 537 (1997); Allan W. Vestal, Advancing the Search for a Compromise: A Response to Professor Hynes, 58 LAW & CONTEMP. PROBS. 55 (1995); Allan W. Vestal, Allan W. Vestal, Fundamental Contractarian Error in the Revised Uniform Partnership Act of 1992, 73 B.U. L. REV. 523 (1993).

[139] Feeley v. NHAOCG, LLC, 62 A.3d 649, 664 (Del.Ch. 2012).

VI. Dissolution

A partner unhappy with the firm's business prospects or the conduct of other partners has relatively few options. The partner's membership in the firm cannot be sold and no market exists for the limited interest that can be assigned. Suits amongst the partners are discouraged by many doctrines, such as the business judgment rule and the co-principal doctrine. Instead, the unhappy partner's chief recourse is to the dissolution remedy.[140]

A.　Dissolution versus Dissociation: The UPA (1914) versus the UPA (1997)

Dissolution of the partnership is not the same thing as going out of business. Under UPA (1914) § 29, a dissolution of the partnership is simply the "change in relationship of the partners caused by any partner ceasing to be associated in the carrying on" of the firm's business. Accordingly, dissolution is only the first step in going out of business. After dissolution, the partnership must be wound up, absent agreement among the partners to carry on the business. Assuming that the business will not be continued, the winding up process generally contemplates that the firm's assets will be distributed to the partners. (See Figure 3.2)

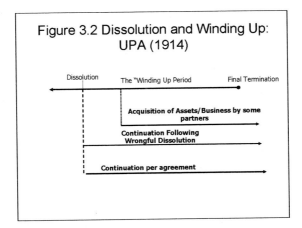

Figure 3.2 Dissolution and Winding Up: UPA (1914)

Obviously, the dissolution and winding up rules can be a significant drawback to the partnership form of doing business. Consider the example of a large national law firm; if the law firm

---

[140] Indeed, under the UPA (1914), it was typically held that "courts will not interfere in internal disputes between members of a partnership, preferring instead that the partners settle their differences among themselves or else dissolve and go out of business settling their affairs at that time by a final and full accounting with all partners joined." Schuler v. Birnbaum, 405 N.Y.S.2d 351, 352 (N.Y.App.Div.1978). UPA (1997) § 405(b) has adopted a more liberal approach, under which courts are authorized to enforce rights amongst the partners during the life of the partnership.

dissolved every time a partner died, retired or jumped ship, operating as a partnership would be highly impractical. Here again, the flexibility of partnership law provides a solution, as the partners can agree that the firm will continue to function even when one member withdraws. Yet, as we shall see below, continuation of a partnership post-dissolution is a complex and technical process.

The UPA (1997) simplified the process by distinguishing between a dissociation and a dissolution. Under it, when a partner ceases to be associated with the firm, one of two things can happen. First, per Article 7, the non-dissociating partners usually may continue the partnership by buying out the dissociating partner's interest. Second, per Article 8, the partners may—and in some cases, must—go forward with a dissolution and winding up of the business. (See Figure 3.3.)

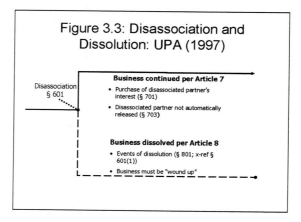

Figure 3.3: Disassociation and Dissolution: UPA (1997)

Disassociation § 601

Business continued per Article 7
- Purchase of disassociated partner's interest (§ 701)
- Disassociated partner not automatically released (§ 703)

Business dissolved per Article 8
- Events of dissolution (§ 801; x-ref § 601(1))
- Business must be "wound up"

B.   Dissolution under the UPA (1914)

1.   *Grounds for Dissolution*

UPA (1914) §§ 31 and 32 specify the actions which cause a dissolution of a partnership. Section 31 sets forth a number of ways in which dissolution can be caused either by acts of one or more of the parties or by operation of law. Section 32 identifies the grounds upon which a court may order a partnership dissolved.

Under § 31, a term partnership—i.e., one in which the partnership agreement provides that the partnership will have a definite term or is to achieve some specific purpose—automatically dissolves when the set term expires or the specific purpose is achieved.[141] Where the partnership is "at will," it is dissolved by the

---

[141] Note that even where the partnership agreement sets a specific time period for the firm's existence or is keyed to achievement of a stated purpose, a partner can

withdrawal of any partner. Either type of partnership is dissolved by expulsion of a partner in accordance with the terms of the partnership agreement. A partnership dissolves by operation of law if it becomes unlawful to carry on the business of the partnership. A partnership also dissolves by operation of law when a partner dies or if either a partner or the partnership itself becomes bankrupt.

Under § 32, a court may order dissolution of the partnership on a number of grounds, including: A partner suffers from an incapacitating mental illness. A partner becomes unable to perform her part of the partnership agreement. A partner's conduct tends to affect prejudicially the carrying on of the business. A partner willfully or persistently breaches the partnership agreement or otherwise so conducts himself so that it is not reasonably practicable to carry on the business in partnership with him. The business of the partnership can only be carried on at a loss. Upon application of the assignee of a partner's interest or of a creditor who has obtained a charging order against a partner's interest pursuant to § 28.[142]

The categories of cases in which dissolution occurs without a prior court order tend to involve definitive events as to which there can be little disagreement as to their occurrence. In contrast, the categories requiring a judicial decree are all premised on rather subjective facts. The necessity of obtaining a judicial decree in such settings helps make sure that there really are good grounds for a dissolution in such cases. It also tends to act as a check on one partner trying to freeze out another.

2.   *Wrongful Dissolution*

Although there are many ways in which a partner can dissolve the partnership without seeking judicial intervention, it frequently is desirable to pursue a judicial decree even if grounds for dissolution under UPA (1914) § 31 appear to exist. Consider, for example, the case of *Owen v. Cohen*.[143] Owen and Cohen became partners in a bowling alley. Owen put up $6,986, which was to be repaid out of the profits of the business. Probably this was treated as a loan. Cohen apparently thought he was entitled to run the show. He belittled and mistreated Owen. After three months, Owen

---

still dissolve the firm before the term expires by express action. However, such a dissolution is regarded as "wrongful" and subjects the wrongful dissolver to damages for breach of the partnership agreement and also results in certain limitations on his or her ability to participate in the winding up process. UPA (1914) §31(2).

[142] Note that the creditor may not do so if the partnership is to have a set duration or is to accomplish a set purpose and the time period has not expired or the purpose is not accomplished. UPA (1914) §32(2).

[143] 119 P.2d 713 (Cal. 1941).

filed an action in equity seeking dissolution and a sale of the partnership assets.

Why did Owen go to court instead of simply withdrawing from the partnership and thereby triggering a dissolution under UPA (1914) § 31(1)(b)? Owen had three good reasons for going to court:

1. Cohen claimed that Owen was not entitled to be repaid his $6,986 before division of the proceeds from a sale of the business, so a judicial determination would have been necessary to resolve this issue.

2. Once Owen announces that he dissolves, there still must be some mechanism for a buy-out or a sale. The practical effect of a dissolution is to force each of the partners to make an effort to buy out the other, possibly after finding a new partner, or to make an effort to find a buyer. Cohen is not likely to be cooperative. So Owen is going to have to go to court anyway to obtain an order for sale and for the appointment of a receiver to operate the business until the sale occurs.

3. The most serious problem is that the partnership might be (and in fact was) a term partnership. A partnership can be dissolved by the unilateral act of any partner at any time where the partnership is "at will," in other words, where its life span is not defined by the partnership agreement. If this partnership had no term, Owen can terminate it by informing Cohen of his intent to dissolve the firm. But if the partnership had a term, dissolution by notice would have been wrongful. A wrongful dissolution by Owen is regarded as a breach of the partnership agreement and Cohen would have been entitled to damages and various other remedies.

Note that filing a lawsuit seeking dissolution under UPA (1914) § 32 does not itself cause a dissolution of the firm.[144] Hence, Owen's filing of the lawsuit could not result in a finding that he had wrongfully dissolved the firm. Given the adverse consequences to the dissolving partner of a wrongful dissolution, this is a critical point.

What constitutes a wrongful dissolution? Curiously, the UPA (1914) does not expressly define the term wrongful dissolution. Instead, § 38(2) refers to a dissolution "caused in contravention of the partnership agreement" and thereafter sets out the consequences of having "dissolved wrongfully." Hence, we infer that

---

[144] Cooper v. Issacs, 448 F.2d 1202 (D.C.Cir.1971); G & S Investments v. Belman, 700 P.2d 1358 (Ariz.App.1984).

a wrongful dissolution is one that breaches the partnership agreement.

Unilateral withdrawal of a partner in a term partnership prior to the expiration of the specified term is the most common way in which a dissolution is deemed to breach the partnership agreement and thus qualify as wrongful. In some cases, however, courts have found that egregious breaches of fiduciary duty also qualify as wrongful. In *G & S Investments v. Belman*,[145] for example, the defendant partner—one Thomas Nordale—began abusing cocaine. He threatened some of the other partners. He sexually propositioned a tenant of an apartment complex owned by the partnership. He occupied an apartment in the complex but refused to pay rent. He made a number of bad business decisions. Eventually the other partners got fed up and sued. The court agreed with them that Nordale's conduct amounted to a wrongful dissolution:

> Contrary to appellant's contention, Nordale's conduct was in contravention of the partnership agreement. Nordale's conduct affected the carrying on of the business and made it impracticable to continue in partnership with him. His conduct was wrongful and was in contravention of the partnership agreement, thus allowing the court to permit appellees to carry on the business. . . .

The other partners doubtless were entitled to a dissolution under UPA (1914) § 32(1)(c), which authorizes a court to dissolve the partnership where: "A partner has been guilty of such conduct as tends to affect prejudicially the carrying on of the business." On these facts, dissolution under § 32(1)(d) likely also was available because Nordale had "so conduct[ed] himself in matters relating to the partnership business that it [was] not reasonably practicable to carry on the business in partnership with him." The court's willingness to treat Nordale's conduct as giving rise to a wrongful dissolution had significant remedial advantages for the other partners, however, as we shall see below.

The Problem of the Implied Term. As we have seen, where the partnership agreement expressly or implicitly provides that the partnership will have a definite term or is to achieve some specific

---

[145] 700 P.2d 1358 (Ariz.App.1984). *See also* Page v. Page, 359 P.2d 41, 44 (Cal.1961) ("plaintiff has the power to dissolve the partnership by express notice to defendant. If, however, it is proved that plaintiff acted in bad faith and violated his fiduciary duties by attempting to appropriate to his own use the new prosperity of the partnership without adequate compensation to his co-partner, the dissolution would be wrongful and the plaintiff would be liable as provided by subdivision (2)(a) of Corporations Code, § 15038 (rights of partners upon wrongful dissolution) for violation of the implied agreement not to exclude defendant wrongfully from the partnership business opportunity.").

purpose, the partnership automatically dissolves when the set term expires or the specific purpose is achieved. This is what is known as a term partnership.

The other major type of partnership (and by far the more common) is the partnership at will. An at will partnership can be dissolved by the unilateral act of any partner at any time, without any of the adverse consequences associated with early dissolution of a term partnership.

Both types of partnership are subject to dissolution by, for example, the unilateral withdrawal of one partner. As courts often say, a partner always has the power to dissolve the firm, but may not always have the right to do so. Hence, in the case of a term partnership, rather than a partnership at will, a partner can still dissolve the firm before the term expires by express action, but there are significant adverse consequences for doing so.

Given the adverse consequences of wrongfully dissolving a term partnership, it is obviously important to know whether you are dealing with a partnership for a term or at will. Sometimes the term is explicit, but often courts will imply a term from the facts surrounding the transaction. In *Owen v. Cohen*, for example, the court held that when a partner loans money to the firm, to be repaid from profits, an implied term is created that does not expire until the loan is repaid. In that case, as you'll recall, Owen had loaned the firm about $7,000 that had not been repaid. Hence, the partnership was one for a term, which is why it was wise for Owen to go to court rather than unilaterally dissolving the firm.

As a general rule, the standard for finding an implied term is linked to the statutory language of UPA (1914) § 31(1)(a): a "definite term or particular undertaking." You look at whether the parties have identified a particular undertaking that is capable of accomplishment at some specific time, even though the exact time may be unknown and even unascertainable at the date of the agreement.[146] Some examples may be helpful. In *Owen v. Cohen*, the partners had borrowed funds to start the business, with an understanding that the loan was to be paid off through partnership profits. In *Vangel v. Vangel*,[147] one partner loaned the business money, with an understanding that it was to be repaid from partnership profits. In *Mervyn Investment Co. v. Biber*,[148] one partner made the entire capital contribution, with an understanding that partnership profits were to be applied to repay his contribution. In each case, the court found an implied

---

[146] Girard Bank v. Haley, 332 A.2d 443 (Pa.1975).

[147] 254 P.2d 919 (Cal.App.1953).

[148] 194 P. 1037 (Cal.1921).

agreement that the partnership remain in business until the specified amount of money had been earned. In *Shannon v. Hudson*,[149] the parties had similarly agreed to operate the motel until it could be profitably sold.

Consequences of Wrongfully Dissolving. As noted, a wrongful dissolution has serious and adverse consequences for the wrongfully dissolving partner. First, the wrongful dissolver is liable for damages for breach of the partnership agreement. Second, the wrongfully dissolving partner is excluded from participating in the winding up process. Third, the remaining partners have the right to continue the business even if the partnership agreement does not so provide. In such a case, however, they must either pay the withdrawing partner the fair value of his or her share in the partnership, minus any damages caused by his or her breach of the agreement, or post a bond for that amount with the court. Finally, in calculating the value of the wrongfully dissolving partner's share of the business, any increment for good will is excluded. As such, the value of the partnership as a going concern is not taken into account; instead, the value is based on what the partnership's assets would bring if the firm was broken up and liquidated.

Pav-Saver Corp. v. Vasso Corp.,[150] is a particularly instructive example of just how severe these consequences can be for the wrongfully dissolving partner. Harry Dale was an inventor and majority shareholder of Pav-Saver Corporation (PSC). PSC held patents and trademarks on concrete paving machines. Moss Meersman was a lawyer and investor, who operated through Vasso Corporation, in which he held all the shares. In 1974, they formed a partnership called Pav-Saver Manufacturing Company to manufacture and sell the paving machines. Their written partnership agreement was drafted by Meersman. Under Paragraph 3 thereof, PSC granted Pav-Saver Manufacturing an exclusive license to use PSC's patents and trademarks. Paragraph 3 stated: "It [is] understood and agreed that same shall remain the property of [PSC] and all copies shall be returned to [PSC] at the expiration of this partnership."

Paragraph 11 of the agreement provided:

It is contemplated that this joint venture partnership shall be permanent, and same shall not be terminated or dissolved by either party except upon mutual approval of both parties. If, however, either party shall terminate or dissolve said relationship, the terminating party shall pay to the other party, as liquidated damages, a sum equal to four (4) times the

[149] 325 P.2d 1022 (Cal.App.1958).
[150] 493 N.E.2d 423 (Ill.App.1986).

gross royalties received by PAV–SAVER Corporation in the fiscal year ending July 31, 1973, as shown by their corporate financial statement. Said liquidated damages to be paid over a ten (10) year period next immediately following the termination, payable in equal installments."

After several years of operation, Dale (acting through PSC) sought to unilaterally dissolve the partnership. Meersman assumed control of Pav-Saver Manufacturing, claiming UPA (1914) § 38 authorized him both to continue to operate the business and to collect damages under the formula in the partnership agreement. Dale then filed suit seeking a return of the patents and trademark.

Section 38 provides, in pertinent part that:

(2) When dissolution is caused in contravention of the partnership agreement the rights of the partners shall be as follows:

(a) Each partner who has not caused dissolution wrongfully shall have . . .

II. The right, as against each partner who has caused the dissolution wrongfully, to damages for breach of the agreement.

(b) The partners who have not caused the dissolution wrongfully, if they all desire to continue the business in the same name, either by themselves or jointly with others, may do so, during the agreed term for the partnership and for that purpose may possess the partnership property, provided they secure the payment by bond approved by the court, or pay to any partner who has caused the dissolution wrongfully, the value of his interest in the partnership at the dissolution, less any damages recoverable under clause (2a II) of this section, and in like manner indemnify him against all present or future partnership liabilities.

(c) A partner who has caused the dissolution wrongfully shall have: . . .

II. If the business is continued under paragraph (2b) of this section the right as against his co-partners and all claiming through them in respect of their interests in the partnership, to have the value of his interest in the partnership, less any damages caused to his co-partners by the dissolution, ascertained and paid to him in cash, or the payment secured by bond approved by the court, and to be released from all existing liabilities of the partnership; but in ascertaining the value of the partner's interest the value of the good-will of the business shall not be considered.

The court held that these provisions governed the case at bar. The partnership agreement created a "permanent" partnership—i.e., one that under the agreement could be dissolved only by the mutual consent of both partners. Dale's attempt to unilaterally dissolve the partnership therefore was a breach of the agreement and, accordingly, a wrongful dissolution.

Meersman therefore prevailed. First, the court held that Meersman was entitled under § 38(2)(b) to continue to operate the business. Under the express terms of Paragraph 3 of their agreement, the trademarks and patents were to be returned to PSC when the partnership terminated (i.e., dissolved). Because the trademarks and patents were essential to carry on the business of the partnership, however, the court refused to enforce their agreement. Given the importance freedom of contract plays in partnership law, this holding seems clearly erroneous. The court's unwillingness to enforce the agreement thus illustrates just how severe the consequences of a wrongful dissolution can be for the dissolving partner.

Yet, things got worse for Dale. The court acknowledged that under § 38(b), Dale was entitled to his share of the value of the partnership. The court held that the value of the patents and trademarks should not be considered in determining Dale's share of the value of the business. Such intangible assets were deemed to be part of the good will of the business, which § 38(b) excludes from calculating the value of the dissolving partner's interest.

Finally, the court rejected Dale's argument that Paragraph 11 was a liquidated damages provision. Applying the damages calculation thereunder, Dale owed Meersman $384,612, which more than off-set the amount owed Dale for his share of the business, albeit Dale only had to pay the damages in installments over 10 years.

Again, the court's interpretation of Paragraph 11 seems clearly erroneous. There are two ways to read that provision. The more plausible reading is that the partnership can be dissolved notwithstanding § 38(2), subject to the damages provision. In other words, it provides that neither party can terminate unless is it willing to pay damages. The second reading, which the court adopted without analysis, is that if either party dissolves, that is a wrongful act, so § 38(2) controls. The court's adoption of the latter interpretation seems especially odd in light of the well-established rule that contracts are to be construed against their drafter, which seems especially relevant here where Meersman was a lawyer.

What is the bottom line? Woe unto those who wrongfully dissolve. All sorts of adverse consequences follow and you are unlikely to get much in the way of judicial sympathy.

3.   *Winding Up*

After dissolution, the partnership must be wound up, absent agreement among the partners to carry on the business. Assuming that the business will not be continued, the winding up process generally contemplates that the firm's assets will be sold and the proceeds distributed to the partners.

As a general rule, the dissolution of a partnership terminates all authority of all partners to transact business on behalf of the firm except for such business as is necessary to wind up the partnership.[151] Partners retain actual authority to enter into only transactions designed to terminate, rather than carry on the business. In effect, they may finish up old business but can't engage in new business.

What about apparent authority post-dissolution? This is dealt with in a rather complicated way by UPA (1914) § 35. As to a creditor who had done business with the partnership prior to the dissolution, a partner retains apparent authority to bind the partnership post-dissolution unless the creditor has knowledge or has been put on individual notice of the dissolution. As to all others, the partnership can destroy apparent authority by advertising the dissolution in a newspaper of general circulation in each place in which the partnership's business was regularly carried on.

4.   *Liquidating the Business*

As noted, assuming that the business will not be continued, the winding up process generally contemplates that the firm's assets will be distributed to the partners. In general, distributions in the winding up of a partnership must be made in cash, unless the partners agree otherwise.[152] As such, the partners are entitled to have the business be sold on either a going concern basis or through liquidation of individual assets. If the other parties refuse, the partner is entitled to a judicial sale of the business under court supervision.[153]

Occasionally, some of the partners may prefer a distribution of the assets in kind. Suppose, for example, that the partnership's sole assets consist of barrels of oil. Some of the partners might want

---

[151] UPA (1914) § 33.

[152] Dreifuerst v. Dreifuerst, 280 N.W.2d 335 (Wisc.1979).

[153] Absent bad faith or breach of fiduciary duty, one or more of the partners are free to bid on the partnership's assets at such a sale. Prentiss v. Sheffel, 513 P.2d 949 (Ariz.App.1973).

physical pro rata distribution of the barrels rather than a sale, such as where they expect the price of oil to rise in the future. Under the general rule set out above, however, most courts will not allow an in-kind distribution unless all the partners agree. If any partner objects, he is entitled to force a sale and get the proceeds distributed in case. A few states have adopted an exception permitting in-kind distributions where: (1) there are no creditors to be paid; (2) nobody but the partners is interested in the firm's assets; and (3) an in-kind distribution is fair and equitable to all of the partners.[154] It is difficult to imagine a partnership in real life that would have no creditors and which holds such unique assets that nobody would be interested in buying them. Accordingly, even in those few states following this rule, it seems unlikely that there will be many in-kind distributions absent agreement by the partners.

5. Settling Up

After the business is liquidated, settling up amongst the partners is controlled by UPA (1914) §§ 18(a) and 40. The former provides:

> The rights and duties of the partners in relation to the partnership shall be determined, subject to any agreement between them, by the following rules:

> (a) Each partner shall be repaid his contributions, whether by way of capital or advances to the partnership property and share equally in the profits and surplus remaining after all liabilities, including those to partners, are satisfied; and must contribute towards the losses, whether of capital or otherwise sustained by the partnership according to his share in the profits.[155]

Section 40(b) provided that, subject to any contrary agreement, upon dissolution liabilities of the partnership should be paid in the following order:

I. Those owing to creditors other than partners,

II. Those owing to partners other than for capital and profits,

III. Those owing to partners in respect of capital,

IV. Those owing to partners in respect of profits.[156]

---

[154] *See, e.g.,* Rinke v. Rinke, 48 N.W.2d 201 (Mich.1951).

[155] CAL. CORP. CODE § 15018(a) (West 1998). Effective January 1, 1999, California repealed the UPA (1914) and replaced it with the 1994 version of the UPA (1996). CAL. CORP. CODE § 16111(b) (West 1998).

[156] CAL. CORP. CODE § 15040(b) (West 1998).

Subsection 40(d) further provides, in pertinent part: "The partners shall contribute, as provided by [§ 18(a)] the amount necessary to satisfy the liabilities [set forth in § 40(b)]. . . ."[157]

What is the order in which payments are made?

Taken together, these provisions establish the following rules governing the order in which the proceeds of the partnership's assets are distributed:

1. Any debts owed the firm's creditors shall be paid.

2. If any amounts remain for distribution after step 1, you pay any amounts owed a partner "other than for capital and profits." Suppose, for example, that A and B each make a capital contribution of $10,000 to their partnership. A then loans the firm $5,000. A is entitled to be repaid the loan amount before the capital contributions are returned. If the firm has only $5,000 left after paying off its creditors, the whole amount goes to A.

3. If any sums remain after steps 1 and 2, the value of the partners' capital accounts are paid them. This step can get complicated where the partners have unequal capital accounts and the firm as a whole has suffered a capital loss. Suppose A, B, and C are partners whose capital accounts stand at $10,000, $5,000 and $2,000 respectively. Upon winding up, amount remaining for distribution with respect to capital is only $5,000. In other words, the firm lost $12,000. Each partner's pro rata share of the loss is $4,000. How will the $5,000 be distributed?

    a) If the remaining cash is insufficient to reimburse the partners for all of their capital contributions, the loss is divided pro rata and the remaining funds are distributed in accord with their capital contributions. Thus, A gets $6,000, B gets $1,000 and C must put $2,000 into the kitty.

4. If any cash remains after the above payments are made, it is distributed among the partners in accord with their agreed division of profits.

The rule set out in step 3 requiring partners in some cases to contribute out-of-pocket to off-set capital losses strikes many observers as unduly harsh. In *Kovacik v. Reed*,[158] carved out an exception to the statutory scheme for the important class of firms

---

[157] CAL. CORP. CODE § 15040(d) (West 1998).

[158] 315 P.2d 314 (Cal. 1957). *See generally* Stephen M. Bainbridge, *Contractarianism in the Business Associations Classroom: Kovacik v. Reed and the Allocation of Capital Losses in Service Partnerships*, 34 GA. L. REV. 631 (2000).

known as service partnerships. Kovacik and Reed entered into a general partnership to operate a kitchen remodeling business. Kovacik made an initial capital contribution of $10,000. Reed made no capital contribution, but did contribute a promise of future services by agreeing to superintend the partnership's work and to estimate the jobs on which the partnership bid. Kovacik and Reed agreed to share profits equally, but made no provision for allocating losses. Reed apparently took no salary. Unfortunately, things did not go as planned and Kovacik dissolved the partnership, after only ten months, on grounds that it was unprofitable. Kovacik claimed that the partnership had lost $8,680 and brought a proceeding for an accounting in which he sought to recover one half of the partnership's capital loss from Reed.

On the face of the statutes, Kovacik had a strong claim. It appears that the partnership had no liabilities falling under UPA (1914) §§ 40(b)(I) or (II). Accordingly, the next set of liabilities to be satisfied were those "owing to partners in respect of capital"; in other words, return of capital was the senior remaining claim on the partnership's assets. Assuming for the sake of simplicity that there had been no adjustments to the initial capital accounts (there being no facts to the contrary), the partnership owed $10,000 to Kovacik "in respect of capital" and nothing to Reed. Kovacik therefore was entitled to the entire $1,320 apparently realized upon the liquidation of the partnership, leaving a capital loss of $8,680. Per § 40(d) both partners were required to contribute to satisfaction of that liability in accordance with the rules laid out in § 18(a). In turn, § 18(a) provides that the $8,680 loss was to be shared among the partners "according to [their] share in the profits," which it will be recalled were shared equally.

On dissolution, the partnership thus had suffered a capital loss, in the form of a capital deficit, of $8,680. Equal sharing of that loss required a debit to each partner of $4,340. Because Reed made no capital contribution, however, he would not bear any share of the capital loss unless he was required to pay in $4,340. Likewise, unless Reed paid him $4,340, Kovacik would bear the entire $8,680 loss. On the face of the statute, Reed is therefore obliged to equalize the losses by paying Kovacik the demanded sum of $4,340.

Courts have strictly applied the UPA provisions in most situations, except those involving a so-called "service partnership," of the sort present in *Kovacik*, in which some partners contribute only services. Although none of the relevant UPA sections make any distinction between general partnerships in which all partners make capital contributions and a service partnership, many courts have refused to apply the statute to firms of the latter type if doing so would mean that the service-only partner would be required to make a cash contribution out of personal assets towards his share of any capital losses.[159]

Kovacik is typical of these decisions. The *Kovacik* court acknowledged the general rule, but held that where the partners had agreed that one was to contribute capital and the other only services, neither partner could be held liable to the other for contribution towards capital losses.[160] "Thus, upon loss of the money the party who contributed it is not entitled to recover any part of it from the party who contributed only services." The California Supreme Court made no effort to ground this exception in the statute. Instead, the court explained its holding as follows:

> The rationale of this rule . . . is that where one party contributes money and the other contributes services, . . . in the event of a loss each would lose his own capital—the one his money and the other his labor. Another view would be that in such a situation the parties have, by their agreement to share equally in profits, agreed that the value of their contributions—the money on one hand and the labor on the other—were likewise equal; it would follow that upon the loss . . . of both money and labor, the parties have shared equally in the losses.

Whatever one makes of this rationale, it has been widely accepted by the courts.[161]

In distinguishing cases following the statutory scheme, however, the *Kovacik* court implicitly limited the newly created exception to the facts of that case. The court observed that in each of the cited cases following the "general rule" each of the partners had made a capital contribution or had been compensated for

---

[159] *See, e.g.,* Kovacik v. Reed, 315 P.2d 314 (Cal. 1957); Becker v. Killarney, 532 N.E.2d 931 (Ill. App. 1988); Snellbaker v. Herrmann, 462 A.2d 713 (Pa. Super. Ct. 1983). The leading precedent to the contrary is Richert v. Handly, 330 P.2d 1079, 1081 (Wash. 1958), in which the Washington Supreme Court (without any analysis) held that where the parties had not agreed upon or specified the basis upon which losses were to be shared, the UPA provisions controlled. Each partner, including the service-only partner, therefore was required to contribute toward the capital loss sustained by the partnership according to his share of the profits. *Richert* perhaps can be reconciled with *Kovacik* by invoking the limitation set forth in the latter that service-only partners who are compensated for their services can be held liable for their share of capital losses. Although this fact did not assume any prominence in the opinion, it appears that the service-only partner in *Richert* was compensated for at least a portion of his services, 330 P.2d at 1080–81, and, therefore, perhaps could be held liable even under *Kovacik* and its progeny.

[160] A later decision made clear that the dispositive fact is that one partner was to provide only services. The *Kovacik* rule therefore still applies even if the partner who contributed the firm's capital also contributes some services, so long as the other partner contributes only services. De Witte v. Calhoun, 34 Cal. Rptr. 491, 494–95 (Cal. App. 1963).

[161] *See* Snellbaker v. Herrmann, 462 A.2d 713, 716 (Pa. Supr. 1983) (collecting cases); David B. Sweet, Annotation, *Joint Venturers' Comparative Liability for Losses, Absence of Express Agreement,* 51 A.L.R.4th 371 (same).

services rendered. Accordingly, so long as the service-only partner makes at least a nominal capital contribution or is compensated for his labor, the court will follow the statutory scheme and hold that partner liable for his share of any capital losses.[162]

Although the *Kovacik* rule strikes many as more fair than the statutory rule, at least as applied to service partnerships, note that it does create a perverse incentive for the services-only partner and a corresponding risk for the capital-only partner. The problem is that the services-only partner, with nothing to lose but his or her time, may make bad decisions from the perspective of the capital-only partner—especially, when there is a strong possibility of failure. Suppose, for example, that there is $10,000 in the partnership bank account, all of which would go to the capital-only partner on dissolution, and that the partnership business is on the verge of failure. The services-only partner has an incentive to spend the money in any way that creates some possibility of survival and ultimate success even if the expenditure has, say, only a 10 percent chance of creating value of $20,000 and no other outcome. Or, once the business's prospects have become bleak, the services-only partner may lose interest and may fail to exert optimal effort to salvage as much as possible.

Further practical complexities arise when considering a partner's contribution of additional capital. Moreover, what happens when a new partner joins or leaves? What if some partners are paid in an alternative form of compensation (rather than through profits)? What if the service partner performs poorly or fails to perform at all? Is it fair to value his or her input at $10,000.00 then? And over what length of time is the service partner's contribution to actually reach the implied value of his contribution? One year? Ten years? Perpetuity?

6.   *Continuing the Business*

Under the UPA (1914), there are three situations in which the business of the partnership may be continued post-dissolution. As discussed above, where the partnership has been wrongfully dissolved, the non-dissolving partners may elect to buy out the dissolving partner and thereafter continue the business. Second, as discussed below, some of the partners may purchase and use the partnership's assets. Finally, as discussed in this section, the

---

[162] *See, e.g.,* Century Universal Enterprises, Inc. v. Triana Dev. Corp., 510 N.E.2d 1260, 1268 (Ill. App. 1987) ("given the fact that defendants were to be compensated for their services, the rule annunciated by the supreme court of California in Kovacik v. Reed . . . does not control the instant case since the exception for compensation which did not apply in that case applies in the instant case.").

partnership agreement properly may provide for the business to be continued without liquidation.

As a technical matter, a provision authorizing continuation of the partnership post-dissolution does not prevent the dissolution from occurring. Instead, a new partnership is formed to which the assets of the old partnership are transferred and which assumes the liabilities of the old partnership. Such a provision therefore is properly structured as a buy-sell agreement, pursuant to which the interest of a withdrawing partner is calculated and then paid. Not infrequently, however, one sees drafters structuring such provisions as so-called denial of dissolution clauses, stating that the death of a partner—to take but one example—does not effect a dissolution of the partnership even though the statute unequivocally is to the contrary.[163] Courts sometimes treat such provisions as valid despite the legal niceties of the statute. Because of the litigation risk posed by the conflict between such provisions and the statute, and because courts routinely enforce properly drafted buy-sell agreements, there is no justification for a lawyer to charge a client for drafting a denial of dissolution agreement.

What are the rights of the firm's old creditors when some of the partners continue the business? First, the withdrawing partners remain liable on all obligations incurred by the partnership while they were members of the firm unless the creditor releases them from that obligation. Second, to boil UPA section 40 down to its basic elements, the firm's old creditors automatically become creditors of the new firm. If a new partner joins the firm when it continues after a dissolution, the new partner is also liable for the firm's old debts, but such liability can only be satisfied out of partnership property. The new partner cannot be held personally liable for the old debts, unless he or she expressly agrees to be so held.

7. *Fiduciary Duties Pre- and Post-Dissolution*

Recall the adage that partners always have the power to dissolve the partnership, but do not always have the right to do so. One of the limitations on the right to dissolve stems from the fiduciary duties partners owe one another:

Even though the Uniform Partnership Act provides that a partnership at will may be dissolved by the express will of any partner, this power, like any other power held by a fiduciary, must be exercised in good faith. . . .

---

[163] HYNES & LOWENSTEIN at 732–33.

A partner at will is not bound to remain in a partnership, regardless of whether the business is profitable or unprofitable. A partner may not, however, by use of adverse pressure "freeze out" a co-partner and appropriate the business to his own use. A partner may not dissolve a partnership to gain the benefits of the business for himself, unless he fully compensates his co-partner for his share of the prospective business opportunity. . . .[164]

As discussed in subsection 2 above, moreover, many courts would treat such conduct as a wrongful dissolution giving rise to all the adverse consequences thereof.

Even after dissolution occurs, the fiduciary obligations partners owe one another do not immediately terminate. The fiduciary duties of loyalty and care continue to apply during the winding up process. Once the winding up process is completed, however, fiduciary obligations terminate. This is true even if the business of the partnership is continued by some of the partners. The remaining partners owe no fiduciary duties to those who have withdrawn.[165]

C. Dissociation and Dissolution under the UPA (1997)

UPA (1997) § 601 identifies the events that result in a partner being disassociated from the firm, which include:

(1) the partnership's having notice of the partner's express will to withdraw as a partner or on a later date specified by the partner;

(2) an event agreed to in the partnership agreement as causing the partner's dissociation;

(3) the partner's expulsion pursuant to the partnership agreement;

(4) the partner's expulsion by the unanimous vote of the other partners if: (i) it is unlawful to carry on the partnership business with that partner; (ii) there has been a transfer of all or substantially all of that partner's transferable interest in the partnership, other than a transfer for security purposes, or a court order charging the partner's interest, which has not been foreclosed; (iii) within 90 days after the partnership notifies a corporate partner that it will be expelled because it has filed a certificate of dissolution or the equivalent, its charter has been revoked, or its right to conduct business has been suspended by the jurisdiction of its incorporation, there is no revocation of

---

[164] Page v. Page, 359 P.2d 41, 44 (Cal.1961).

[165] Bane v. Ferguson, 890 F.2d 11 (7th Cir. 1989).

the certificate of dissolution or no reinstatement of its charter or its right to conduct business; or (iv) a partnership that is a partner has been dissolved and its business is being wound up;

(5) on application by the partnership or another partner, the partner's expulsion by judicial determination because: (i) the partner engaged in wrongful conduct that adversely and materially affected the partnership business; (ii) the partner willfully or persistently committed a material breach of the partnership agreement or of a duty owed to the partnership or the other partners under Section 404 [i.e., fiduciary duties]; or (iii) the partner engaged in conduct relating to the partnership business which makes it not reasonably practicable to carry on the business in partnership with the partner;

(6) the partner's: (i) becoming a debtor in bankruptcy; (ii) executing an assignment for the benefit of creditors; (iii) seeking, consenting to, or acquiescing in the appointment of a trustee, receiver, or liquidator of that partner or of all or substantially all of that partner's property; or (iv) failing, within 90 days after the appointment, to have vacated or stayed the appointment of a trustee, receiver, or liquidator of the partner or of all or substantially all of the partner's property obtained without the partner's consent or acquiescence, or failing within 90 days after the expiration of a stay to have the appointment vacated;

(7) in the case of a partner who is an individual: (i) the partner's death; (ii) the appointment of a guardian or general conservator for the partner; or (iii) a judicial determination that the partner has otherwise become incapable of performing the partner's duties under the partnership agreement;

(8) in the case of a partner that is a trust or is acting as a partner by virtue of being a trustee of a trust, distribution of the trust's entire transferable interest in the partnership, but not merely by reason of the substitution of a successor trustee;

(9) in the case of a partner that is an estate or is acting as a partner by virtue of being a personal representative of an estate, distribution of the estate's entire transferable interest in the partnership, but not merely by reason of the substitution of a successor personal representative; or

(10) termination of a partner who is not an individual, partnership, corporation, trust, or estate.

Upon dissociation of a partner on any of these grounds, per § 602, the dissociated partner's rights to participate in management of the firm terminate. The partner's fiduciary obligation to refrain from competing with the partnership terminates. The partner's other statutory fiduciary duties remain applicable only with respect to matters that arose before the disassociation or those arising in connection with the winding up of the partnership.

What happens next depends on the reason the partner was dissociated and the nature of the partnership. In a partnership at will, dissociation per § 601(2) through 601(10) is governed by Article 7 of the UPA (1997), which provides for removal of the dissociating partner without dissolution or winding up. In contrast, per § 801(1), dissociation under § 601(1)—i.e., the dissociating partner gives the partnership notice of his express will to withdraw—triggers a dissolution and the "business must be wound up" in accordance with the provisions of Article 8.

Note that several key events that would have resulted in dissolution under the UPA (1914) not merely result in disassociation of the affected partner. Among these are the death and bankruptcy of a partner. In the event of such occurrences, the partnership does not dissolve unless a majority of surviving partners vote to wind up the business within 90 days after the disassociation. This makes large partnerships—in which such events occur often—far more stable under the UPA (1997).

A term partnership must be dissolved and wound up at the expiration of the specified term or completion of the specified undertaking. It also must be dissolved if all the partners agree. Finally, a dissociation under § 601(6) through 601(10) or a wrongful dissociation triggers a dissolution, unless a majority of the remaining partners, including any partners who rightfully dissociated, agree to continue the partnership.

Either type of partnership must be dissolved if an event occurs that is identified in the partnership agreement as causing a dissolution. Second, they also must be dissolved if the business of the partnership becomes illegal. Third, both types of partnerships can be dissolved by court order where "(i) the economic purpose of the partnership is likely to be unreasonably frustrated; (ii) another partner has engaged in conduct relating to the partnership business which makes it not reasonably practicable to carry on the business in partnership with that partner; or (iii) it is not otherwise reasonably practicable to carry on the partnership business in conformity with the partnership agreement."[166] Finally, upon application by an assignee of a partner's interest or a creditor with a charging order on such interest, a court may dissolve the partnership if "it is equitable to wind up the partnership business."

---

[166] UPA (1997) § 801(5).

1.   Wrongful Dissociation

Unlike UPA (1914), which failed to define the key term wrongful dissolution, UPA (1997) § 602(b) sets out an exclusive list of events constituting a wrongful dissociation:

(b) A partner's dissociation is wrongful only if:

(1) it is in breach of an express provision of the partnership agreement; or

(2) in the case of a partnership for a definite term or particular undertaking, before the expiration of the term or the completion of the undertaking: (i) the partner withdraws by express will, unless the withdrawal follows within 90 days after another partner's dissociation by death or otherwise under Section 601(6) through(10) or wrongful dissociation under this subsection; (ii) the partner is expelled by judicial determination under Section 601(5); (iii) the partner is dissociated by becoming a debtor in bankruptcy; or (iv) in the case of a partner who is not an individual, trust other than a business trust, or estate, the partner is expelled or otherwise dissociated because it willfully dissolved or terminated.

Note that in a partnership at will, breach of fiduciary duty does not give rise to a wrongful dissolution. Recall that there was case law to the contrary under the UPA (1914).

As with the UPA (1914), a partner who wrongfully dissociates is liable to the partnership for any damages caused by his dissociation. If the business is to be dissolved, the wrongfully dissociating partner is not allowed to participate in the winding up process or to vote on certain other matters. A key difference between the two statutes, however, is the treatment of good will. Recall that under UPA (1914), good will is not included in valuing the interest of a partner who wrongfully dissolves the business. Under UPA (1997), by contrast, good will is included in that valuation.

2.   Dissociation without Dissolution

Article 7's treatment of situations in which a partner dissociates without causing a dissolution of the partnership is quite complex, but the gist is pretty simple: the other partners buy out the dissociating partner's interest and then continue the business on their own. Under UPA (1997) § 701(b):

The buyout price of a dissociated partner's interest is the amount that would have been distributable to the dissociating partner . . . if, on the date of dissociation, the assets of the partnership were sold at a price equal to the greater of the liquidation value or the value based on a sale of the entire business as a going concern without the dissociated partner and the partnership were wound up as of that date.

Interest must be paid from the date of dissociation to the date of payment. If the parties are unable to agree on the correct valuation of the dissociating partner's interest, the dissociating partner may go to court for a judicial appraisal of the value of his interest.[167] If the dissolution is wrongful, any resulting damages "and all other amounts owing, whether or not presently due, from the dissociated partner to the partnership, must be offset against the buyout price."[168]

Dissociation terminates the dissociating partner's actual authority to conduct partnership business. Under § 702(a), however, there is a two-year grace period during which the dissociating partner has some lingering apparent authority. During the first two years following the dissociation, the dissociated partner still can bind the firm by transactions with third parties who reasonably believed he was still a partner and who had neither notice nor knowledge of the dissociation. A dissociated partner is liable to the partnership for any damages caused by such transactions.

Because the partnership continues without legal change, a dissociation has no effect on the rights of creditors vis-à-vis the business or the continuing partners. As for the disassociating partner, he remains liable for debts and other obligations incurred prior to the dissociation unless released by the firm's creditors. In addition, the dissociating partner may be personally liable for debts and obligations incurred by the firm for two years following the dissociation vis-à-vis creditors who reasonably believed the dissociated partner was still a member of the firm and had neither notice nor knowledge of the dissociation.

Either a dissociating partner or the partnership can file with the state a "statement of dissociation" under UPA (1997) § 704. Such a statement is deemed to put creditors on notice of the dissociation. The statement thus cuts off the dissociating partner's otherwise lingering apparent authority and, conversely, insulates the dissociated partner from post-dissociation debts.

3.   *Dissolution and Winding Up*

The UPA (1997)'s process for winding the business up where there is to be a dissolution is substantially similar to that under the UPA (1914). A few key points should be noted, however.

---

[167] UPA (1997) § 701(i).

[168] UPA (1997) § 701(c).

Continuing the business. Recall that § 103 provides that the statute consists mainly of default rules that are subject to be trumped by provisions of the partnership agreement. Under it, some—but not all—of the events of dissolution under § 801 can be trumped by either a buy-sell agreement or a denial of dissolution clause:

> The partnership agreement may not: . . . .
>
> (8) vary the requirement to wind up the partnership business in cases specified in Section 801(4), (5), or (6). . . .

Accordingly, the business must be wound up when the dissociation was caused by:

> (4) an event that makes it unlawful for all or substantially all of the business of the partnership to be continued, but a cure of illegality within 90 days after notice to the partnership of the event is effective retroactively to the date of the event for purposes of this section;
>
> (5) on application by a partner, a judicial determination that:
>
> > (i) the economic purpose of the partnership is likely to be unreasonably frustrated;
> >
> > (ii) another partner has engaged in conduct relating to the partnership business which makes it not reasonably practicable to carry on the business in partnership with that partner; or
> >
> > (iii) it is not otherwise reasonably practicable to carry on the partnership business in conformity with the partnership agreement; or
>
> (6) on application by a transferee of a partner's transferable interest, a judicial determination that it is equitable to wind up the partnership business:
>
> > (i) after the expiration of the term or completion of the undertaking, if the partnership was for a definite term or particular undertaking at the time of the transfer or entry of the charging order that gave rise to the transfer; or
> >
> > (ii) at any time, if the partnership was a partnership at will at the time of the transfer or entry of the charging order that gave rise to the transfer.

In contrast, when the dissociation is triggered by the following events, a buy-sell agreement or denial of dissolution clause will be valid:

(1) in a partnership at will, the partnership's having notice from a partner, other than a partner who is dissociated under Section 601(2) through(10), of that partner's express will to withdraw as a partner, or on a later date specified by the partner;

(2) in a partnership for a definite term or particular undertaking:

(i) within 90 days after a partner's dissociation by death or otherwise under Section 601(6) through (10) or wrongful dissociation under Section 602(b), the express will of at least half of the remaining partners to wind up the partnership business, for which purpose a partner's rightful dissociation pursuant to Section 602(b)(2)(i) constitutes the expression of that partner's will to wind up the partnership business;

(ii) the express will of all of the partners to wind up the partnership business; or

(iii) the expiration of the term or the completion of the undertaking;

(3) an event agreed to in the partnership agreement resulting in the winding up of the partnership business. . . .

Even absent a denial of dissolution clause in the partnership agreement, moreover, the partners "may waive the right to have the partnership's business wound up" by unanimous vote.[169] Partners who rightfully dissociated are entitled to vote on that decision; partners who wrongfully dissociated are not.

Where there is neither a unanimous waiver of dissolution not an applicable buy-sell agreement or denial of dissolution clause, the statutory winding up process is mandatory. In *Corrales v. Corrales*,[170] for example, brothers Rudy and Richard Corrales formed RC Electronics (RCE) in 1989. They entered into a written partnership agreement with an indefinite term, which contained the following buy-sell provision:

In the event of retirement, expulsion, bankruptcy, death or insanity of a general partner, the remaining partners have the right to continue the business of the partnership under the same name by themselves, or in conjunction with any other persons they select.

The brothers had a falling out over an allegedly competing business started by Rudy and in 2005 Richard dissolved the partnership by

---

[169] UPA (1997) § 802(b).
[170] 129 Cal.Rptr.3d 428 (Cal.App. 2011).

written notice. At trial, the court attempted to value the business so that one of the brothers could buy the other out.

On appeal, the appellate court noted that none of the events triggering the buy-sell agreement had occurred. Accordingly, there was no basis for one partner to buyout the other. Instead, the statutory winding up process must be followed:

> The procedure to be followed upon dissolution . . . differs from the buyout procedure of section [701]. There is no buyout. Instead, the partnership's creditors are paid, and then the partners settle accounts between or among themselves, pursuant to section [807].

> When Richard withdrew from RCE, the partnership dissolved by operation of law; by definition, a partnership must consist of at least two persons. A person cannot dissociate from a dissolved partnership, and the buyout rule of section [701] does not apply to a two-person partnership when one partner leaves. When that happens, the dissolution procedures take over. The partnership is wound up, its business is completed, and the partners make whatever adjustments are necessary to their own accounts after paying the creditors.

The court explained that this rule was necessary in order to protect the partnership's creditors. It prevents partnership assets from being used to buyout one of the partners and thus preserves those assets for the benefit of creditors. Note, however, that neither the rule as set forth by the court—nor the rationale behind it—would preclude a partner from using personal assets to purchase the partnership business when it is sold in the winding up process.

Service partnerships. Recall that *Kovacik v. Reed*[171] carved out an exception to the statutory scheme for allocating losses in the class of firms known as service partnerships. Although the drafters of the UPA (1997) explicitly rejected *Kovacik* by name in their official comment to § 401(b), the situation under the UPA (1997) in fact is somewhat more complicated. The difficulty is that § 401(b) deals with charging profits and losses to the partners' capital accounts on a going concern basis. Division of profits and losses in the event of a dissolution, the situation with which *Kovacik* was concerned, is addressed by UPA (1997) § 807(b). The requirement therein that a partner contribute to the partnership an amount equal to any excess of charges over credits appears to continue the UPA (1914) rule and, hence, to confirm the rejection of *Kovacik*. This impression arguably is undermined, however, by the comment

---

[171] 315 P.2d 314 (Cal. 1957). *See generally* Stephen M. Bainbridge, *Contractarianism in the Business Associations Classroom: Kovacik v. Reed and the Allocation of Capital Losses in Service Partnerships*, 34 GA. L. REV. 631 (2000).

to this section, which provides: "The partners may . . . agree to share 'operating' losses differently from 'capital' losses, thereby continuing the UPA distinction." Here is a loophole through which a court could drive *Kovacik*—the court could find an implied agreement that the service-only partner would not be responsible for any share of capital losses, just as the California Supreme Court did in *Kovacik* itself. As yet, there is no definitive case law.

VII. Limited Partnerships

In a general partnership there is usually only one type of investor, a general partner having full rights of management, control, and profit-sharing. Limited partnerships create two classes of partners: general partners, whose rights are largely the same as in a general partnership; and limited partners, who have much less expansive rights, but whose obligations are correspondingly limited.

A. Creation

Most states have adopted the Uniform Limited Partnership Act (ULPA) or the more recent Revised Uniform Limited Partnership Act (RULPA). Under both statutes, creating a limited partnership requires compliance with certain statutory formalities, including filing a limited partnership certificate with the appropriate state official. In states that retain the ULPA, these formalities are especially burdensome because of the substantial amount of information required in the certificate and the resulting need for frequent amendments to update the certificate. The RULPA retains the filing requirement, but the amount of information that must be contained in the certificate is considerably reduced.[172]

B. Separation of Ownership and Control

The ULPA does not actually forbid limited partners from participating in management of the business. A limited partner who does so, however, gives up the principal advantage of being a limited partner; namely, limited liability:

> A limited partner shall not become liable as a general partner unless, in addition to the exercise of his rights and powers as a limited partner, he takes part in the control of the business.[173]

As the statutory language suggests, the general partner has almost unfettered control over the operation of the business.[174] The

---

[172] In addition, a limited partnership interest may be deemed to be a security and thus be subject to the extensive disclosure and filing requirements of the federal and state securities laws.

[173] ULPA § 7.

[174] *See* ULPA § 9 ("A general partner shall have all the rights and powers and be subject to all the restrictions and liabilities of a partner in a partnership without limited partners. . . ."; subject to specified exceptions).

downside for the general partner is that he is fully personally liable for debts and other obligations of the firm, just as in a general partnership. In any case, it is the statutory creation of a class of partners with strong incentives to remain purely passive that probably explains the continuing attractiveness the limited partnership form. Where business considerations advise barring some of the members from participating in control, the limited partnership can be an effective choice of form.

The key issue under these provisions was the extent to which limited partners could provide advice or guidance to the general partners without crossing the line into taking "part in control of the business." The leading case is *Holzman v. De Escamilla*.[175] James Russell and H.W. Andrews formed a limited partnership with Ricardo de Escamilla as the general partner. The partnership operated a farm whose products were marketed through a produce concern controlled by Andrews. In 1943, the partnership entered bankruptcy. The bankruptcy trustee sued Russell and Andrews, claiming they were held liable as general partners by virtue of having taken part in the control of the business of the firm.

The evidence left no doubt that Russell and Andrews in fact controlled the partnership. When decisions were to be made as to what crops to plant, they always participated in the discussions. In at least two cases, they overruled de Escamilla's planting decisions and ordered him to plant other crops. The firm's checking account required that at least two of the three partners sign checks. At least 20 checks were drawn solely on the signatures of Russell and Andrews. In any case, de Escamilla had no power to withdraw funds from the firm's accounts without the consent of at least one of the two partners. Finally, when Russell and Andrews asked de Escamilla to resign as manager, he did so. The court deemed these indicia of participation in control more than adequate to treat Russell and Andrews as general partners who would be personally liable on the firm's debts.

Holzman v. De Escamilla is a very easy case. Russell and Andrews went way over the line. This leaves open, however, the question of exactly where the line is to be drawn. Guidance is provided by the oft-cited decision in *Mount Vernon Savings and Loan Association v. Partridge Associates*,[176] in which the court held that:

> [T]he law does not confine the role of a limited partner to that of a passive investor . . . To the contrary, . . . a limited partner may be actively involved in the day to day operation of the

---

[175] 195 P.2d 833 (Cal.App.1948).
[176] 679 F. Supp. 522 (D.Md.1987).

partnership's affairs, provided that he does not have ultimate decision making responsibility. Thus, the question is not whether [the limited partner] provided advice and counsel to [the general partner] . . . but whether it exercised at least an equal voice in making partnership decisions so as, in effect, to be a general partner.

RULPA § 303(a) provides that: "a limited partner is not liable for the obligations of a limited partnership unless the limited partner is also a general partner or, in addition to the exercise of his rights and powers as a limited partner, he takes part in the control of the business." Although control of the firm basically remains vested in the general partner under the RULPA, the new statute does give limited partners some voting and management rights. RULPA § 303(b), for example, clarifies that "a limited partner does not participate in control . . . solely by . . . (2) consulting with and advising a general partner with respect to the business of the limited partnership."

Under both the ULPA and the initial version of the RULPA, the limited partner apparently was liable without regard to whether creditors believed the limited partner to be a general partner or not. As the *Mount Vernon* decision explained:

> [A] limited partner who disregards the limited partnership form to such an extent that he becomes substantially the same as a general partner has unlimited liability regardless of a plaintiff's knowledge of his role. At the same time, a limited partner may have unlimited liability for exercising less than a general partner's power if the fact that he acted as more than a limited partner was actually known to the plaintiff.[177]

In 1985, however, the RULPA was amended to limit a limited partner's personal liability to those creditors "reasonably believe, based upon the limited partner's conduct, that the limited partner is a general partner."[178]

---

[177] Mount Vernon Savings and Loan Association v. Partridge Associates, 679 F. Supp. 522, 527 (D.Md.1987).

[178] RULPA § 303(a). A New Jersey appeals court has held that the corporate law doctrine known as piercing the corporate veil may be applied to limited partnerships, a step that could significantly increase the liability exposure of limited partners:

> We agree that corporate veil-piercing principles can be applied to a New Jersey limited partnership under appropriate circumstances. However, to pierce the veil there must be evidence that the limited partner participated in the control of the limited partnership's business by taking or attempting action not within the safe harbor of N.J.S.A. 42:2A–27b or dominated the limited partnership and used the limited partnership to perpetrate a fraud or injustice, or otherwise circumvent the law. Both prongs of the domination test must be established by clear and convincing evidence.

Canter v. Lakewood of Voorhees, 22 A.3d 68, 75 (N.J. App. 2011).

C. Insulating the General Partner from Personal Liability

As just discussed in the preceding section, the liability of the general partner of a limited partnership is the same as that of a partner in a regular partnership. General partners thus remain subject to unlimited liability for the business' obligations. Suppose Jane Doe wants to set up a limited partnership that she will control. At the same time, however, Jane is loath to expose her personal assets to liable for the firm's debts. Is there a solution? Sure. Although the ULPA did not expressly address the issue, it was widely held that a corporation could serve as the general partner of a limited partnership.[179] This result was confirmed by RULPA § 101, which defines the term "person" to include a corporation. Jane therefore can set up a corporation, of which she will be the sole shareholder, to serve as the general partner. In order for a creditor of the limited partnership to hold Jane personally liable, the creditor would have to be able to pierce the corporate veil of the incorporated general partner.

The insulation from personal liability thereby provided was expanded significantly by the leading decision in *Frigidaire Sales Corp. v. Union Properties, Inc.*[180] Commercial Investors was a limited partnership. Leonard Mannon and Raleigh Baxter were limited partners therein. Commercial Investors' general partner was Union Properties, which in turn was a corporation of which Mannon and Baxter were shareholders, officers, and directors. After Commercial Investors breached a contract with Frigidaire, the latter sued Mannon and Baxter personally. The court explained:

> We first note that petitioner does not contend that respondents acted improperly by setting up the limited partnership with a corporation as the sole general partner. . . . In Washington, parties may form a limited partnership with a corporation as the sole general partner. . . . Petitioner's sole contention is that respondents should incur general liability for the limited partnership's obligations, because they exercised the day to day control and management of Commercial. Respondents, on the other hand, argue that Commercial was controlled by Union Properties, a separate legal entity, and not by respondents in their individual capacities.

It seems undisputed that Mannon and Baxter did manage CI's business. As a formal matter, however, they did not do so in their individual capacities. Instead, they did so in their capacity as

---

[179] *See, e.g.,* Frigidaire Sales Corp. v. Union Properties, Inc., 562 P.2d 244 (Wash.1977); Port Arthur Trust Co. v. Muldrow, 291 S.W.2d 312 (Tex.1956).

[180] 562 P.2d 244 (Wash.1977).

officers and directors of Union Properties. Accordingly, "because respondents [Mannon and Baxter] scrupulously separated their actions on behalf of the corporation from their personal actions, petitioner never mistakenly assumed that respondents were general partners with general liability." *Ex ante*, if the creditor wanted to hold Mannon and Baxter personally liable, it should have insisted that they personally guarantee Union Properties' debts. *Ex post*, if the creditor wants to reach Mannon's and Baxter's personal assets, it will have to pierce the corporate veil. They can be both limited partners and active officers of the corporate general partner without losing the benefit of limited liability applicable to them in both such capacities.

Given the ease with which a corporate general partner can be created, it seems anachronistic to continue insisting that general partners bear full personal liability for a limited partnership's debts. As we have seen, moreover, there is a general trend towards expanding the realm of limited liability. Limited liability companies and limited liability partnerships, for example, now provide limited liability for many firms that previously would have organized as general partnerships. In light of these developments, many states have now adopted limited liability limited partnership statutes. The so-called LLLP is identical to the traditional limited partnership, except that the general partner gets the benefit of limited liability. Existing limited partnerships may freely convert into LLLPs by filing the appropriate paperwork with the state government.

D. Fiduciary Duties

Given the separation of ownership and control created by the respective rights of general and limited partners under the statute, it should come as no surprise that the former owe fiduciary duties of case and loyalty to the latter.

1. *Waiver of the Duty of Loyalty*

The duties of loyalty owed by a general partner in a limited partnership are largely identical to those present in a general partnership. In the limited partnership context, however, it is critical that those duties be subject to limitation or waiver by contract. In many settings, a single investor or company may act as a general partner in numerous limited partnerships. In real estate, for example, a developer typically sets up a new limited partnership for each new development project. In oil and gas, an exploration firm might have a separate limited partnership for each drilling operation. And so on. As a result, questions can arise as to whether work done by the general partner for one partnership competes with the business of another partnership.

In general, as with partnership law, courts give significant deference to the parties' agreement, but there are important precedents suggesting that while the agreement may modify the duty of loyalty, the agreement may not eliminate that duty. In *Jerman v. O'Leary*,[181] for example, the O'Learys were general partners in a limited partnership formed to develop a mobile home park. After the park was developed and sold, the limited partnership retained ownership of 36 acres, 11 of which were later transferred to the county government in connection with a re-zoning of the property. The O'Learys offered to purchase the remaining 25 acres from the partnership for $110,250. After Jerman objected on grounds that the land was worth considerably more, the O'Learys asked the other limited partners to approve the sale. When they did so, the O'Learys went forward with the transaction. Jerman sued.

The limited partnership statute then in effect held that a general partner could not, without consent of the limited partners, possess partnership property for non-partnership purposes. The limited partnership agreement signed by all members allowed the general partner, without consent of the limited partners, to acquire "less than substantially all" of the partnership property "upon terms which the General Partner shall determine in its sole discretion." The issue presented thus was whether that provision trumped the statute.

The court held that the consent required by the statute could be inferred from the agreement. In dicta, the court went even further, quoting an earlier decision holding "in the absence of an express prohibition, the Act leaves the members of a limited partnership free to determine their rights with respect to each other by any contractual agreement which does not contravene public policy or run afoul of the common law." On the other hand, however, the court strongly suggested that limited partnership law does not provide complete freedom of contract. It held that the general partners had a fiduciary duty to disclose all material information relating to the value of the property, even though the agreement seemed to give the general partner sole discretion to set the terms of the deal.

A third Uniform Limited Partnership Act was promulgated in 2001. Section 110(b)(5) thereof adopts the modify but do not eliminate formulation used in the UPA (1997):

A partnership agreement may not: . . . eliminate the duty of loyalty . . . , but the partnership agreement may: (A) identify specific types or categories of activities that do not violate the

---

[181] 701 P.2d 1205 (Ariz.App.1985).

duty of loyalty, if not manifestly unreasonable; and (B) specify the number or percentage of partners which may authorize or ratify, after full disclosure to all partners of all material facts, a specific act or transaction that otherwise would violate the duty of loyalty. . . .

In contrast, Delaware's limited partnership statute provides that fiduciary "duties may be expanded or restricted or eliminated by provisions in the partnership agreement."[182]

2. *The Duty of Care and the Business Judgment Rule*

Although it is well settled that a general partner owes the limited partners a duty of care, it is sharply debated whether a general partner can be held liable for simple negligence. The majority views seems to be that a version of the corporate law business judgment rule applies to protect the general partner from liability for mere negligence.[183] The rationale, at least in a limited partnership context, appears to rest on the notion that a limited partnership is similar to a corporation with its limited investor liability, delegation of authority to management, and fiduciary obligation owed by management.[184]

E. Duration and Dissolution

The limited partnership has an indefinite duration, with the rules governing dissolution of the limited partnership largely tracking those of a general partnership. One important

---

[182] DEL. CODE ANN., tit. 6, § 17–1101(d). The statute, however, further provides "that the partnership agreement may not eliminate the implied contractual covenant of good faith and fair dealing." *Id.* Interpreting that proviso, the Delaware Chancery Court has explained that:

> The implied covenant is not a substitute for fiduciary duty analysis. "The covenant is 'best understood as a way of implying terms in the agreement'. . . . Existing contract terms control, however, such that implied good faith cannot be used to circumvent the parties' bargain, or to create a free-floating duty unattached to the underlying legal documents." Dunlap v. State Farm Fire & Cas. Co., 878 A.2d 434, 441 (Del.2005) (quoting E.I. DuPont de Nemours & Co. v. Pressman, 679 A.2d 436, 443 (Del.1996)) (other citations omitted). The Court must focus on "what the parties likely would have done if they had considered the issues involved." Cincinnati SMSA Ltd. P'ship v. Cincinnati Bell Cellular Sys. Co., 708 A.2d 989, 992 (Del.1998). It must be "clear from what was expressly agreed upon that the parties who negotiated the express terms of the contract would have agreed to proscribe the act later complained of ... had they thought to negotiate with respect to that matter." Katz v. Oak Indus. Inc., 508 A.2d 873, 880 (Del.Ch.1986) (Allen, C.). "The doctrine thus operates only in that narrow band of cases where the contract as a whole speaks sufficiently to suggest an obligation and point to a result, but does not speak directly enough to provide an explicit answer." Airborne Health, Inc. v. Squid Soap, LP, 984 A.2d 126, 146 (Del.Ch.2009).

Lonergan v. EPE Holdings, LLC, 5 A.3d 1008, 1117–18 (Del. Ch. 2010).

[183] *See, e.g.,* Weinberg v. Lear Fan Corp., 627 F. Supp. 719, 723 (S.D.N.Y 1986) ("the decision of the general partners ... would probably be considered a direct benefit to the limited partners and a decision entitled to protection under the business judgment rule.").

[184] *See* Wyler v. Feuer, 85 Cal. App. 3d 392, 402 (1978).

qualification is that a limited partnership is not deemed to end when a limited partner withdraws or transfers his or her interest.[185]

F.   Transferability of Membership Interest

A limited partnership interest is freely assignable, just as is the case with a general partnership interest. Determining the rights of the assignee is somewhat more complicated in the limited partnership setting then in the general partnership context, however. Under ULPA § 19, the assignee of a limited partnership interest may become a limited partner if (a) the limited partnership certificate authorizes transfers of membership or (b) all other partners consent. RULPA § 704 is essentially identical. Under ULPA § 19(5) transferring a limited partnership interests is somewhat burdensome because it requires filing an amendment to the partnership certificate. The RULPA eliminates that requirement, making limited partnership interests much more liquid.

---

[185] RULPA § 801.

Chapter 4

LIMITED LIABILITY COMPANIES

One of the most important ways in which transactional lawyers can create value for their clients is by helping them choose appropriate organizational structures for their businesses. In considering the problems that arise in this area, it again proves useful to think of the statutes governing different types of business organizations as standard form contracts. When two or more persons enter into a business relationship, they are undertaking an inherently contractual act. They must specify a host of rules to govern their relationship: what are their respective rights and duties, powers and obligations. If the parties choose to structure their relationship as a particular type of business organization, much of this work will already have been accomplished. The statute provides a sort of standardized contract, which lowers bargaining and other transaction costs by providing a set of default rules the parties can adopt off the rack. At the same time, because most statutory rules in this area are merely default rules, it is possible to modify the standard form contract when and as necessary to more closely tailor the firm to the clients' needs.

Until recently, the only important standard form contracts provided by most states were the corporation and the general partnership. During the 1990s, however, most states have added a third standard form contract to this short list of options: the limited liability company (LLC).[1] To be sure, LLCs have been around for a couple of decades. Prior to 1988, however, only a few states had adopted LLC statutes and very few had been formed. In that year, the situation changed dramatically because the Internal Revenue Service concluded that LLCs could be classified as a partnership for federal tax purposes.[2] With that development, the concept took off. LLCs provide a standard form contract that incorporates many of the most attractive features of partnerships and corporations. In particular, they combine the latter's limited liability with the former's pass through tax treatment.

---

[1] See generally William J. Carney, Limited Liability Companies: Origins and Antecedents, 66 U. COLO. L. REV. 855 (1995); Wayne M. Gazur, The Limited Liability Company Experiment: Unlimited Flexibility, Uncertain Role, 58 LAW AND CONTEMP. PROBS. 135 (1995); Robert R. Keatinge et al., The Limited Liability Company: A Study of the Emerging Entity, 47 BUS. LAW. 375 (1992); Larry E. Ribstein, The New Choice of Entity for Entrepreneurs, 26 CAP. U. L. REV. 325 (1997); Larry E. Ribstein, The Emergence of the Limited Liability Company, 51 BUS. LAW. 1 (1995).

[2] Rev. Rul. 88–76, 1988–2 Cum. Bull. 360. *See generally* William A. Klein & Eric Zolt, *Business Form, Limited Liability, and Tax Regimes: Lurching Toward a Coherent Outcome?*, 66 U. COLO. L. REV. 1001 (1995).

The rapid growth of the LLC phenomena has resulted in a considerably more complex legal environment than is the case with partnership law. The Uniform Limited Liability Company Act (ULLCA) was not promulgated until 1995, by which time many states had already adopted LLC codes. In many states, moreover, the liberalization of the tax regulations when the check-the-box system was adopted (see Chapter 1) triggered a second wave of amendments and recodifications of the LLC statute. As a result, there is considerable variation among LLC statutes. As of 2013, only 9 states had adopted the ULLCA. A Revised Uniform Limited Liability Company Act (RULLCA) was promulgated in 2006, but had been adopted by only two states as of 2013. In this text, we therefore focus mainly on general principles rather than specific statutes.[3]

I. Origins

The first LLC statute was passed by Wyoming in 1977. Why Wyoming? A fine state, to be sure, but not one normally thought of as a source of cutting edge business organization law. The answer seems to be the importance of oil and gas to the Wyoming economy.

At that time, oil & gas companies were eligible for a number of special tax deductions, especially for those for intangible drilling costs. As a result, oil and gas drilling projects were popular tax shelter investments for high-bracket taxpayers. Because the risk of drilling a dry hole is high, however, such investments easily could become worthless or even end up with substantial liabilities. Because passive investors generally wish to avoid taking on any additional liabilities beyond their original investment, oil & gas drilling ventures had to be structured in a way that would (1) allow them to get the tax benefits attributable to the drilling operation and (2) limit investor liability.

Before LLCs were developed, the only vehicles by which one could accomplish both goals were S corporations and limited partnerships. S corporations are not as flexible or useful as partnerships because the tax attributes of the corporation get attributed to the shareholders in proportion to their shares, whereas in a partnership it is possible to provide in the partnership agreement how the tax attributes are going to be allocated. For example, if you wanted to set up the business so that the passive

---

[3] The question of whether a membership interest in an LLC is a security for purposes of the federal or state securities laws is beyond the scope of this text. *See generally* Larry Ribstein, *Form and Substance in the Definition of a "Security": The Case of Limited Liability Companies,* 51 WASHINGTON & LEE L. REV. 807 (1994); *see also* J. William Callison, *Changed Circumstances: Eliminating the Williamson Presumption that General Partnership Interests are not Securities,* 58 BUS. LAW. 1373 (2003).

investors got certain deductions allocated solely to them rather than to the general partner, you could do so. Indeed, this ability to allocate tax benefits was critical to how these investments were marketed.

Limited partnerships therefore long were the vehicle of choice for most oil and gas drilling ventures that were marketed to passive investors as tax-sheltered investments. One of the problems with a limited partnership, however, was that it had to have at least one general partner, which would not be protected from the partnership's liabilities. The answer to that problem was easy, of course; one simply created a corporation to serve as the general partner. (Today, one could use a limited liability limited partnership, as well.) Under the tax code of that era, however, there were a number of cumbersome restrictions on a tax shelter limited partnership's ability to use a incorporated general partner.

The idea behind the LLC was that it could be treated as a partnership for tax purposes without either having to have a general partner or worrying about whether an incorporated general partner would pass muster with the IRS. The Wyoming legislature wanted to attract investors to invest in Wyoming oil & gas production, so it enacted the first LLC act to make it easier for the promoters to organize the investment entities. All of this depended, of course, on the IRS' willingness to treat the LLC as a partnership for tax purposes. Once it did so, however, the rest was history. Today every state has an LLC statute and the number of LLCs is skyrocketing. Indeed, it seems fair to say that the LLC has become the organizational form of choice for most small businesses. (See Figure 1.1)

II. Formation

In most states, filing articles of organization with the appropriate state official creates an LLC.[4] The articles of organization are comparable to corporate articles of incorporation and are treated as such by the statute with respect to such questions as amendment and filing. In addition, the LLC may adopt an operating agreement, which fulfills many of the same functions as a partnership agreement or corporate bylaws.[5] As is also true of corporations and limited partnerships, the LLC must comply with various additional formalities, such as maintaining a registered office and keeping certain records.

---

[4] *See* ULLCA § 202(b) ("Unless a delayed effective date is specified, the existence of a limited liability company begins when the articles of organization are filed.").

[5] The operating agreement need not be in writing. See, e.g., ULLCA § 103(a).

A.   Choosing the State of Formation

Although most corporations are organized under the laws of the state in which the LLC has its principal place of business, there is no legal requirement that one do so. Instead, as with corporations, one may choose to form an LLC in the state that offers the most attractive package of statutory provisions, case law, taxes, and other considerations. As with corporations, moreover, Delaware is increasingly dominating the market for LLC formations:

> Where are LLCs formed if they are not formed locally? For out-of-state formations, Delaware emerges as the destination of choice. Of all LLCs in our sample that are formed outside their PPB state, no less than 54 percent have chosen Delaware as their state of formation. Moreover, we find strong size effects .... Of those LLCs that have between 20 and 99 employees and that are formed outside their PPB state, about 41 percent are formed in Delaware. That percentage increases as the number of employees increases. Indeed, for LLCs with 5,000 or more employees, Delaware attracts roughly 95 percent of those firms that are formed outside their PPB state. . . .

> Incidentally, the dominance of Delaware in the market for out-of-state LLC formations also becomes obvious if one compares Delaware's numbers to those of the runner-up states. Whereas Delaware attracts 54.44 percent of all out-of-state LLC formations, the next most successful states are Florida and Nevada (each of which has a modest 3.14 percent of such LLC formations), followed by Texas (2.46 percent), Georgia and New York (2.19 percent each), Ohio and Virginia (2.12 percent each), Illinois (1.91 percent), California (1.84 percent), and North Carolina (1.84 percent).[6]

As is also true of corporations, the choice of state in which to form an LLC matters because of the choice of law rule known as the internal affairs doctrine. Under it, the law of the state in which the LLC law was organized governs disputes over LLC governance and related matters.[7]

---

[6] Jens Dammann & Matthias Schündeln, Where are Limited Liability Companies Formed? An Empirical Analysis, 55 J. L. & Econ. 741, 745–46 (2012).

[7] *See, e.g.,* Fusion Capital Fund II, LLC v. Ham, 614 F.3d 698, 700 (7th Cir.2010) (whether a corporation's investors are liable for its debts "is an aspect of the internal affairs doctrine," which dictates application of the law of the state of formation); In re Mervyn's Holdings, LLC, 426 B.R. 488 (Bkrtcy. D.Del. 2010) ("The internal affairs doctrine directs federal courts sitting in Delaware to apply the law of the state of organization to claims that implicate an organization's internal affairs."); Ritchie Capital Management, L.L.C. v. Coventry First LLC, 2007 WL 2044656 at *4 (S.D.N.Y. 2007) (applying Delaware law to a corporate veil piercing claim brought against a Delaware limited liability company, citing the internal affairs doctrine as the basis therefor); *see also* ULLCA § 1001(a) ("The laws of the State or other jurisdiction under which a foreign limited liability company is organized govern its

B.   Content of the Articles of Organization

The name of the newly formed LLC, which must be set out in the articles of organization, must include the words limited liability company, the abbreviation LLC, or a sufficiently similar phrase to alert third parties that the entity with which they are dealing has limited liability for its owners.[8] The ULLCA requires that the articles specify if the LLC is to be managed by a manager rather than its members.[9] Neither the RULLCA nor the DLLCA contain such a requirement.

C.   Non-Profit and Low Profit LLCs

Unlike a partnership, a LLC need not be a for profit business. RULLCA § 104(b), for example, provides that an LLC "may have any lawful purpose, regardless of whether for profit." The comment to that section explains that:

> The subsection does not bar a limited liability company from being organized to carry on charitable activities, and this act does not include any protective provisions pertaining to charitable purposes. Those protections must be (and typically are) found in other law, although sometimes that "other law" appears within a state's non-profit corporation statute.

Several states now also have separate statutes authorizing formation of "low profit limited liability companies" (L3Cs):

> These statutes are intended to facilitate investments by private foundations that seek exemptions as nonprofits under § 501(c)(3) of the Internal Revenue Code. The foundations may be assessed excise taxes if they make investments that jeopardize their charitable purposes. Congress enacted provisions in the Tax Reform Act of 1969 for "program related investments" (PRIs) that would exempt these foundations from the excise taxes. However, forty years after the birth of the concept, few foundations were using PRIs—perhaps because of ambiguity of the definition of PRIs. L3C statutes are intended to solve this problem by creating a form of entity that is clearly limited to charitable-type purposes. . . .
>
>   . . . [T]he L3C provides default rules that, even apart from the PRI rules, address the difficulty of contracting for hybrid profit/nonprofit entities. This particularly includes defining the

---

organization and internal affairs and the liability of its managers, members, and their transferees.").

[8] ULLCA § 105. Typically, the name of the LLC and the identity of its owners also must be disclosed in a fictitious business name filing.

[9] ULLCA § 203(a)(6).

fiduciary duties of managers who must serve both society and markets. Although existing business associations let managers of essentially for-profit firms mingle profit-making with social responsibility and permit contracting to alter the mix of these objectives, the L3C adds clear structural rules for defining the duties in such hybrid firms. These rules not only provide guidance for managers, but also help signal the firm's objectives to investors and customers.[10]

D.   Single Member LLCs

Early LLC statutes tracked partnership law by requiring that the LLC have at least two members and be formed for the purpose of pursuing a business for profit. More recent LLC statutes have relaxed both requirements. As a result, most states now allow the LLC to be formed for any lawful purpose. Sole proprietorships thus may now form LLCs in most states:

> Since most states do not restrict ownership, members may include individuals, corporations, other LLCs and foreign entities. There is no maximum number of members. Most states also permit "single member" LLCs, those having only one owner. . . .[11]

E.   Shelf and Series LLCs

A growing number of states allow the organizer to form a so-called shelf LLC, which has no members as of the time it is formed. RULLCA § 201, for example, provides that:

> (b) A certificate of organization must state: . . .
>
> (3) if the company will have no members when the [Secretary of State] files the certificate, a statement to that effect.
>
> (e) If a filed certificate of organization contains a statement as provided in subsection (b)(3), the following rules apply:
>
> (1) The certificate lapses and is void unless, within [90] days from the date the [Secretary of State] files the certificate, an organizer signs and delivers to the [Secretary of State] for filing a notice stating:
>
> (A) that the limited liability company has at least one member; and

---

[10] Bruce H. Kobayashi & Larry E. Ribstein, *Law as Product and Byproduct*, 9 J.L. ECON. & POL'Y 521, 552–53 (2013).

[11] Baltimore Street Builders v. Stewart, 975 A.2d 271, 274 n.2 (Md.App. 2009).

(B) the date on which a person or persons became the company's initial member or members.

(2) If an organizer complies with paragraph (1), a limited liability company is deemed formed as of the date of initial membership stated in the notice delivered pursuant to paragraph (1).

(3) Except in a proceeding by this state to dissolve a limited liability company, the filing of the notice described in paragraph (1) by the [Secretary of State] is conclusive proof that the organizer satisfied all conditions to the formation of a limited liability company.

Once formed, an LLC whose certificate contains such a provision waits "on the shelf" for someone to join it. A number of service companies now routinely form shelf LLCs that they maintain in inventory for sale to business persons who thus avoid the need to go through the formalities of creation. Neither the ULLCA nor the DLLCA contain a shelf LLC provision.

The DLLCA does, however, permit formation of a so-called "series LLC":

A limited liability company agreement may establish or provide for the establishment of 1 or more designated series of members, managers, limited liability company interests or assets. Any such series may have separate rights, powers or duties with respect to specified property or obligations of the limited liability company or profits and losses associated with specified property or obligations, and any such series may have a separate business purpose or investment objective.[12]

DLLCA § 215(b) provides that debts and obligations of a series LLC "shall be enforceable against the assets of such series only, and not against the assets of the limited liability company generally or any other series thereof," provided that "the records maintained for any such series account for the assets associated with such series separately from the other assets of the limited liability company" and "notice of the limitation on liabilities of a series as referenced in this subsection is set forth in the certificate of formation of the limited liability company." Each series can have the same or different membership and management. The series LLC thus allows one to operate several distinct businesses under a single legal umbrella, which may reduce franchise taxes, filing fees, and other expenses, while ensuring that the liabilities of each series LLC are limited to the series that incurred the debt or obligation. In light of

---

[12] DLLCA § 215(a). Neither the ULLCA nor the RULLCA contain provisions for series LLCs.

the judicial willingness to adapt the doctrine of piercing the corporate veil to the LLC context, however, the purported advantages of the series LLC seem somewhat dubious.

F.   Conversion from Other Organizational Forms

ULLCA § 902 authorizes conversion of partnerships or limited partnerships to LLCs. The pre-conversion debts of the partnership automatically become debts of the LLC.[13] Per § 902(g), however, members remain liable as partners vis-à-vis pre-conversion partnership debts. The IRS typically treats such a conversion as a nonrecognition event, so that there are no tax consequences for the new LLC's owners.

There is no provision in the ULLCA for converting a corporation into an LLC. If such a reorganization is desired, it is typically affected by merging the corporation into a shell LLC, with the LLC as the surviving entity. The IRS treats such a merger as a potential tax recognition event to which the tax free reorganization provisions generally do not apply. As a result, such a reorganization often has adverse tax consequences for the owners of the business.

G.   Liability for Pre-Formation Transactions

Just as promoters of a corporation can run into legal difficulties for conducting business on behalf of a corporation during the formation process, so may members of a newly formed LLC. In *Water, Waste & Land, Inc. d/b/a Westec v. Lanham*,[14] Larry Clark and Donald Lanham formed Preferred Income Investors, LLC (P.I.I.), a Colorado LLC. Clark then entered into an oral contract with Westec, a land development and engineering company, pursuant to which Westec was to perform engineering work in connection with construction of a fast food restaurant. Clark's business card had the letters "P.I.I." above the business address, but there was no indication that P.I.I. was an LLC. Westec did the work for which Clark had hired it, but was never paid. Westec sued both the LLC and Clark and Lanham in their individual capacities.

Under Colorado's LLC statute, filing of the articles of organization is deemed to serve of constructive notice to third parties that the business is an LLC. Lanham and Clark relied on that provision to claim that Westec had constructive notice that it was dealing with an LLC. In turn, they claimed that as members of the LLC they were entitled to limited liability. In their view, Westec

---

[13] ULLCA § 903 (b)(2). In C & J Builders and Remodelers v. Geisenheimer, 733 A.2d 193 (Conn.1999), the court applied the partnership-to-LLC conversion rules by analogy to creation of an LLC by a sole proprietor. Accordingly, the LLC had successor liability for the obligations of the proprietorship.

[14] 955 P.2d 997 (Colo.1998).

could only pursue the LLC for payment. The court rejected that argument:

> We hold . . . that the statutory notice provision applies only where a third party seeks to impose liability on an LLC's members or managers simply due to their status as members or managers of the LLC. When a third party sues a manager or member of an LLC under an agency theory, the principles of agency law apply notwithstanding the LLC Act's statutory notice rules.

The court then held that Clark had acted as an agent on behalf of both the LLC and Lanham. Since Westec knew that Clark was Lanham's agent, Clark was excused from liability on the contract. As for Lanham, however, the court held (1) that Lanham had acted as an agent on behalf of the LLC in executing the contract and (2) that Lanham had not informed Westec he was acting on behalf of an LLC. As we saw in Chapter 2, an agent of an undisclosed principal is liable on the contract. Since Lanham was the LLC's agent, but the LLC was undisclosed to Westec, Lanham was personally liable on the contract.

In some such cases, courts have considered whether the corporate law doctrines of de facto corporation and corporation by estoppel should be applied to the LLC context. If the promoter failed to form a legal corporation because of some technical defect in the incorporation process, a court may nevertheless treat the business as a de facto corporation.[15] The rationale seems to be a concern that imposing full personal liability on the promoter may amount to a windfall for the other party to the transaction, which probably believed it was dealing with a corporation having limited liability. If so, the rule makes good economic sense.[16] As long as the creditor thought it was dealing with a de jure corporation, the firm's defective incorporation is irrelevant. Personal liability would constitute a windfall the creditor did not expect and has done

---

[15] A de jure corporation is a true corporation: A legal entity that has been validly formed by complying with all statutory requirements. The term is also sometimes used for corporations that substantially complied with the statutory requirements for incorporation, but failed to comply with some very minor technical requirement. In the latter case, neither the state nor nonstate parties may contest the corporation's existence. If a defect in the incorporation process prevents the business from being treated as a de jure corporation, but the promoter made a good faith effort to incorporate the business, and carried on the business as though it were a corporation, some courts treat the firm as a de facto corporation. The state may contest the existence of the corporation, but nonstate parties who transact business with a de facto corporation may not hold the firm's promoters or investors personally liable for the firm's obligations.

[16] The economic argument for not allowing creditors of a de facto corporation to hold shareholders personally liable is essentially the same as that for granting limited liability to shareholders of de jure corporations. For an analysis of the economics of limited liability, see Stephen M. Bainbridge, *Abolishing Veil Piercing*, 26 J. Corp. L. 479 (2001).

nothing to earn. Put another way, giving a second bite at the apple to people who could have cheaply protected themselves creates perverse incentives, promotes litigation, and discourages investment.

The basic standard for invoking the de facto corporation doctrine is whether (1) there was a good faith effort to incorporate the business and (2) the putative shareholders carried on the business as though it were a corporation, especially with respect to the transaction in question.[17] Some jurisdictions use an alternative three-part test: (1) a statute must exist under which incorporation was legally possible; (2) there was a "colorable" (a.k.a. "bona fide") attempt to incorporate the business; and (3) there was an actual use or exercise of corporate powers and privileges.[18] The difference between the two tests is largely semantic. Both tend to collapse into the question of whether there was a good faith effort to incorporate the business.

The de facto corporation doctrine does not forbid the state from contesting the corporation's existence in a quo warranto proceeding brought to terminate the putative corporation's existence.[19] It simply holds that private parties who transact business with a de facto corporation may not hold the firm's promoters or investors personally liable for the firm's obligations.[20] In other words, investors in a de facto corporation get the benefit of limited liability, just as though the business were a de jure corporation.[21]

---

[17] *See, e.g.,* Cantor v. Sunshine Greenery, Inc., 398 A.2d 571 (N.J. App. Div. 1979).

[18] Fred S. McChesney, *Doctrinal Analysis and Statistical Modeling in Law: The Case of Defective Incorporation*, 71 WASH. U.L.Q. 493, 498–99 (1993).

[19] If the defect in the incorporation is minor, the court may treat the business as a de jure corporation. If so, the business' corporate existence may not even be challenged by the state.

[20] In Cantor v. Sunshine Greenery, Inc., 398 A.2d 571 (N.J. 1979), for example, the promoter mailed articles of incorporation to the secretary of state's office. The articles were officially filed only after some unexplained delay. In the meanwhile, assuming that the articles had been filed and that the corporation existed, the promoter entered into a lease on the corporation's behalf. The lessor had considerable business experience, but did not require the promoter to guarantee the lease personally. Instead, the lessor knew and expected that the corporation would be responsible for the lease. When the corporation failed to perform, lessor sought to hold the promoter personally liable. The court held that, because of the delay in filing the articles, the business was not a legal corporation at the time the lease was made. The promoter's execution of articles of incorporation, the good faith effort to file them, and the carrying on of business in the corporation's name, however, justified treating the firm as a de facto corporation. The promoter therefore could not be held personally liable. Id.

[21] The case against imposing personal liability on shareholders of a defectively incorporated business is stronger yet when the third party seeks to hold liable participants other than the promoter. Courts have been willing to invoke the de facto corporation doctrine to protect an investor who actively participates in the firm's business in the honest and reasonable belief that the firm was properly incorporated. Inactive investors present an even stronger case for invoking the de facto corporation doctrine and are rarely held personally liable for the firm's obligations. *See, e.g.,*

Cases occasionally arise in which the promoter made no good faith effort to incorporate the business. This failure precludes one from invoking the de facto corporation doctrine. As noted, however, imposing full personal liability on the firm's would-be shareholders gives the other party to the transaction a windfall. Courts developed the corporation by estoppel doctrine to deal with such cases. The corporation by estoppel doctrine differs from the more familiar concept of equitable estoppel. There is no requirement of a misrepresentation, of reasonable reliance, or of a change in position. Instead, someone who deals with the firm as though it were a corporation is estopped later to deny the corporation's existence.[22]

Several cases have applied these doctrines to LLCs. In *In re Hausman*,[23] for example, both the majority and dissent agreed that New York law recognized a de facto LLC doctrine analogous to the de facto corporation doctrine. The majority held that the test for de facto status was not met on the facts of the case, because there was no good faith effort to form the corporation prior to entering into the transaction in question, while the dissent thought a sufficient effort had been made.[24]

Flanagan v. Jackson Wholesale Bldg. Supply Co., 461 So.2d 761, 765 (Miss. 1984) (declining to hold inactive investor personally liable).

[22] A leading example of the doctrine in action is Cranson v. Int'l Business Machines Corp., 200 A.2d 33 (Md. 1964), in which the defendant was asked to invest in a corporation that was about to be created. Defendant was advised by an attorney that the business had been incorporated. Defendant bought shares, received a stock certificate, was shown the corporation's seal and minute book. Defendant was elected an officer and director of the corporation. The firm operated as though it were a corporation and conducted business in its corporate name. Due to an oversight by the attorney, of which defendant was unaware, the firm was not incorporated until about seven months after Defendant invested in the firm. During that period the corporation entered into a contract to purchase typewriters from a supplier. The supplier dealt with the firm as though it were a corporation, and dealt with Defendant as an agent of the firm. When the corporation defaulted, the supplier sought to hold Defendant personally liable. The court held that the supplier was estopped to deny the corporation's existence and, accordingly, could not hold Defendant personally liable.

In *Cranson*, the Maryland Court of Appeals distinguished the corporation by estoppel doctrine from the de facto corporation doctrine by holding that the latter could be invoked only if articles of incorporation were filed. A corporation by estoppel, however, could be found because the third party had dealt with the firm as though it were a corporation and relied on the firm, not the individual defendant, for performance. While there is general agreement that the de facto corporation doctrine requires a good faith effort to incorporate, opinion is divided as to whether *Cranson* correctly held that a failure to file articles of incorporation—standing alone—precludes application of the de facto corporation doctrine.

[23] 858 N.Y.S.2d 330 (N.Y. App. 2008).

[24] *See also* Duray Development, LLC v. Perrin, 792 N.W.2d 749 (Mich.App. 2010) (holding that both the corporation by estoppel and de facto corporation doctrines apply equally to LLCs); Ruggio v. Vining, 755 So.2d 792, 795 (Fla. App. 2000) (holding that "traditional defenses" of de facto corporation and corporation by estoppel apply to LLCs).

On the other hand, in *Stone v. Jetmar Properties, LLC*,[25] an intermediate state appellate court held that because Minnesota's corporation statute had abolished the doctrines of corporation by estoppel and de facto corporation, that the LLC statute must also prohibit their use. The court also explained that because "the LLC statute provides organizers with an indisputably simple route to formal organization" "it is doubtful that one could actually make an unsuccessful 'colorable attempt' to organize a de jure LLC."

In light of the persistence of the doctrines in their corporate law home, despite the efforts of some reformers to abolish them, one suspects that they will continue to be adapted by most state courts to the LLC context.

H.   Fiduciary Duties of Organizers

In addition to potential liability for LLC obligations, the organizers of an LLC have fiduciary duties to its eventual members. In *Roni LLC v. Arfa*,[26] for example, LLC investors brought an action against the LLC's promoters for accounting, breach of fiduciary duty, and constructive fraud, arising from allegations that the promoters made secret profits from a series of business transactions in which the LLCs purchased and managed multi-family residential buildings in Harlem and the Bronx. The court held that "the organizer of a limited liability company is a fiduciary of the investors it solicits to become members. . . . The fiduciary duty includes the obligation to disclose fully any interests of the promoter that might affect the company and its members, including profits that the promoter makes from organizing the company."

III. Members' Interests

One of the great advantages of the public corporation as an investment vehicle is the free transferability of shares. In contrast, an ownership interest in a partnership is essentially nontransferable. In this respect, the LLC more closely resembles the partnership. Admission of a new member requires unanimous consent, unless the operating agreement provides to the contrary. The assignee of an ownership interest receives only an entitlement to the assignor's share of profits.[27]

The degree to which ownership interests are freely transferable, however, rarely will be dispositive of the choice of form issue. Although shares of stock in a closely held corporation are

---

[25] 733 N.W.2d 480 (Minn.App.2007).

[26] 903 N.Y.S.2d 352 (N.Y. App. Div. 2010).

[27] Absent contrary agreement, most statutes allocate profits and losses on the basis of the value of members' contributions. ULLCA § 405(a), however, uses a partnership-like equal shares rule.

freely transferable in theory, the lack of a readily available secondary trading market for such shares means that in practice they are seldom easily transferable. Moreover, investors in a closely held corporation will often prefer to restrict transferability. Like any other personal relationship, the success or failure of a small business often depends upon maintaining a rather delicate balance between the owners. Free transferability of ownership interests can threaten that balance. In closely held corporations, accordingly, the standard form contract is often modified in ways that make it closely resemble partnerships or LLCs.

Conversely, the partnership and LLC rules are merely default rules. In both cases, the rules restricting transferability are subject to any contrary agreement the founders wish to make. If your clients want free transferability, you can thus provide it within the partnership or LLC context, subject of course to tax considerations and the practical limitations imposed by the absence of a secondary trading market.[28]

IV. Governance

The decisionmaking processes of business enterprises fall on a spectrum between two poles that might be labeled consensus and authority. In small business firms, those who own the firm usually also are the firm's decisionmakers. Their decisionmaking processes tend to be based on consensus, lacking formality or hierarchy. This is possible because there is a limited number of owner managers who share the same basic goal and have more or less the same level of information about the firm. Equality of information ensures that each partner can correctly determine the course of action that best advances his interests; commonality of interest ensures that the partners usually will agree on the course of action to be pursued.

As firms become larger, however, consensus becomes increasingly impractical. By the time we reach the public corporation, it becomes essentially impossible. At the most basic level, the sheer mechanics of achieving consensus amongst thousands of decisionmakers preclude an active role for shareholders. Yet, even if those mechanical obstacles could be overcome, active shareholder participation in corporate decisionmaking would still be precluded by the shareholders' widely divergent interests and distinctly different levels of information. The decisionmaking processes of large corporation are thus based

---

[28] In setting up a partnership or closely held corporation, the transaction planner should normally ask the client to consider an appropriate buyout agreement. Unlike its corporate and partnership counterparts, the LLC statute includes a default buyout provision pursuant to which a member who resigns is entitled to the fair value of his interest in the firm. *See, e.g.,* ULLCA §§ 701–02.

on authority models. Formality and hierarchy are the orders of the day.

This economic reality is reflected in the default rules provided by the various statutes. State law allows one to choose between off the rack governance systems ranging from an almost purely consensus based model to an almost purely authority based model. At one extreme, the default decisionmaking structure provided by partnership law is a consensus model. Partners have equal rights to participate in management of the firm on a one vote per partner basis. This rule makes sense for most small businesses because all partners are also entitled to share equally in profits and losses, giving them essentially identical interests (namely higher profits), and are entitled to equal access to information, giving them essentially identical levels of information.

At the other extreme, a publicly held corporation's decisionmaking structure is principally an authority based one. As a practical matter, most public corporations are marked by a separation of ownership and control. Shareholders, who are said to "own" the firm, have virtually no power to control either its day to day operation or its long term policies. Instead, the statutory model contemplates that the vast majority of corporate decisions shall be made by the board of directors (or their subordinates) acting alone. The default corporate decisionmaking model thus is one in which the board acts and shareholders, at most, react. This statutory framework is given teeth by the rules governing corporate limited liability. Under state corporate law, failure to comply with corporate formalities of this sort is one of the factors to be considered when a creditor seeks to pierce the corporate veil.

Both the corporation and partnership statutes provide substantial flexibility to vary from the default rules provided by statute. Under partnership law, the statutory one partner/one vote model is subject to "any" contrary agreement amongst the partners.[29] A general partnership thus can have any decisionmaking structure upon which its members are able to reach agreement. This flexibility is particularly valuable for mid-sized firms, in which formal corporate like decisionmaking remains inappropriate but some degree of centralized decisionmaking is nevertheless desirable. Similarly, under many corporation statutes, a shareholder agreement may treat the corporation as though it were a partnership for this purpose.

The LLC statute provides similar flexibility. The default rule is comparable to the general partnership form, vesting management in the LLC's members, except that a member's proportional share

---

[29] UPA (1914) § 18.

in the aggregate book value of the firm's membership interests determines the number of votes cast by each member.[30] In general, both of these rules are subject to any contrary provisions of the articles of organization and operating agreement. The LLC thus provides substantial flexibility in structuring the firm's decisionmaking processes. If desired, for example, one could establish a virtual dictatorship. If the articles of organization so provide, the members may elect a manager who shall have such authority and responsibility as the members may delegate in the operating agreement or articles of organization.[31] Unless specifically retained by them therein, the members thereby lose control over areas delegated to the manager. Alternatively, because one can have multiple managers, it is be possible to operate by committee or even to set up a corporate like board of managers. Unfortunately, however, the flexibility provided by the LLC statute is achieved at the cost of specificity. If the LLC's decisionmaking structure is to vary from the standard form contract, detailed contractual provisions are thus essential if later disputes are to be avoided.

V. Limited Liability and Veil Piercing in the LLC Context

In corporate law, the doctrine of limited liability holds that shareholders of a corporation generally are not liable for debts incurred or torts committed by the firm. Shareholder losses when the firm faces financial difficulties are limited to the amount the shareholder has invested in the firm—i.e., the amount initially paid by the shareholder to purchase his stock.

Despite the statutory guarantee of limited liability for shareholders of a corporation, however, unlimited personal liability may be involuntarily thrust upon a shareholder via the equitable remedy known as piercing the corporate veil. "The 'veil' of the 'corporate fiction,' or the 'artificial personality' of the corporation is 'pierced,' and the individual or corporate shareholder exposed to personal or corporate liability, as the case may be, when a court determines that the debt in question is not really a debt of the corporation, but ought, in fairness, to be viewed as a debt of the individual or corporate shareholder or shareholders."[32]

---

[30] ULLCA § 404. This is not true of all LLC statutes. In a number of states, the LLC code's default allocation of voting power follows the partnership rule of one-person/one-vote.

[31] ULLCA § 404.

[32] STEPHEN B. PRESSER, PIERCING THE CORPORATE VEIL § 1.01 at 1–6 (1991 and supp.) (footnotes and emphasis omitted). Shareholders may also face personal liability in connection with watered stock or unlawful dividends. In some states, special statutory provisions impose personal liability on shareholders with respect to

LLC statutes likewise provide limited liability for LLC members. ULLCA § 303, for example, states that:

> The debts, obligations, and liabilities of a limited liability company, whether arising in contract, tort, or otherwise, are solely the debts, obligations, and liabilities of the company. A member or manager is not personally liable for a debt, obligation, or liability of the company solely by reason of being or acting as a member or manager.

Given the corporate precedent, the question inevitably arose whether corporate law's veil piercing rules carried over to the LLC context. Courts and commentators have uniformly concluded that the LLC form does not provide truly unlimited limited liability; rather, the LLC veil may be pierced in appropriate circumstances.[33] In some cases they were compelled to this result by statute, but they have done so even when the statute was silent.[34]

A. Statutes Invoking Veil Piercing

Minnesota's LLC statute provides that "case law that states the conditions and circumstances under which the corporate veil of a corporation may be pierced under Minnesota law also applies to limited liability companies."[35] In *Tom Thumb Food Markets, Inc. v. TLH Properties, LLC*,[36] one Hartmann, acting for TLH, agreed to build a building for Tom Thumb on property owned by Smith.

---

certain corporate debts. New York and Wisconsin, for example, do so with respect to employee wages. *Id.*

[33] *See* Kaycee Land and Livestock v. Flahive, 46 P.3d 323, 327–28 (Wyo. 2002) (citing authorities). In some regulatory settings, veil piercing-like standards are mandated by statute or rule. In plant closing litigation arising under the federal Worker Adjustment and Retraining Notification Act (the "WARN Act"), 29 U.S.C. § 2101 et seq., for example, the issue often arises as to whether corporate or LLC subsidiaries should be treated as a "single employer" along with their parents. The federal Department of Labor has promulgated a standard closely resembling corporate veil piercing for use in making that determination. UAW Local 157 v. OEM/Erie Westland, LLC, 203 F.Supp.2d 825, 832–33 (E.D. Mich. 2002). In addition, courts often supplement the DOL standard with ordinary corporate veil piercing principles. *Id.* at 833.

Courts also often use veil piercing-based theories in procedural settings. *See, e.g.,* Hesni v. Williams & Boshea, LLC, 2002 WL 373273 (E.D. La. 2002) (holding that because plaintiff would be able to pierce the LLC's veil to hold an individual personally liable consent of that individual was required in order for the case to be removed federal court).

[34] The statutory language governing LLC member liability "varies significantly among the states." Rebecca J. Huss, *Revamping Veil Piercing for all Limited Liability Entities: Forcing the Common Law into the Statutory Age,* 70 U. Cin. L. Rev. 95, 101 (2001). For a useful taxonomy of the various approaches states have taken to the question of LLC member liability, albeit one whose assignments of individual states to particular approaches is now out-of-date, see Robert B. Thompson, *The Limits of Liability in the New Limited Liability Entities*, 32 Wake Forest L. Rev. 1, 14–18 (1997) (analyzing the various state LLC statutes).

[35] Minn. Stat. § 322B.303(2). At one time, a number of other states had similar provisions, although these have largely faded away.

[36] 1999 WL 31168 (Minn. App. 1999).

Hartmann represented that he owned the property. In fact, Hartman did not own the property, but believed that he had a deal with one Smith to develop it. After the project fell through, Tom Thumb sued, seeking to pierce TLH's LLC veil and hold Hartmann personally liable. On appeal, the appeals held that, under express terms of the Minnesota LLC statute, the law relating to piercing the corporate veil applies to LLCs. On the facts, however, the court held that Tom Thumb had failed to establish the element of injustice or fundamental unfairness necessary to pierce the veil.[37]

B. Silent Statutes

Absent a Minnesota-like statute mandating the use of corporate veil piercing precedents in determining the personal liability of members of an LLC, should a court import the corporate law doctrine into the LLC arena?

Given the availability of corporate law doctrines as a ready made body of law close at hand, doing so has proven an irresistible impulse.[38] Some courts even refer to the relevant cause of action as being one to "pierce the corporate veil" of an LLC.[39] The analysis in most of these cases is perfunctory, at best; most simply assume the corporate law standard applies and have done with it.[40]

---

[37] *Id.* at *3. Minnesota's corporate veil piercing standard is a two-pronged one, requiring proof both that (1) the corporation is a mere alter ego of the shareholder and (2) that failing to pierce would allow some injustice or fundamental unfairness to the plaintiff to go unremedied. Gallinger v. North Star Hospital Mutual Assurance, Ltd., 64 F.3d 422, 427 (8th Cir. 1995).

[38] *See, e.g.,* Hollowell v. Orleans Regional Hospital LLC, 217 F.3d 379, 385 n.7 (5th Cir. 2000); International Bancorp LLC v. Societe des Bains de Mer et Du Cercle des Estrangers a Monaco, 192 F. Supp.2d 467, 477–78 (E.D. Va. 2002); GMAC Comm. Mortgage Corp. v. Gleichman, 84 F. Supp.2d 127, 145 (D. Me. 1999); Ditty v. Checkrite, Ltd., Inc., 973 F. Supp. 1320, 1335 (D. Utah 1997); NetTech Solutions LLC v. ZipPark.com, 2001 WL 1111966 at *11 (S.D.N.Y. 2001); In re Sanner, 218 B.R. 941, 947 (Bankr. D. Az. 1998); Litchfield Asset Management Corp. v. Howell, 799 A.2d 298, 309–16 (Conn. App. 2002); Bonner v. Brunson, 585 S.E.2d 917, 918 (Ga. App. 2003); Hamilton v. AAI Ventures, L.L.C., 768 So.2d 298, 302 (La. App. 2000); Stauffacher v. Lone Star Mud, Inc., 54 S.W.2d 810, 815–16 (Tex. App. 2001).
Some courts have done even stranger things when it comes to veil piercing in the LLC context. In New Horizons Supply Cooperative v. Haack, 590 N.W.2d 282 (Wis.App.1999), the trial court decided to treat the LLC as though it were a partnership, and imposed personal liability on the members, mainly because the LLC was treated as a partnership for tax purposes. The appeals court reversed that holding, but imposed personal liability on the alternative grounds that the member did not follow proper procedures for dissolution and did not prove that the amounts distributed to her on dissolution were less than the amount of the debt to New Horizons. *Id.*

[39] *See, e.g.,* Stone v. Frederick Hobby Associates II, 2001 WL 861822 at *6 (Conn. Super. 2001); Advanced Telephone Sys. Inc. v. Com-Net Professional Mobile Radio LLC, 59 Pa. D. & C.4th 286, 289 (Pa. Com. Pl. 2002).

[40] In Rafferty v. Noto Brothers Const., LLC, 2001 WL 459073 (Conn. Super. 2001), for example, the court simply stated: "The protection afforded by the L.L.C. is not unlimited and may be disregarded, as in the case of a corporation, when the L.L.C. is the alter ego or business conduit of individuals." *Id.* at *1 (citing other unpublished opinions). In Ditty v. Checkrite, Ltd., Inc., 973 F. Supp. 1320 (D. Utah 1997), the court contented itself with the observation that "most commentators *assume* that the [veil piercing] doctrine applies to limited liability companies. *Id.* at

The Connecticut statute, for example, provides that "a person who is a member or manager of a limited liability company is not liable, *solely* by reason of being a member or manager . . . for a debt, obligation or liability" of the LLC. Connecticut courts have read the word "solely" as permitting imposition of unlimited personal liability on grounds other than mere LLC membership and, moreover, have invoked the corporate veil piercing rules to supply the requisite grounds.[41]

The statute admittedly does not preclude the interpretation given it by the Connecticut courts. Yet, other interpretations were readily available, The legislature's use of the word "solely" could be understood as suggesting only that an LLC member or manager may be held personally liable on some basis other than his mere status as such.[42] For example, a member who guarantees an LLC debt may be held personally liable if the LLC fails to perform. Likewise, a member can be held personally liable where he committed a tort for which the entity is also liable. Similarly, if the member or manager fraudulently induced a creditor to lend to the LLC, the member or manager could be held personally liable for committing fraud. Perhaps the legislature used the word "solely" to avoid foreclosing the prospect of direct personal liability of a member or manager arising out of his own conduct in cases such as those just described. If so, there was no need to import the corporate veil piercing rules. Yet, the Connecticut courts have failed to seriously examine this alternative interpretation of their statute.

Securities Investor Protection Corp. v. R.D. Kushnir & Co.[43] offers an even more example of just how poor the analysis in many

---

1335 (emphasis supplied). *See also* NetTech Solutions LLC v. ZipPark.com, 2001 WL 1111966 at *11 (S.D.N.Y. 2001) (applying corporate standard without analysis of difference in entities); Great Neck Plaza, L.P. v. Le Peep Restaurants, LLC, 37 P.3d 485, 489–90 (Colo. App. 2001) (affirming trial court's piercing of the LLC veil without analysis of the LLC issues); Collins v. E-Magine, LLC, 739 N.Y.S.2d 15, 17 (App. Div. 2002) (rejecting plaintiff's alter ego liability theory for failure of proof rather than as legally insufficient).

[41] *See, e.g.,* Bastan v. RJM & Associates, LLC, 2001 WL 1006661 at *1 (Conn. Super. 2001) (citing the relevant statute and holding that it did not foreclose veil piercing); *see also* Thompson, *supra* note 34, at 19 (arguing that "the use of 'solely' leaves room for other grounds [for setting aside the protections of limited liability] based on traditional common-law corporate principles for piercing the veil").

[42] In Pepsi-Cola Bottling Co. of Salisbury, Md. v. Handy, 2000 WL 364199 (Del. Ch. 2000), Delaware Vice Chancellor Jacobs reviewed the similar Delaware LLC statute. Interestingly, Jacobs did not seize on the word "solely" to justify veil piercing. Instead, he parsed the facts and determined that the individual defendants had engaged in at least some of the challenged wrongdoing before the LLC was formed. As such, their liability did not arise solely from their status as LLC members, and plaintiff was entitled to proceed against them individually. *Id.* at *3–4. This is precisely the sort of analysis which courts ought to undertake in the face of such statutes, as compared to the simplistic assumption that corporate veil piercing standards apply.

[43] 274 B.R. 768 (Bankr. N.D. Ill. 2002).

of these cases has been. The original Illinois LLC statute contained a provision pursuant to which members of an LLC were "personally liable for any act, debt, obligation, or liability of the limited liability company or another member or manager to the extent that a shareholder of an Illinois business corporation is liable in analogous circumstances under Illinois law." This phrasing plausibly can be interpreted as inviting courts to extend the corporate veil piercing doctrine to the LLC context. Illinois subsequently repealed that statute, however, and replaced it with one tracking ULLCA § 303, providing in pertinent part that:

> (a) Except as otherwise provided in subsection (d) of this Section, the debts, obligations, and liabilities of a limited liability company, whether arising in contract, tort, or otherwise, are solely the debts, obligations, and liabilities of the company. A member or manager is not personally liable for a debt, obligation, or liability of the company solely by reason of being or acting as a member or manager. . . .

> (c) The failure of a limited liability company to observe the usual company formalities or requirements relating to the exercise of its company powers or management of its business is not a ground for imposing personal liability on the members or managers for liabilities of the company.

If the original wording permitted a pro-veil piercing inference, perhaps one should infer that the subsequent legislative action was intended to preclude extension of the veil piercing doctrine to the LLC setting. The legislature repealed a statute inviting such an extension, replacing it with one containing a flat prohibition of imposing liability on the members of an LLC. The bankruptcy judge, however, failed even to address this interpretation. Instead, the judge simply quoted the relevant statutes and then opined:

> It would seem from the foregoing that "members" or "managers" of an Illinois limited liability company cannot be held liable for the mere failure to observe corporate formalities or repayment, but nothing in the statute bars piercing of the "corporate veil" for other grounds on which that may be done for ordinary corporations.

Why does the statute have to explicitly bar veil piercing? What else does the judge think the legislature was doing? Granted, the legislative action is not dispositive, because the statutory change in question here was part of a larger package of amendments. In addition, because failure to comply with organizational formalities is a much criticized factor weighed under the corporate veil piercing standard, the legislature's efforts to ensure that failure to observe organizational formalities is not used as a basis for imposing personal liability on LLC members may implicitly recognize the possibility of otherwise applying corporate veil piercing rules to LLCs. At the very least, however, the judge should have joined issue with the alternative interpretation suggested above.

C.   The Leading Case

Appropriately enough, the leading case to undertake a substantial analysis, *Kaycee Land and Livestock v. Flahive,*[44] comes from Wyoming, which is the state in which the LLC was born. The Wyoming LLC statute is one of the silent statutes, providing no express authorization for courts to pierce the LLC veil. To the contrary, the statute's text seems clearly to preclude the imposition of personal liability: "Neither the members of a limited liability company nor the managers of a limited liability company managed by a manager or managers are liable under a judgment, decree or order of a court, or in any other manner, for a debt, obligation or liability of the limited liability company." Not even the hedge word "solely," on which the Connecticut courts seized, appears in what looks like a flat prohibition of personal liability. Yet, the Wyoming supreme court concluded that the LLC veil may be pierced.

This result was predetermined when the court began its analysis by immediately conflating the LLC with the corporation: "To answer this question, we must first examine the development of the doctrine within Wyoming's corporate context." Apparently anticipating this move, Flahive had tried to avoid extension of the corporate doctrine to the LLC by contrasting the LLC statute to the relevant provision of the Wyoming corporation code, which stated: "Unless otherwise provided in the articles of incorporation, a shareholder of a corporation is not personally liable for the acts or debts of the corporation except that he may become personally liable by reason of his own acts or conduct." Flahive pointed out that the LLC statute lacks a comparable proviso for personal liability arising from an LLC member's "own acts or conduct."

The court rejected this argument. At the outset of its opinion, the court had noted that veil piercing evolved as an equitable doctrine. In response to Flahive's argument, the court then opined that because veil piercing "is an equitable doctrine" the paucity of statutory authority for piercing the LLC veil was not surprising. Finally, the court invoked the hoary canon of statutory construction under which statutes in derogation of the common law are to be strictly construed. Because the court saw no evidence of legislative intent to preclude application of the common law veil piercing to the LLC context, the court held that the LLC veil could be pierced.

---

[44] 46 P.3d 323 (Wyo. 2002).

The flaws in this analysis are many and obvious. Most significantly, there was no common law of LLCs. The interpretative canon in question is invoked typically when the legislature adopts a statute in an area of the law where there is pre-existing common law.[45] The LLC, however, was an entirely new statutory creation. There was no background of common law against which it was to be implemented. Corporate common law was relevant to the problem at bar only by virtue of judicial fiat.

Even if the court was correct in opining that corporate common law was relevant, moreover, its invocation of the canon in question was suspect. Karl Llewellyn, of course, famously demonstrated that canons of construction are essentially indeterminate.[46] The canon requiring strict construction of statutes in derogation of the common law, however, is particularly suspect. The canon "can work to ossify an obsolete status quo and, in any event, is probably rooted historically in a selfish desire by English judges to limit Parliament's" power.[47] The authors of the passage just quoted further opine that "the derogation canon . . . is usually treated as anathema by contemporary commentators."

D.　The Emerging Standards for Piercing the LLC Veil

Several formulations of the veil piercing standard compete in corporate law. In light of the predominant trend for courts to import the corporate law regime into the LLC context, it is not surprising that a similar multitude of standards is emerging in the latter setting.

Control is the common (if sometimes implicit) feature of all the concepts used to describe cases in which veil piercing is appropriate. LLC members who do not actively participate in the firm's business or management are rarely held liable on a veil piercing theory.[48] Hence, it seems clear that control is an essential prerequisite for holding an LLC member or manager liable.

Standing alone, however, control cannot be a sufficient ground for piercing the veil of either a corporation or an LLC. Granted, *Walkovszky v. Carlton,*[49] the leading corporate law decision,

---

[45] *See, e.g.,* Augusta & Savannah Railroad v. McElmurry, 24 Ga. 75, 78 (Ga. 1858) (holding that "[a]cts relative to railroads cannot be in derogation of the common law, for railroads were unknown to the common law."); *see also* Gottling v. P.R. Inc., 61 P.3d 989, 995 (Utah 2002) (declining to follow the canon where there was no relevant common law when the statute in question was enacted).

[46] Karl Llewellyn, *Remarks on the Theory of Appellate Decision and the Rules or Canons About How Statutes Are To Be Construed,* 3 Vand. L. Rev. 395 (1950).

[47] WILLIAM N. ESKRIDGE ET AL., LEGISLATION AND STATUTORY INTERPRETATION 332 (2000)

[48] *See* New England Nat'l LLC v. Kabro of East Lyme LLC, 2000 WL 254590 at *6 (Conn. Super. 2000).

[49] 223 N.E.2d 6 (N.Y. 1966).

indicates that veil piercing is appropriate where the corporation is "a 'dummy' for its individual shareholders who are in reality carrying on the business in their personal capacities for purely personal rather than corporate ends."[50] The problem with this analysis, however, is that a close corporation with, say, one to three dominant shareholders has no "corporate ends" separate from those of its owners. In apparent recognition of this fact, courts generally require plaintiffs to show something more than mere control in the corporate law context.[51]

Courts are likewise developing multi-pronged standards for the LLC context. A common formulation, for example, asks whether the LLC member to be held personally liable (1) controlled the LLC and (2) abused his control of the firm "in order to defeat justice or perpetrate fraud."[52] Another common formulation adapts the three-pronged instrumentality doctrine used in corporate law, under which plaintiff must show: (1) control of the corporation by defendant that is so complete as to amount to total domination of finances, policy, and business practices such that the controlled corporation has no separate mind, will or existence; (2) such control is used to commit a fraud, wrong or other violation of plaintiff's rights; and (3) the control and breach of duty owed to plaintiff was a proximate cause of the injury.[53]

As with corporate law cases, the analysis in LLC litigation frequently collapses into a mere litany of factors considered by the court. In *Bonner v. Bruson*,[54] for example, the Georgia Court of

---

[50] *Id.* at 8. *See* Franklin A. Gevurtz, *Piercing Piercing: An Attempt to Lift the Veil of Confusion Surrounding the Doctrine of Piercing the Corporate Veil*, 76 ORE. L. REV. 853, 864 (1997) ("No corporation in the world has a mind of its own; they are fictitious entities. People control corporations.").

[51] Luis v. Orcutt Town and Water Co., 22 Cal. Rptr. 389 (Cal. App. 1962) ("It is not true that any wholly owned subsidiary is necessarily the alter ego of the parent corporation."); Shafford v. Otto Sales Co., Inc., 260 P.2d (Cal. App. 1953) ("complete stock ownership and actual one-man control will not alone be sufficient").

[52] *See, e.g.,* Bonner v. Bruson, 2003 WL 21730686 at *1 (Ga. App. 2003) (holding that: "A court may disregard the separate LLC entity and the protective veil it provides to an individual member of the LLC when that member, in order to defeat justice or perpetrate fraud, conducts his personal and LLC business as if they were one by commingling the two on an interchangeable or joint basis or confusing otherwise separate properties, records, or control."); *see also* Gallinger v. North Star Hospital Mutual Assurance, Ltd., 64 F.3d 422, 427 (8th Cir. 1995) (adopting similar two-pronged standard).

[53] *See, e.g.,* Zaist v. Olson, 227 A.2d 552, 558 (Conn. 1967); Collett v. American Nat'l Stores, Inc., 708 S.W.2d 273, 284 (Mo. App. 1986). A number of decisions, especially in Connecticut, have extended the instrumentality rule to the LLC setting. *See, e.g.,* Bastan v. RJM & Associates, LLC, 2001 WL 1006661 (Conn. Super. 2001); Stone v. Frederick Hobby Associates II, 2001 WL 861822 (Conn. Super. 2001); Rafferty v. Noto Brothers Const., LLC, 2001 WL 459073 (Conn. Super. 2001).

[54] 2003 WL 21730686 (Ga. App. 2003). *See generally* Eric Fox, Note, *Piercing the Veil of Limited Liability Companies*, 62 GEO. WASH. L. REV. 1143, 1167–77 (1994) (setting out a list of potentially relevant factors and arguing that the relevance of any given factor will depend on the extent to which the LLC's governance and financial structures resembles those of a corporation or an unincorporated firm).

Appeals set out its "defeat justice or perpetrate fraud" standard, but then ignored that standard to focus on various specific transactions to determine whether there was "any evidence that [defendant] Bruson abused the form of the LLC by commingling or confusing LLC business with his personal affairs."

The *Bonner* decision is particularly troubling because the Georgia court seemingly imported into the LLC context not only the corporate veil piercing doctrine but also the fetish for formalities so often found in corporate veil piercing cases. Limited liability is a social concern mainly because it permits equity investors to externalize risk. As such, failure to observe organizational formalities is largely irrelevant. Setting aside the rare cases in which failure to observe organizational formalities misleads a creditor into believing it is dealing with an individual rather than an LLC, there simply is no causal link between the creditor's injury and the member's misconduct.

The ULLCA's drafters recognized the desirability of getting away from an emphasis on compliance with formalities by providing, in § 303(b), that:

> The failure of a limited liability company to observe the usual company formalities or requirements relating to the exercise of its company powers or management of its business is not a ground for imposing personal liability on the members or managers for liabilities of the company.

So too did the *Kaycee* court, which noted that because the LLC is intended to be "much more flexible" in operation than corporations the standard for piercing the LLC veil should not emphasize disregard for operational formalities to the extent the corporate law version does.[55] Unfortunately, as *Bonner* illustrates, not all courts are getting it right; instead, these courts are importing corporate law's insistence on compliance with organizational formalities into the LLC context.[56]

---

[55] Kaycee Land and Livestock, 46 P.3d 323, 328 (Wyo. 2002). *See also* Hollowell v. Orleans Regional Hospital LLC, 1998 WL 283298 at *9 (E.D. La. 1998), *aff'd*, 217 F.3d 379 (5th Cir. 2000) (holding that "analyses between corporate veil piercing and limited liability companies veil piercing may not completely overlap . . . '[b]ecause the Louisianan LLC law requires fewer formalities' then does corporate law").

[56] *See, e.g.*, Martin v. Freeman, 272 P.3d 1182 (Colo. App. 2012) (piercing the LLC veil where personal and business assets were commingled, the company had minimal books and records, and various legal formalities were ignored); Lincoln Diversified Systems, Inc., 2000 WL 1880338 (S.D.N.Y. 2000) (citing lack of evidence that formalities were ignored in explaining its refusal to pierce); Litchfield Asset Management Corp. v. Howell, 799 A.2d 298, 315–16 (Conn. App. 2002) (discussing defendant's failure to observe formalities); Stone v. Frederick Hobby Associates II, 2001 WL 861822 at *10 (Conn. Super. 2001) (piercing the corporate veil on grounds, *inter alia*, that defendants "affirmatively acted with disregard for Hobby II's existence as an entity that is separate and distinct"); Hamilton v. AAI Ventures, L.L.C., 768 So.2d 298, 302 (La. App. 2000) (invoking corporate standard of "failing to

E.   Enterprise Liability Involving LLCs

Veil piercing-like issues are frequently presented in cases involving groups of affiliated corporations, including those involving parent and subsidiary corporations. In the leading corporate law decision, *Walkovszky v. Carlton*,[57] the defendant was the principal shareholder of a number of corporations operating taxicabs. The plaintiff, who had been injured by a cab owned by one of those companies, claimed that the multiple corporations had no separate existence, but rather were just components of a single business enterprise. The court held that the corporate veil may not be pierced simply because the defendant corporation is part of a larger enterprise. Instead, proof that multiple corporations are simply part of a single corporate group may give rise to enterprise liability.

If correctly (and successfully) invoked, enterprise liability permits a creditor to reach the collective assets of all of the corporations making up the enterprise. Obviously, this theory is most useful when the responsible corporation is insolvent, but the enterprise as a whole has sufficient assets to satisfy the creditor's claim. Given that enterprise liability is well-established in corporate law, and that borrowing from corporate law is a well-established pattern in LLC cases, it comes as no surprise that courts are extending enterprise liability to corporate groups including LLCs.[58]

F.   Summation

In the leading Kaycee decision, the Wyoming supreme court concluded: "We can discern no reason, in either law or policy, to treat LLCs differently than we treat corporations." Admittedly, there is a certain intuitive logic to treating LLCs the same way we do corporations. Yet, why privilege the assumption that corporations and LLCs are to be treated the same? Indeed, why not see the creation of the LLC form of business organization as an opportunity to rethink the doctrine of limited liability and its application to the various forms of business entities?[59]

---

follow statutory formalities for incorporating and transacting corporate affairs" in LLC setting); Advanced Telephone Sys. Inc. v. Com-Net Professional Mobile Radio LLC, 59 Pa. D. & C.4th 286, 305 (Pa. Com. Pl. 2002) (citing the absence of evidence that "necessary formalities [were] ignored").

[57] 223 N.E.2d 6 (N.Y. 1966).

[58] *See, e.g.,* Litchfield Asset Management Corp. v. Howell, 799 A.2d 298, 315–16 (Conn. App. 2002).

[59] *See* J. William Callison, *Rationalizing Limited Liability and Veil Piercing*, 58 BUS. LAW. 1063, 1072 (2003) ("The entity rationalization movement provides the opportunity for scholars, practitioners, and legislators to take a step back and to consider the various rationale for offering limited liability protection to firm owners and to determine the extent to which such protection should be given.").

Granted, there is little direct evidence that legislatures intended to treat LLCs and corporations differently. Yet, if legislatures had intended to incorporate the corporate law doctrines, they easily could have done so explicitly. Indeed, as we have seen, Minnesota did exactly that. So did a number of other early LLC statutes. Given the ready availability of such models, one could infer that subsequently adopted statutes were not intended to incorporate corporate law rules in the absence of explicit Minnesota like language. As we have seen, this argument is especially compelling for states like Illinois, which moved away from a Minnesota-like formulation to a more neutral model that neither expressly nor impliedly invokes corporation law's veil piercing rules. Yet, as we have seen, the courts have blindly followed the corporate law precedent.

Where does this leave the law of LLC veil piercing? Benjamin Cardozo long ago observed that veil piercing is a doctrine "enveloped in the mists of metaphor,"[60] a complaint that remains true today. On the one hand, corporate veil piercing cases are highly fact-specific. On the other hand, the facts often tell us little about the likely outcome. Successful corporate veil piercing claims seem to differ only in degree, but not in kind, from unsuccessful claims. Unfortunately, there is no evidence to date that matters will improve as the vague corporate law standards are exported to the LLC setting.

VI. Freedom of Contract and Fiduciary Obligation

A. The Policy of Freedom of Contract in LLC Law

Many LLC statutes stand as exemplars of freedom of contract; they consist mostly of default rules that the parties are free to vary or even derogate. The ULLCA, for example, allows variations on and departures from the statute in all but a handful of areas.[61] The

---

[60] Berkey v. Third Ave. Ry. Co., 155 N.E. 58, 61 (N.Y. 1926).

[61] ULLCA § 103(b) provides that the operating agreement may not:

(1) unreasonably restrict a right to information or access to records under Section 408;

(2) eliminate the duty of loyalty under Section 409(b) or 603(b)(3), but the agreement may:

(i) identify specific types or categories of activities that do not violate the duty of loyalty, if not manifestly unreasonable; and

(ii) specify the number or percentage of members or disinterested managers that may authorize or ratify, after full disclosure of all material facts, a specific act or transaction that otherwise would violate the duty of loyalty;

(3) unreasonably reduce the duty of care under Section 409(c) or 603(b)(3);

(4) eliminate the obligation of good faith and fair dealing under Section 409(d), but the operating agreement may determine the standards by which the performance of the obligation is to be measured, if the standards are not manifestly unreasonable;

Delaware statute goes even further, expressly providing that: "It is the policy of this chapter to give the maximum effect to the principle of freedom of contract and to the enforceability of limited liability company agreements."[62]

In *Elf Atochem North America, Inc. v. Jaffari*,[63] Elf and Jaffari formed a joint venture formally structured as a Delaware LLC. The operating agreement contained an arbitration clause requiring that any arbitration (and/or any judicial proceeding to enforce an arbitral award) take place in California. Elf claimed that Jaffari had breached his fiduciary obligations and filed a derivative suit against Jaffari in Delaware. Citing the Delaware statutory provision on freedom of contract, and the social policies favoring arbitration as a mode of dispute resolution, the court held that the operating agreement was binding on both the LLC and its several members. "The basic approach of the Delaware Act is to provide members with broad discretion in drafting the Agreement and to furnish default provisions when the members' agreement is silent." Analogizing LLCs to limited partnerships for this purpose, and noting the policy of freedom of contract recognized by Delaware limited partnership law, the court further noted that "[o]nce partners exercise their contractual freedom in their partnership agreement, the partners have a great deal of certainty that their partnership agreement will be enforced in accordance with its terms."[64]

The *Jaffari* result makes sense not only in light of the statutory policy of freedom of contract, but also efficiency considerations. Default statutory rules provide cost savings comparable to those provided by standard form contracts, because both can be accepted without the need for costly negotiation. At the same time, however, because the default rule can be modified by

---

(5) vary the right to expel a member in an event specified in Section 601(6);

(6) vary the requirement to wind up the limited liability company's business in a case specified in Section 801(3) or (4); or

(7) restrict rights of a person, other than a manager, member, and transferee of a member's distributional interest, under this [Act].

[62] DLLCA § 1101(b). In general, however, the Delaware LLC code is a bare bones statute, which puts a high premium on preformation planning and creates a strong incentive for the use of detailed operating agreements. In contrast, the ULLCA lends itself to "off the rack" use by virtue of its numerous and highly detailed default rules.

[63] 727 A.2d 286 (Del. 1999).

[64] The specific application of this principle in the *Jaffari* case, however, has been overruled by statute. Both the limited partnership and LLC statutes were amended post-*Jaffari* to provide that the partners or LLC members cannot waive their right to sue in Delaware courts. DEL. CODE ANN., tit. 6, §§ 17–109(d) (limited partnerships), 18–109(d) (LLCs). Presumably the Delaware legislature did not want Delaware courts to lose business.

contrary agreement, idiosyncratic parties wishing a different rule can be accommodated. Given these advantages, a fairly compelling case ought to be required before we impose a mandatory rule. Indeed, mandatory rules seem justifiable only if a default rule would demonstrably create significant negative externalities or, perhaps, if one of the contracting parties is demonstrably unable to protect itself through bargaining.

B. Fiduciary Duties in the LLC

The default rules under the ULLCA § 409 depend on whether the LLC is managed by its members or by a manager. In manager-managed LLCs, the managers have a duty of care and loyalty to the members. In contrast, members of a manager-managed LLC have no duties to the LLC or its members by reason of being members.[65] Where the LLC is managed by its members, however, all members of a member-managed LLC have a duty of care and loyalty to the organization and fellow members.

Although fiduciary duties traditionally had been principally defined by case law, the ULLCA—like the UPA(1997)—sought to limit the scope of fiduciary duties in the LLC context to those defined by statute. Section 409(b), for example, provided that:

> A member's duty of loyalty to a member-managed company and its other members is *limited* to the following:
>
> (1) to account to the company and to hold as trustee for it any property, profit, or benefit derived by the member in the conduct or winding up of the company's business or derived from a use by the member of the company's property, including the appropriation of a company's opportunity;
>
> (2) to refrain from dealing with the company in the conduct or winding up of the company's business as or on behalf of a party having an interest adverse to the company; and
>
> (3) to refrain from competing with the company in the conduct of the company's business before the dissolution of the company.

Likewise, subsection (c) limited the duty of care to "refraining from engaging in grossly negligent or reckless conduct, intentional misconduct, or a knowing violation of law."

With respect to the distinction between member-managed and manager-managed LLCs, RULLCA § 409 is essentially similar. With respect to the content of fiduciary duties, however, the

---

[65] ULLCA § 409(h).

RULLCA abandoned the effort to limit the scope of those duties to their statutory definition:

> In an effort to respect freedom of contract, bolster predictability, and protect partnership agreements from second-guessing, the Conference decided that RUPA should fence or "cabin in" all fiduciary duties within a statutory formulation. That decision was followed without re-consideration in ULLCA and ULPA (2001).

> This Act takes a different approach. After lengthy discussion in the drafting committee and on the floor of the 2006 Annual Meeting, the Conference decided that: (i) the "corral" created by RUPA does not fit in the very complex and variegated world of LLCs; and (ii) it is impracticable to cabin all LLC-related fiduciary duties within a statutory formulation.

> As a result, this Act: (i) eschews "only" and "limited to"—the words RUPA used in an effort to exhaustively codify fiduciary duty; (ii) codifies the core of the fiduciary duty of loyalty; but (iii) does not purport to discern every possible category of overreaching. One important consequence is to allow courts to continue to use fiduciary duty concepts to police disclosure obligations in member-to-member and member-LLC transactions.[66]

In addition, the RULLCA struck out in a new direction with respect to the content of the duty of care. Section 409(c) provides that:

> Subject to the business judgment rule, the duty of care of a member of a member- managed limited liability company in the conduct and winding up of the company's activities is to act with the care that a person in a like position would reasonably exercise under similar circumstances and in a manner the member reasonably believes to be in the best interests of the company. In discharging this duty, a member may rely in good faith upon opinions, reports, statements, or other information provided by another person that the member reasonably believes is a competent and reliable source for the information.

The comment to that section explains that:

> This subsection, therefore, seeks "the best of both worlds"—stating a standard of ordinary care but subjecting that standard to the business judgment rule to the extent circumstances warrant. The content and force of the business judgment rule vary across jurisdictions, and therefore the

---

[66] RULLCA § 409 cmt.

meaning of this subsection may vary from jurisdiction to jurisdiction.

That result is intended. In any jurisdiction, the business judgment rule's application will vary depending on the nature of the challenged conduct. There is, for example, very little (if any) judgment involved when a person with managerial power acts (or fails to act) on an essentially ministerial matter. Moreover, under the law of many jurisdictions, the business judgment rule applies similarly across the range of business organizations. That is, the doctrine is sufficiently broad and conceptual so that the formality of organizational choice is less important in shaping the application of the rule than are the nature of the challenged conduct and the responsibilities and authority of the person whose conduct is being challenged.

This Act seeks therefore to invoke rather than unsettle whatever may be each jurisdiction's approach to the business judgment rule.

C.   Private Ordering of Fiduciary Obligations

Should the fiduciary duties of an LLC's members or managers be subject to contractual variation and/or derogation? The ULLCA permits modification, but not elimination, of the duty of loyalty. The operating agreement thus may not "eliminate the duty of loyalty" but may "identify specific types or categories of activities that do not violate the duty of loyalty, if not manifestly unreasonable. . . ."[67] In addition, the operating agreement may "specify the number or percentage of members or disinterested managers that may authorize or ratify, after full disclosure of all material facts, a specific act or transaction that otherwise would violate the duty of loyalty."[68] The agreement also may modify, but not "unreasonably reduce the duty of care. . . ."[69] In contrast, the Delaware LLC statute far more permissively provides that fiduciary "duties and liabilities may be expanded or restricted *or eliminated* by provisions in a limited liability company agreement."[70]

---

[67] ULLCA § 103(b)(2). Note the parallel to how the UPA (1997) allows for modification but not waiver of fiduciary duties.

[68] ULLCA § 103(b)(2)(ii).

[69] ULLCA § 103(b)(3).

[70] DLLCA § 1101(c)(2) (emphasis supplied). In Auriga Capital Corp. v. Gatz Properties, LLC, 40 A.3d 389 (Del. Ch. 2012), the Court examined the history of this provision and concluded that:

> The statute incorporates equitable principles. Those principles view the manager of an LLC as a fiduciary and subject the manager as a default principle to the core fiduciary duties of loyalty and care. But, the statute allows the parties to an LLC agreement to entirely supplant those default principles or to modify them in part. Where the parties have clearly supplanted default principles in full, we give effect to the parties' contract choice. Where the

Courts appear to be giving full effect to the principle of freedom of contract even in this controversial area. A widely cited Ohio decision, *McConnell v. Hunt Sports Enterprises*,[71] for example, involved the formation of an LLC to buy a NHL hockey expansion franchise to be located in Columbus, Ohio. After the LLC's members failed to obtain public financing of a hockey arena, Nationwide Insurance offered to build an arena that would be leased to the LLC. LLC member Lamar Hunt, purporting to act on the LLC's behalf but without authority to do so, rejected the offer. In a series of meetings over the next several weeks, Hunt and his cronies among the LLC's members persisted in rejecting that offer, while LLC member John McConnell and his supporters wanted to accept it. McConnell and his supporters thereupon formed a separate team ownership group that accepted Nationwide's offer and, moreover, was awarded the franchise. Hunt sued, alleging breach of fiduciary duty and contract claims.

The court noted that the LLC operating agreement expressly allowed members to compete with the LLC. Focusing on the plain language of the relevant provision, which authorized LLC members to engage in "any other business venture of any nature," the court held that McConnell's group was free to pursue their own bid for the NHL franchise despite being members of an LLC that had been formed for that same purpose. Unfortunately, in going on to discuss Hunt's contract based claims, the court muddied the waters somewhat by implying that the result might have been different if Hunt had not rejected the Nationwide proposal. The opinion is nevertheless significant for its strong "affirmative" answer to "the question [of whether] an operating agreement of a limited liability company may, in essence, limit or define the scope of the fiduciary duties imposed upon its members."

As with *Jaffari*, this result is consistent not only with the statute but also with economic theory. Fiduciary duties function as gap-fillers; they provide rules to govern the parties' conduct in the absence of agreement. Where the parties have gone to the effort of bargaining over specific matters, however, there is no gap to be filled. Instead, absent negative externalities or other forms of market failure, the basic principle of freedom of contract mandates that courts respect the bargain struck by the parties. Consequently, to invoke fiduciary obligation to trump actual contracts sets the process on its head. Worse yet, doing so often results in an

---

parties have clearly supplanted default principles in part, we give effect to their contract choice. But, where the core default fiduciary duties have not been supplanted by contract, they exist as the LLC statute itself contemplates.
Id. at 852 (footnotes omitted).

[71] 725 N.E.2d 1193 (Ohio App. 1999).

unjustified windfall. When the parties entered into their bargain, the price paid by each member for an LLC interest (or what have you) reflected their estimate of the trade offs inherent in that investment, including the protections (or lack thereof) provided by the operating agreement. Allowing parties to subsequently invoke fiduciary obligation to escape a bargain that turned out badly gives them an undeserved second bite at the apple. Put another way, the parties made their bed and courts ought to let them—indeed, make them—lie in it.

D. What Is Both the Statute and the Operating Agreement Are Silent?

In August 2013, the Delaware legislature amended § 1104 DLLCA by adding the italicized words to the existing text: "In any case not provided for in this chapter, the rules of law and equity, including *the rules of law and equity relating to fiduciary duties and* the law merchant, shall govern." As noted above, the DLLCA is a bare bones statute that leaves many issues for the parties to fill by private ordering. Where the parties fail to do so, such that neither the statute nor the operating agreement provide guidance, § 1104 takes the commonsense approach of directing the parties to the case law.

The 2013 amendment was occasioned by the Delaware Supreme Court's decision in *Gatz Properties, LLC v. Auriga Capital Corp.*[72] In the case, the Chancery Court had opined that the DLLCA imposes default fiduciary duties upon an LLC's members and managers unless operating agreement specifies that such duties shall not apply. The Supreme Court rejected that conclusion as one "that the trial court should not have reached or decided":

> Where, as here, the dispute over whether fiduciary standards apply could be decided solely by reference to the LLC Agreement, it was improvident and unnecessary for the trial court to reach out and decide, sua sponte, the default fiduciary duty issue as a matter of statutory construction. The trial court did so despite expressly acknowledging that the existence of fiduciary duties under the LLC Agreement was "no longer contested by the parties."

The Supreme Court then held that the Chancery Court's "statutory pronouncements must be regarded as dictum without any precedential value."

In *Graz Properties*, the Supreme Court suggested that the Delaware legislature ought to consider resolving "any statutory

---

[72] 59 A.3d 1206 (Del. Supr. 2012).

ambiguity on this issue." The amendment to § 1104 provided the Legislature's answer to that suggestion. The adopting bill's synopsis explains that the amendment was intended:

> [T]o to confirm that in some circumstances fiduciary duties not explicitly provided for in the limited liability company agreement apply. For example, a manager of a manager-managed limited liability company would ordinarily have fiduciary duties even in the absence of a provision in the limited liability company agreement establishing such duties. Section 18–1101(c) continues to provide that such duties may be expanded, restricted or eliminated by the limited liability company agreement."

VII.   Dissociation and Dissolution

The process of dissociation and dissolution under the ULLCA is quite similar to that under UPA (1997). AN LLC member is dissociated by withdrawal or expulsion of a member.[73] As with the UPA (1997), dissociation does not necessarily lead to dissolution. If the business is to be continued without dissolution, the dissociated member's interest must be purchased by the LLC or the other members.[74] If they are unable to agree to a price, a judicial appraisal proceeding is available.[75] Dissociation terminates a member's right to participate in firm business terminates, except where the firm is to be dissolved, in which case the dissociating member is entitled to participate in the winding up process.

The LLC must be dissolved and its business wound up upon the occurrence of any event specified in LLC operating agreement as triggering dissolution. A vote of the members, as specified in operating agreement, also can require a dissolution. A court may order a dissolution upon request by one or more of the members where the economic purpose of the business has been frustrated or there has been serious misconduct by one or more of the members. Note that the ULLCA thus departs from the UPA (1997) in one very significant respect. Under it, the unilateral withdrawal of a member does not result in a dissolution. The ULLCA thus is designed to confer a corporate-like stability on the LLC by making it far harder for a member to force a dissolution and winding up than is the case in a partnership. RULLCA § 701 is essentially similar.

---

[73] ULLCA § 601. Interestingly, the Delaware LLC statute provides no mechanism for expelling an LLC member. *See* Walker v. Resource Development Co., 2000 WL 1336720 (Del.Ch.2000).

[74] ULLCA § 701.

[75] ULLCA § 702.

VIII.   LLCs in Transactional Planning

One of the great advantages of thinking of business firms in a contractual sense is that one quickly realizes that the standard form contracts provided by statute almost always can be manipulated into a result that meets the client's needs. From this perspective, the LLC offers little that was not already achievable under the existing corporation and partnership statutes. To be sure, the LLC combines pass through taxation with limited liability, thereby achieving two of the transaction planner's key goals, but such a structure could be created under the prior statutes.

Having said that, the LLC statute nevertheless can play a useful role in transaction planning. While we could provide clients with pass through taxation, relatively informal decisionmaking, restricted membership, and limited liability, we could do so only by substantially modifying the default rules governing corporate operation. From the client's perspective, extensive modifications of the default statutory rules are always problematic. Acceptable modifications must be bargained out, which is costly and may result in disagreements that prevent the relationship from ever getting off the ground. Agreed upon modifications must be spelled out in detail to reduce the risk of future disagreements and, even if this is done, disputes over the parties' intent may nevertheless arise. By providing a set of default rules meeting these four criteria, the LLC statutes allow many small business relationships to adopt the statutory rules "off the rack."

TABLE OF CASES

INDEX